BOUND FEET, YOUNG HANDS

BOUND FEET, YOUNG HANDS

*Tracking the Demise of Footbinding
in Village China*

Laurel Bossen and Hill Gates

STANFORD UNIVERSITY PRESS
STANFORD, CALIFORNIA

Stanford University Press
Stanford, California

Printed in the United States of America on acid-free,
archival-quality paper

Library of Congress Cataloging-in-Publication Data

Names: Bossen, Laurel, author. | Gates, Hill, author.
Title: Bound feet, young hands : tracking the demise of foot-
    binding in village China / Laurel Bossen and Hill Gates.
Description: Stanford, California : Stanford University Press,
    2017. | Includes bibliographical references and index.
Identifiers: LCCN 2016020136| ISBN 9780804799553
    (cloth : alk. paper) | ISBN 9781503601079 (electronic)
Subjects: LCSH: Footbinding—China. | Footbinding—
    Economic aspects—China. | Rural girls—Employment—
    China. | Rural women—Employment—China. | Handi-
    craft industries—China. | Rural girls—China—Social life
    and customs. | Rural women—China—Social life and
    customs. | China—Rural conditions.
Classification: LCC GT498.F66 B67 2017 | DDC 391.4/
    130951—dc23
LC record available at https://lccn.loc.gov/2016020136

Typeset by Newgen in 10/14 Sabon

*To Annika and Seraphina, who passed through the age
of footbinding while this book was in progress*
—Laurel Bossen

For Arthur Wolf
—Hill Gates

CONTENTS

MAPS, FIGURES, AND TABLES

Maps

Figures

Tables

ACKNOWLEDGMENTS

This book is the fruit of many years of effort and has received support from many institutions and more people than we will be able to thank personally. We are fortunate to have been able to undertake this quest to understand how footbinding, an accepted part of everyday life for millions of people, could have declined so precipitously. We hope that it will stimulate a re-evaluation of the way explanations for cultural practices are accepted and transmitted.

First, we thank the nearly two thousand elderly village women and their family members who invited us into their homes, patiently answered our questions, described their experiences in the early twentieth century, and often showed us their surviving handmade items and tools. They made great efforts to help us understand the conditions in which they were raised. Having the opportunity to interview them was truly remarkable.

We thank the institutions that have provided funding and support for this project: the National Science Foundation, Award Number BCS 0613297; the Harry Frank Guggenheim Foundation Program on Violence and Aggression Toward Women; the Silk Road Foundation; the Radcliffe Institute for Advanced Study at Harvard University; the Carl and Lily Pforzheimer Foundation Fellowship; the Social Science and Humanities Research Council of Canada; the National Museum of Ethnology, Osaka; Chinese University of Hong Kong Universities Service Centre; the Lee Hysan Foundation Fellowship; McGill University; and Stanford University.

Among the many libraries that we have consulted and that have assisted us we thank the McGill University Humanities and Social Science Library; the Harvard Yenching, Baker, and Widener Libraries; the Radcliffe Institute's Schlesinger Library; the National Museum of Ethnology Library; the

Chinese University of Hong Kong Universities Service Centre Library; the Lowell Museum of Technology; Stanford University Library; Yunnan Provincial Library; and libraries at the Yunnan Academy of Social Sciences, Shaanxi Academy of Social Sciences, Zhengzhou University, Anhui University, and Yunnan University.

Institutions and conferences where we have presented parts of this research include the Radcliffe Institute of Advanced Study at Harvard University; the University of Chicago; the Shorenstein Center of Stanford University; STANDD (Society for Technology and Development) and the Redpath Museum at McGill University; State University of New York at Albany; State University of New York at Plattsburgh; the National Museum of Ethnology; Chinese University of Hong Kong; Fudan University, Shanghai; Yunnan Academy of Social Sciences, Kunming; Minzu University of China, Beijing; the American Anthropological Association; the Association for Asian Studies; the European Association of Chinese Studies; and the International Congress of Anthropological and Ethnological Sciences.

In China, a great many people have facilitated our research over the years. Among those who were particularly helpful were Cheng Shaozhen, Leng Yunli, Li Chaodong, Fan Chengdiao, Hu Jing, Pan Zhao, Sun Liping, Tong Qunxia, Wang Xurui, Xiong Jingming (Jean Hung), Yang Shengwen, Zhang Haiyang, Zhang Liren, Zheng Baohua, and Zhu Xia. In each site, with the help of Chinese friends and colleagues and often through the good offices of local Women's Federation cadres, village leaders, university professors, graduate students, and local teachers, we found and trained interviewers. Members of these diverse teams, too numerous to name, have our warm thanks for their patience and genuinely hard work.

Many colleagues and friends helped in other phases with suggestions, criticisms, advice, draft reading, encouragement, and support. Among them we thank Donald W. Attwood, Kathryn Bernhardt, Liz Cohen, Mark Elvin, Jacob Eyferth, Mareile Flitsch, Grace Fong, Suzanne Friedberg, Amy Goldstein, Susan Greenhalgh, Ralph Hanna, Xiong Jingming, Gal Kaminka, Nobuhiro Kishigami, Li Li, Ishaq Ma Jianfu, Anthony Masi, Joseph P. McDermott, John Plotz, Jan Rindfleisch, John Shepherd, Benny Shilo, Matt Sommer, Janice Stockard, Judith Vichniac, Deborah Winslow, Robin Yates, and Macy Zheng. We thank Melissa J. Brown, co-participant for the initial years of the project, for her many insights and efforts on its behalf. We also thank Adela C. Y. Li of the Silk Road Foundation for kick-starting the project, traveling across North China with Hill Gates to evaluate possibilities and set up contacts for our different research sites.

In addition, we acknowledge the help of research assistants Cynthia Tan, Emilio Dirlikov, and Rafael Charron-Chenier at McGill and research partners Xiao Fu and Justine Liu at Harvard and thank them for their contributions. We also thank McGill University Geographic Information Centre and Shi Ruilan, who worked patiently on the maps. We appreciate the helpful suggestions of the anonymous readers and thank editor Jenny Gavacs for suggestions and encouragement.

Finally, our deepest gratitude belongs to our families. Ever supportive behind the scenes were Nathan Bossen and the late Arthur Wolf.

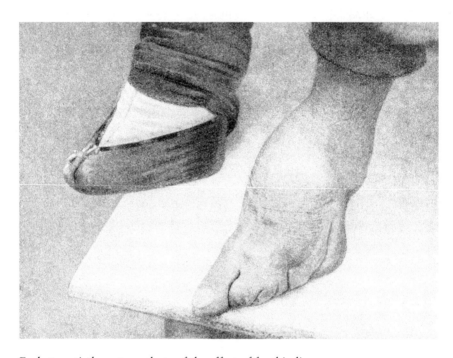

Early twentieth-century photo of the effect of footbinding

SOURCE: Arthur Corbett-Smith, "China: How Its Teeming Millions Toil and Live," in *Peoples of All Nations: Their Life Today and Story of Their Past*, ed. J. A. Hammerton (London: Fleetway House, 1923), 2:1350. Photo by B. T. Prideaux.

CHAPTER ONE

Questions About Footbinding

I was seven years old when my mother took me out to the fields. There, while the buckwheat was in bloom, Mother bound my feet, tightly winding the cloth around them. She used a binding cloth to bind them tightly; it would [eventually] break the bones. When I cried, my mother just hit me. Ma said that my feet were too big; no one would want me, and I would not find a pojia *[literally, mother-in-law family]. In the buckwheat fields, after she had bound them well, she made me walk back to the house. I did not rest. When we got back to the house, she just made me sit down and spin thread. At that time, they did not let girls go outside. When I was smaller, I could still go outside to run around, but when I grew, then I could not go out; I had to stay at home and work, spinning thread and weaving cloth. The yarn that I spun was very good. I also spun yarn for other people, earning money. Other people brought cotton to me, and when I had finished spinning, they came to take the cotton thread that I had spun. They gave me money or gave me* mantou *[steamed bread]. When I was young, I also wove straw hats. My father took them to market to sell.*

> —"Lovely Flower" (eighty years old), interview by the authors and team, Luochuan, Shaanxi, October 19, 2008

In the recent past, the debilitating custom of footbinding affected millions of Chinese girls and women.[1] Footbinding forcibly compressed growing girls' foot bones, toes, and arches so that the foot bones could not grow forward or outward. In its most extreme form, the binding permanently and painfully deformed girls' feet and hindered their mobility throughout their life. Reaching this fixed shape took years. These "lotus feet" were essentially irreversible. When political movements required that women remove their binding tapes and allow the feet to spread beyond their previous confines, walking on these "let out" feet was painful or even impossible without rebinding. The bony architecture had been destroyed. Less demanding traditions of binding only narrowed the foot by bending the four lesser toes beneath the sole. These "cucumber" or "half-sloped" feet were easier to let out, although for many who removed their bindings, the toes remained embedded in the sole. Footbinding was widespread within the Chinese empire for centuries, lasting into the Republican period (1912–1949). Although binding young girls' feet came to an end in the mid-twentieth century, many grown women with bound feet survived into the twenty-first. During this same era, ending at the Republican period, most Chinese practiced labor-intensive family farming. But how did rural Chinese women work with bound feet? Were they merely idle consumers—surplus labor in an over-populated agrarian empire—or did they mainly raise children? This seems extremely unlikely for most poor families. This puzzle piqued our interest and motivated our research.

China scholars, missionaries, historians, and novelists have offered many perspectives on Chinese women's bound feet. Questions about life and work with bound feet, however, have been either ignored or given superficial treatment. Few researchers asked the women themselves. The reasons for this may spring from old assumptions about women—for example, that peasant women rarely had bound feet, and if they did, they were merely housewives who did not contribute to the commercial economy. Additional reasons may be that the women's limited mobility proved both a physical and a language barrier to interacting with researchers, mainly unrelated men, since women were kept so close to home. Finally, because most women's work took place within the household's private spaces of home and courtyard, women's lives and labor were simply less visible to outsiders, even to the men in their own community. Our research instead focuses on the ways that the labor of women and girls is related to footbinding. We ask whether footbinding and its demise can be better understood by taking the changing patterns of girls' and women's labor into account.

The political instability of the late imperial and early Republican periods (1850–1949) produced radical disruptions of daily life across wide swaths of China's territory.[2] Disasters, natural and human made, and chronic warfare punctuated the lives of most ordinary people. Migrations and invasions, international and civil wars, and monstrous upwellings of popular dissent in the form of millenarian movements reshuffled people, possessions, and cosmologies. Among the major nineteenth-century political conflicts were the Opium Wars, the Taiping Rebellion, and numerous, lengthy regional rebellions. The early twentieth century was marked by the 1911 revolution, the Anti-Japanese War, and the Chinese Civil War that brought the Communists to power.[3] Ecological disasters compounded political and military conflicts. North China in particular experienced extended droughts, famines, and floods that killed many millions.[4] These dreadful events caused masses of villagers to uproot themselves and flee natural disasters, banditry, and warfare. Despite the rebellions and displacements, the dissolution of the empire, and rise of competing regional warlords, women continued to bind their daughters' feet. Footbinding survived an enormous amount of disruption up to the third and fourth decades of the twentieth century.

While many writers have portrayed footbinding as an urban, elite practice in pursuit of beauty, historians of footbinding find that reliable records concerning its distribution and spread are scarce. The historian Dorothy Ko notes that from the twelfth century on, when Chinese male scholars mentioned footbinding, they did so in the form of fragmentary "jottings," generally "origin discourses" in which "myths, hearsay, and history share the same page." Up to the nineteenth century, footbinding was "taboo in such official genres as public history, local gazetteers, and didactic texts" (Ko 2005, 2, 110–111). Separating trustworthy eyewitness evidence from armchair speculation is extremely difficult. As a result, contemporary historians glean little specific information on the timing, regions, or social and economic associations of the practice. Nonetheless, Chinese scholars who mentioned it, whether admiringly or critically, contributed to the belief that early on it was an elite practice, particularly in cities and towns where elites tended to live and where agricultural work was uncommon. Elite Chinese women writers sometimes referred to their own bound feet, but female farmers, servants, and artisans were rarely authors. Nineteenth-century Western observers' comments on footbinding were largely based on sightings of women working outdoors, usually commoners. The prevalence of footbinding among urban women, elite or commoner, who labored invisibly indoors is difficult to assess.[5] The written record has produced few observations linked to specific places and socioeconomic situations. Despite impressions and generalizations made in good faith, the limited information currently available does not allow any confident assertions about the prevalence of footbinding among elites or lower classes in China's cities and towns before the end of the nineteenth century.

Our study differs in important respects from most writing about footbinding. First, we write about villagers. We interviewed thousands of rural women in disparate parts of China, from the northeast to southwest. Second, we focus on footbinding in relation to the work performed by girls in the household economies in which they were raised and trained. Third, we provide firsthand, large-scale comparative information on the decline of footbinding, offering new insights into the forces that propelled families to reject a practice that had spread and stubbornly persisted for centuries. This project has taken us across China to uncover the scope of this painful and enduring custom that so constrained the bodies of young Chinese girls. Our intention is to correct current beliefs about footbinding and to reconnect girls' and women's lives to their livelihoods.

We interpret Chinese women's homebound labor and footbinding by exploring their links to China's changing rural economy. By examining how footbinding coexisted with heavy demands for female labor and how footbinding came to an end, we contribute to larger discussions concerning China's economic transition. Our findings challenge current renderings of China's economic history by reassessing assumptions about the productivity of labor in the preindustrial era. They also dispute current explanations for the end of footbinding that fail to consider the economic underpinnings of this change.

THE EMERGENCE AND SPREAD OF FOOTBINDING

To examine the economic aspects of footbinding, we would ideally sketch out its origins, identifying the regions and populations in which it first took hold. Yet footbinding originated and expanded within China's empire along paths we cannot trace with confidence. Its original purpose and the patterns of its spread are essentially unknown, although most scholars believe it started among the elite in the heartland of the Song dynasty and diffused to other regions over the centuries.[6] According to Dorothy Ko, drawing on the mid-Qing historian Zhao Yi, the eighteenth century was the zenith for footbinding, which was "practiced all over the empire," although less in the four "peripheral" southern provinces (2005, 131).[7] Zhao Yi's example of footbound women within the walls of Suzhou City and barefoot women working in the field beyond the city gates points to the variability within a region (131). Contrary to the impression Zhao Yi gives, footbinding was not then confined to urban or elite populations. Evidence from nineteenth- and twentieth-century eyewitness and literary sources shows footbinding occurring across China in rural as well as urban areas, among the wealthy and the poor. China scholars have proposed that it spread to lower classes and rural communities by emulation of elite practices, much as any elite fashion may be copied by other classes. In actuality, there is no reliable documentary evidence about when or where footbinding began or how it spread. Agreeing that downward diffusion is possible, even likely, other motivations for its spread must also be considered.

In an effort to determine the geographic extent of footbinding, sociologist Christena Turner uses anecdotal evidence from travel writings and diaries to create a map or "rough sketch" of the distribution of footbinding in China's old core (1997, 447). Although many large rural areas lacked sufficient information to generalize reliably, she suggests that footbinding was present but uncommon south of the Yangzi River and common between the Yangzi and the Yellow Rivers. It was nearly universal north of the Yellow River except for Hebei and, perhaps counterintuitively, in the southwestern province of Yunnan. Yet within a region where footbinding was common, pockets of nonbinding existed, and vice versa. Juxtaposing the footbinding regions with China's agricultural regions, Turner shows that footbinding tapers off in environments where cold winters, deserts, or mountains were less hospitable to settled agriculture (448).[8] The environments where footbinding flourished and persisted were predominantly the agricultural zones occupied by the Han, the dominant ethnic group within China. Ke Jisheng, a Taiwan connoisseur of footbinding, has also concluded that the custom followed sinification or, more precisely, the spread of Han culture (Ke 2003, 15–16).

The Han account for 92 percent of the population. Through the expansion of imperial control, Han Chinese colonized and intermarried with other groups on the frontiers, with the result that in many regions Han and local cultural practices are blended. Despite considerable variation among the customs across a vast territory with differing regional ecologies, languages, and subcultures, Han Chinese culture is strongly associated with an economy that Burton Pasternak and Janet Salaff describe as based on "dense settlement and intensive farming" by smallholders who provided taxes and tribute to support an imperial state and its administrative cities and towns (1993, 3–4). Consolidated by a long sequence of Chinese states, the Han found "an adaptation that worked most of the time"—one Pasternak and Salaff label the "Chinese Way" (3–4). Historically, the limits to the spread of the Chinese Way were found in the environments of China's frontier regions where settled, intensive agriculture did not flourish and where neither the state taxation/distribution system nor a dense local marketing system was an important shaper of local custom and identity (Gates 1996, 72–75).

Footbinding was adopted by some of China's ethnic minorities, especially those living in close proximity to the Han and with similar lifestyles. In general, footbinding came late or not at all to border peoples, and its meaning has become entangled with larger questions of *hanhua* (sinicization). In ethnically mixed regions women in culturally distinctive groups (e.g., Hui, Tujia, Bai, Yi, and the typically nonbinding Hakka[9]) practiced footbinding in varying degrees.[10] Consequently, footbinding was not always a definitive ethnic marker. An important exception to this generalization occurred among the Manchu people who founded the Qing dynasty (1644–1911). These northern rulers firmly identified footbinding as a Han ethnic custom. Although Qing rulers failed to squelch it in the population at large (Ko 1998; Elliott 2001; Shepherd 2012), they were mostly successful in prohibiting it among the Manchu.[11] Suggesting that Han Chinese maintained bound feet as an identity marker to distinguish themselves from other ethnic groups may have explanatory value in some contexts other than Manchu, but it would have been a rather severe measure compared to other methods of marking identity, such as different clothing, hairstyles, or body tattoos.[12] The argument does not explain why footbinding was widely adopted and maintained in central regions where Han people had little contact with non-Han.[13] Sorting out how a recent or distant non-Han past may have affected rates of footbinding is beyond the scope of this study.[14] We can say with confidence that the environments where footbinding flourished and persisted were predominantly the agricultural zones and cities occupied by the Han.

The distribution of footbinding also changed with time. Toward the end of the nineteenth century, Christian missionaries and Chinese reformers initiated anti-footbinding media campaigns, peppering their speeches and articles with claims that it was painful, ugly, unhealthy, unproductive, sexually indulgent, humiliating, and crippling and it weakened the nation (Broadwin 1997, 422, 426–427, 435). They founded anti-footbinding societies such as the Natural Feet Society (Tianzu hui) in Shanghai in 1895, the Chinese-run Anti-footbinding Society (Bu chanzu hui) in Guangzhou in 1896, and the Letting Out Feet Society (Fangzuhui) in Hangzhou in 1903. Anti-footbinders argued that footbound women were lazy and unproductive; they spent their time "either sitting and eating all day or embroidering or doing some other utterly useless thing. Even for those who work they are weak. . . . Five of them cannot match the work of one woman without bound feet" (Broadwin 1997, 426, quoting Zhang Zhidong, a late Qing reformer). Notably, these critics did not consider whether footbound women performed gainful economic activity with their skilled hands. Most anti-footbinding societies were short-lived and encountered stiff resistance, as suggested by a quotation from an American missionary's letter of the 1910s: "I've talked myself hoarse to these freakish, foggish, old-time, undentable, unbendable . . . women, & I simply can't cajole them into the unbinding of their pesky daughters' blooming bound feet" (418, citing Graham 1994, 39). Nonetheless, Julie Broadwin gives them credit: "Collectively they brought down the custom very rapidly in China's urban centers" (420).

According to Turner, "That the demise of footbinding followed a class hierarchy in its early phases is no surprise given the importance of foreign pressure and concern on the part of China's most powerful and wealthy men to create a modern nation" (1997, 465). Noting that footbinding was declining in urban areas along the coast, reformers were eager to claim credit (456–457). "By the 1910s the binding of a daughter's feet virtually disappeared among the urban upper-classes" (Broadwin 1997, 419). Ironically, as Turner noted, "observers not commenting on anti-footbinding efforts usually report that elites bind more universally and to greater extremes than did the lower classes. On the other hand, those commenting on anti-footbinding efforts usually mention that its greatest success was with the elites and that footbinding was still practiced by the lower classes and in rural areas" (1997, 456–457).

FARMING, HANDCRAFTS, AND COMMERCIALIZATION

The rough correlation between footbinding and settled agriculture provides a first step in our efforts to understand women's labor in preindustrial China. The division of labor in households is another. The imperial maxim "men plow, women weave" persisted for centuries and endorsed the interdependence of household grain and cloth production in the preindustrial economy.[15] However, this maxim speaks only to gender, not to age and life-course changes in capability and work. The phrase all-too-neatly hides the contribution to household economy of young girls (Gates 2015, 128–130). Small boys also worked for their families but, until fairly well grown, could not plow or do the many other heavy jobs that fell to men. Nor was the plowman's task dependent on prior work best done by boys. Weavers depended absolutely on girl spinners, who, as the epigraph to this chapter illustrates, could begin their task very early in life. It is precisely this difference between typical girls' and boys' lives that prompted us to reach beyond the proverbial gender division of labor to pursue the significance of phases in the female life course as critical to understanding footbinding.

Considering the economic significance of women's textile labor, we propose that in localities where girls' handcraft production of commodities (goods produced for exchange, not only for family use) was common, footbinding rates would be higher and more persistent than in places where girls made few or no such commercial goods. We believe that family decisions to bind little girls' feet were heavily influenced by their need for particular types of girls' labor and the expectation that girls might be put to useful handwork at an early age. The harsh constraint of footbinding limited a little girl's ability to escape work and taught her that she could no longer run and play. She learned to endure a painful restriction inflicted by her own mother. The pain and difficulty of walking on newly bound feet left her little choice but to remain seated obediently at home or within the courtyard. Girls were commonly told that bound feet would help them achieve marriage and possibly a better life in the future. This promising outcome was combined with the admonition that, if a girl was not bound, no family would want her as a bride for their son.[16] These explanations enlisted the daughter's own willpower in a long-term investment toward married life, preparing her through painful bodily reconstruction for a future life as a daughter-in-law and wife. In the meantime, working for her family put her mind, hands, and upper body to use and trained her in skills valuable to her current as well as future household. When she resisted, harsh punishments ensued.

By this logic, when the market for handcrafted goods produced by domestic female labor contracted after the influx of industrial goods, the incentive to bind feet should also have declined. We interpret the expected effect of economic change as follows: When income from women's hand labor declined or women ceased to produce handcrafts for the market, we expect families to gradually stop initiating bindings on daughters as they reached binding age. When sedentary handcrafts continued to sustain family income and help meet economic obligations, we expect footbinding to persist. A decline in need for girls' labor that would discourage parents from footbinding would not be just a seasonal or one-year drop in prices; it would have to be seen as a trend, a more permanent shift away from the kinds of skilled handwork that footbound girls and women had long performed. Moreover, the rapidity of the shift would depend on whether or not women could find alternative forms of handwork that could be practiced at home and contribute to the family. Where alternative income-producing handcrafts were not available, daughters might still be taught to produce traditional womanly handcrafts for family use if the raw materials were readily available. However, such production would not give parents a very strong incentive to impose footbinding on their daughters.

MOTHERS' REASONS FOR FOOTBINDING

Mothers were the direct agents in binding their daughters' feet. Francesca Bray notes, "One can imagine that many decisions about children were extremely painful. We may often be shocked by what the Chinese expected of a good mother, or a good parent" (1997, 336). As we show in the following chapters, it was most often a girl's mother who bound her feet unless the mother died before a child reached binding age. Sometimes, particularly when a girl was married young, her mother-in-law or future mother-in-law demanded binding or even bound the girl's feet herself. In the early twentieth century some fathers opposed the practice, while mothers continued to insist it was necessary. Why did mothers bind their daughters' feet? We consider two kinds of explanations: reasons the mothers gave their daughters to persuade them to endure it and reasons that were not discussed.

We cannot always expect people to reveal uncomfortable motives or to deeply probe the rationale for an accepted social practice. We suggest that footbinding harmed the daughter to help the mother and, by extension, the future mother-in-law. If mothers explained that they bound their daughters' feet to make them concentrate on handwork, however, it might poison mother-daughter relations. Especially where farm plots were small and crop yields could feed the family for only part of the year, footbinding ensured that young daughters sat still and worked at various forms of tedious hand labor. It may also have helped mothers retain the daughters for indoor work against pressure from fathers and brothers to have them help in the fields.

We believe that mothers and older women bound the feet of the girls in their households to assert control over their labor and then shifted the blame for its bodily costs from the mother they lived with to an unknown mother-in-law who would treat them badly if they did not have bound feet and could not work with their hands.[17] Many women we interviewed repeated what their mothers had told them: it was necessary to bind their feet so they could marry into a good family or marry at all. Implicit was the threat that if they had big feet, they might have to marry into a poor family that would make them work in the fields or do heavy labor, possibly as a hired hand. Such work was associated with lack of assets and family insecurity as well as the pain, exhaustion, risk of pregnancy complications, and rapid aging that heavy farm labor caused. The threat of such hardship was doubtless a convincing argument and helped quell young girls' howls of pain and efforts to loosen the bindings.

Although daughters of wealthy or elite families might have less reason to believe their parents would contract marriage into a poor family, they did worry about their acceptance, respect, and treatment by their future husband and mother-in-law. Bound feet and embroidered dowry goods signaled to a mother-in-law that her son's bride had learned useful hand skills. Daughters in elite families were not exempt from training in hand skills, often dismissively labeled by modern writers as "pastimes" without any information regarding the economic worth of these endeavors.

As we examine competing arguments and present our data on footbinding practices in rural areas across a dozen different provinces, we must keep in mind the problems faced by Chinese mothers. Until the late 1960s, Chinese women bore many more children than they do today. Demographers have debated how much control women had over their fertility and have come to conflicting conclusions about the role of Malthusian checks on population. The estimated average number of live births per rural woman was six.[18] Whether the size of Chinese families was "natural fertility" (by which demographers mean childbearing uncontrolled by effective methods of contraception),[19] the result of abstinence, or the consequence of infanticide, women carried a heavy burden of pregnancies, infants, and small children who distracted them and increased their workload.

The bodily demands on women in addition to long hours of work included dealing with frequent pregnancies, risking miscarriage, hemorrhage, uterine prolapse, and incontinence; the physical demands of breast feeding each child for one to three years; and the physical costs of menstruation.[20] Mothers with young children, like modern working women, faced serious conflicts between work and child care even when the work took place within the household. Feeding and monitoring children seriously interrupted highly skilled jobs such as weaving. Ancient technologies made exhausting the tasks of fetching water, pushing a stone grain mill, preserving foods, cooking over finicky fires, growing garden vegetables, raising courtyard animals, washing clothes at a stream or in a basin, and making quilts, clothing, and shoes for home use. Many women also spun thread to sell or to weave into cloth for summer and winter clothing, bedding, and cloth shoes; they also handcrafted products (ropes, mats, straw hats, sacks, nets) to be sold or exchanged for cash, grain, oil, or raw materials such as cotton. Bray quotes a description of peasant women's labor in homespun cloth as follows: "Whole peasant families assemble, young and old: the mother-in-law leads her sons' wives, the mother supervises her daughters; when the wicker lantern is lit and the starlight and moonlight come slanting down, still the clack-clack of the spindle wheels comes from the house" (1997, 219).[21]

How does a mother convince a seven-year-old girl to work at a boring, sedentary task for many hours each day? In Chinese villages, parents did not treat young children as rational beings or partners in negotiation (Eastman 1988, 22; M. Wolf 1970, 1972, 70–71; A. Wolf 1964). Children were expected to do what their parents told them to do, and if they did not, they were often beaten. Children, however, could be rebellious and run away. A mother who needed to complete her work at the loom did not have time to chase down her daughters to make them spin. Unless a woman stopped her weaving to spin thread, she depended on what others could spin. Chinese mothers were motivated to bind their young daughters' feet because it was an efficient way to make them stay seated and work with their hands. Acquiescing to whatever a parent required, even the torture of footbinding, earned a girl a reputation for obedience that enhanced her worth as a future daughter-in-law.

The temptation to constrain children to keep them still would not have been unusual for busy mothers (Pruitt 1945; Bossen 2002; Gates 1989). Limiting children's activity via footbinding may not seem so extreme in light of more recent Chinese efforts to restrain children. In the 1990s, when parents abandoned tens of thousands of babies, mostly girls, understaffed, underfunded Chinese orphanages were filled to overflowing ("Foreign Parents" 2003).[22] Orphanage workers were overwhelmed with too many babies and too few diapers. In some orphanages, babies and toddlers were bound for long hours to their potty chairs with plastic packaging tape. For the woman cleaning up after forty to eighty babies, this early toilet training saved time and mess. Economist Steven Levitt (2011) described his adopted daughter as having "scars on her legs from where she had been tied down, I think to keep her on the potty."[23] Binding girls' feet may reflect similar motives. If mothers had an overwhelming workload, binding the child's feet, though painful, sped the child's training.

FOOTBINDING AND GIRLS' LABOR IN CHINA STUDIES

Our interest stands at the crossroads of two significant areas in China studies: women's and gender studies and economic history. Within women's and gender studies we focus on the changes in rural women's lives that led to the decline and abandonment of footbinding. Current beliefs about footbinding are highly misleading, particularly in regard to rural women.[24] This portion of China's population was largely illiterate and the least able to record their own experiences. Hence, much of the writing about footbinding has been fueled by literary imagination rather than by direct evidence from footbound women. At the same time, most writing about women's work, from the artistry of elite women to the farmwork and cottage industries of rural women and the poor, says very little about footbinding.

In regard to economic history we examine the way rural household economies encountered industrial competition from the late nineteenth through the early twentieth century. Studies of rural productivity especially have neglected or fudged questions about the labor of girls. The impact of footbinding is one such omission. When painful newly bound feet confined young girls to the house, the work they performed behind closed doors was easy to overlook. Expectations about a young daughter's work for her family were shaped by many background factors, some universal to Chinese life, others very local. However, we can show that confining the girl-child's feet to small shoes and training her hands to make salable products such as yarn, cloth, nets, and mats were common and economically significant in preindustrial China. Our study thus augments current theories about China's industrialization and about ways to change entrenched and debilitating practices affecting girls and women.

Recent contributions to China's history of women have been largely shaped by the prevailing image of pre-Communist Chinese women as oppressed, passive victims. Whether the oppressive forces were defined as patriarchy, feudalism, capitalism, or all three, the prevailing view in the West and among Chinese reformers was that in traditional patriarchal society Chinese women had miserable lives.[25] In the 1990s, attention to new sources written by or about women sought to rescue women from the image of unremitting victimhood by drawing on new literary sources to show that women found ways to express "agency" despite their many social and economic constraints. Some women were writers, poets, or artists; some traveled or supported their families through their own efforts; some took pride in their small bound feet and the artful production of shoes for them. This new branch of women's history shows that women had personalities and personal histories. They developed spheres of activity that, despite the constraints of propriety, might be called a "women's culture."

Elite Bias

Historians who study Chinese women have been largely limited to literary sources. The shortcoming of analyzing literary representations is precisely that they do not "represent" most women in China. They derive from a very thin layer of society in which privileged women were likely to be freed from the drudgery of household labor by female servants and staff. Elite women writers devoted themselves to "higher" literary and artistic pursuits that brought more respect, sometimes grudging, from men. Their discourses on beauty, joy, sadness, and sacrifice for family are testaments to human spirit yet are far removed from the economic difficulties faced by most women.[26] Nonetheless, even elite and educated women's writings are replete with references to their work at embroidery, weaving, and needlework that formed part of the gift economy, especially at marriages and other life-cycle events.[27] Perhaps it was considered déclassé to mention the monetary value of their textile labors.

Many China scholars have assumed that footbinding symbolized the seclusion and leisure of China's elite women and have interpreted its spread as emulation by the poorer classes competing among themselves for status (Ebrey 1993, 37–43, 266; Ko 1994,147–151; Mann 1997). Given the wide distribution of binding we found among poor rural populations, it seems unlikely that elite emulation was the main consideration.[28] From our labor-oriented perspective, footbinding might be imagined instead to have spread as a disciplinary practice among harried mothers struggling to meet their quotas of spun yarn or woven cloth for imperial taxes. Assumptions about family wealth or status aspirations as a motive for binding feet seem to be inspired by the Western "small-foot-Cinderella-marries-a-prince" fable rather than by the daily lives of peasant women who married peasant men in arranged marriages and did manual work throughout their lives.[29] It is unlikely that small feet were bound to please a future groom; young men generally accepted what their parents arranged for them. The intrusion of a sexy bride into the mother-son relationship could hardly have pleased the older woman (Gates 2008, 2015). A more pressing concern may have been to please or reassure the mother-in-law, who would govern the work of young women who married into her household and made up her labor team. The critical senior women of the groom's family and neighbor-kin would want to ensure that the new girl knew her place and her work. Their own status and dreams of possible leisure depended on it.

Historians working with sources by and about the elite sometimes broach the topic of women's and girls' labor in relation to footbinding, but labor quickly drops from sight. For example, Ko writes, "The materials needed for footbinding were themselves products of 'womanly work' (*nügong*)—weaving, sewing, needlework. By using them, a girl would soon be taught to master these skills" (1994, 149). Ko does not pursue this link any further, missing the opportunity to discuss the training, labor, products, and economic value of young girls. This deficiency undoubtedly stems from the literature itself, perhaps because elite women preferred (and still prefer) to write about loftier subjects than work for economic reward.

Links Between Handcrafts and Footbinding

The few scholars of Chinese women's lives who have linked footbinding with women's work have always done so with extreme caution. Historian Susan Mann asks, "Did the spread of home handicraft industries in the eighteenth century—a phenomenon consciously associated with female cloistering—encourage farm families to bind their daughters' feet?" but concludes, simply, that "we have no evidence to prove this" (1997, 167). Citing a nineteenth-century travel report (by Fortune [1847] 1972) that some women did heavy work even with bound feet, Mann repeats that "it cannot be proved that the expansion of women's home handicrafts accompanied the spread of footbinding down the status hierarchy" (168). This observation of the incongruity of footbound women doing heavy work ignores the fact that as economic conditions fluctuated, whether in the prices for cotton textiles or in families' need for outdoor field labor, women could be called on to perform heavier tasks even with irreversibly bound feet. But just as the footbound woman was disadvantaged during the peak seasons of outdoor labor, women whose hands became tough and calloused through fieldwork might find their hands less adept at the fine motor skills required for efficient textile work. Like many others, Mann *assumes* footbinding trickled *down* to commoners, in emulation of elite seclusion and in aid of respectability. Although Mann recognizes that binding may have been convenient for families where women spun and wove, she does not consider the possibility of a reverse causal order: that expanding commercial production of handcrafted textiles might have spurred the spread of footbinding. Limited to literary sources, Mann cautiously proposes some kind of link: "We can plausibly assume that the desirability of footbinding and the spread of women's home handicrafts in peasant households were systematically related" (168). In contrast, we maintain that intensified demand for daughters' labor in textiles and other salable handcrafts gave mothers a strong incentive to bind their feet.

Historian Francesca Bray pays considerable attention to women's handwork (*nügong*), particularly to women's importance in textile production from the Song to the Qing dynasties (roughly nine centuries).[30] Noting that labor started in girlhood, Bray writes,

> When a little girl was taught to spin and weave, she was not only acquiring the skills to produce useful goods—through them she was learning diligence,

orderliness, and respect for labor, the dignity of a wife and the responsibility of a subject of the state. In the cloth that she produced, her skills were transmuted into worth and virtue. This is one reason why so many social reformers and moralists of the late imperial period were anxious to revive women's weaving skills. (1997, 242)

In the late imperial period taxes changed from demands for cloth to demands for currency, which took away the explicitly recognized value women's work previously had enjoyed (Bray 1997, 214, 257). As commerce developed, men specialized in skilled weaving with complex looms in urban workshops, while rural women's textile work in their homes became less visible and its value less recognized (257–260). Here, Bray evidently means that scholars began to ignore women's work. Bray points to a deskilling and "gradual loss of control" in a sphere once recognized as women's domain and in which vast numbers of women continued to labor (239).[31] Bray also focuses on a change in the way women's textile work was perceived by a very narrow segment of the Chinese population.

> Philip Huang remarks that the commercialization of the Chinese peasant economy in the late imperial period increased the involvement of all family members in production, including women. This may seem to contradict the arguments I have been making about marginalization, but it does not, for Huang is talking about the facts of economic activity, and I am interested in its representations. (257)

It is useful to distinguish between the "facts of economic activity" and the "representations" by literate authorities. Literary sources have fostered the tendency among China scholars to disregard the intensity of textile work routinely performed by rural women and to overlook the possibility of a relationship between handwork and footbinding. Indeed, Bray's (1997) impressive contribution to the study of women and technology barely mentions footbinding.

Footbinding was common among the landless as well as landowners (Brown et al. 2012; Gates 2015, chap. 4). Its presence or absence was not a simple reflection of family wealth. Despite widespread interest in footbinding, few studies have seriously attempted to analyze its spatial and class variations or what kinds of work women could and did perform when their feet were bound.[32] Our evidence from China's interior explicitly addresses the relationship between female labor and footbinding. By examining the distribution of rural hand labor and footbinding across a broad sweep of China's immense territory and population, we find that a new picture of gender relations in China's preindustrial economy emerges. This picture includes the work of little girls, which involved costly, painful body deformation at an early age.

FEMALE TEXTILE LABOR IN CHINA'S ECONOMIC HISTORY

In contrast to historians focusing on women and gender, economic historians debating China's place in world history have recognized the importance of the textile industry in Chinese economic transformation. These historians have paid more attention to the organization of women's textile labor and less attention to bound feet.

Long before foreign factory-made goods began to appear in village markets in the nineteenth century, China's impressive indigenous transport network was important to the small-farm economy. The late imperial marketing network that grew from largely separate regional entities to the beginning of a truly national one has been examined by G. William Skinner (1964, 1965).[33] Skinner posited and refined a model of China's preindustrial regional networks and central places that operated on market principles. The importance of girls' and women's labor in producing commodities varied regionally, influenced not just by environment and location but also by the shifting demand for specific commodities both locally and far outside their standard marketing area. Goods also flowed in nonmarket channels: conscripted armies had to be fed and clothed, bureaucrats and the imperial household supported. Until the early twentieth century, China was predominantly an agrarian empire with a vast rural population knit together by a market system and imperial taxation. The peasant woman's textile labor was an important part of both.

The global expansion of trade driven by the Industrial Revolution was closely intertwined with women's labor in rural and urban China. In the nineteenth and twentieth centuries, new modes of transportation, such as steamships and railroads, began to reach regional and local markets. As these new technologies reduced shipping costs overseas, along navigable rivers, and overland on railroads, merchants rapidly set out to reach new markets. Industrial goods appeared in Chinese market towns and villages many decades before entrepreneurs established factories in nearby areas. By the early twentieth century, China had begun to establish its own industries. Coastal cities industrialized first, creating new jobs that undercut traditional livelihoods. For the tiny proportion of girls who took factory jobs in the coastal cities like Shanghai, Tianjin, or Canton (Guangzhou), this marked an economic and social revolution of great import (Hershatter 1986; Honig 1986; Stockard 1989).

Small-scale domestic producers found their local markets increasingly supplied with new machine-made cotton yarn from Manchester, Bombay, or Yokohama. As industrial textiles penetrated urban and rural markets, they changed Chinese girls' lives, lowering the value of their spinning and weaving labor and rendering their skills obsolete. Chinese families everywhere had to reconsider how their daughters should work and how to respond to the dwindling value of female labor. The interaction between women's home-based handcrafts and competing industrial products is an important part of our analysis.

Examining China's development in the late imperial period, economic historians agree on the predominance and persistence of small-scale family farms and cottage industries, particularly textiles. Recently, two camps have disputed the degree of intensification and involution (increased production through increased labor inputs rather than through increased productivity) that characterized China's development in that period.[34] Claims about the changing productivity of rural women's labor in textile production have taken on a central importance. But the estimates of women's and girls' labor and productivity in this debate are problematic; little information comes directly from women or from systematic observation of them. We are convinced that our ethnographic study of the demise of footbinding and associated textile arts will ground the debate in a much closer approximation to reality.

Efforts to calculate the productivity of female handcraft labor in the heyday of China's preindustrial textile trade have been particularly controversial. Central to the exceedingly complex claims and counterclaims, calculations and recalculations, and back-and-forth exchanges are the works of Philip Huang (1985, 1990, 2002, 2003, 2011) and Kenneth Pomeranz (2000, 2002, 2003a, 2003b, 2005). We concentrate on these two central figures who have taken opposing positions regarding women's work.

Huang links the expanding commercial production of silk and cotton cloth to labor intensification in the North China Plain from the sixteenth century to the 1930s and in the Yangzi delta (also known as Jiangnan) over a period of six centuries (1985, 1990). In Jiangnan, nonfood crops such as silk and cotton required more labor to grow and process into cloth than did growing grain. Through the late imperial period the economy of Jiangnan, China's most developed region, grew in absolute terms but "at the cost of declining returns per workday" because it required more family labor (Huang 1990, 77). Commercialization helped peasants maintain subsistence levels as the population grew, but family production of labor-intensive crops on ever-smaller farms, combined with work on labor-intensive cotton and silk handcrafts, meant that productivity remained low. Huang insists that peasant women, children, and the elderly were working more without obvious improvements in their standard of living.[35]

In an effort to estimate earnings from women's cotton handcrafts, Huang notes the work of children. Although he uses the gender-neutral terms "children" and "elderly," there is little doubt that in regard to textile work these terms almost always refer to girls and older women.[36] He calculated that a cotton spinner's daily earnings were less than one *jin* (1.1 pounds) of husked rice per day and "only enough to sustain a pre-teen child. It is not surprising that spinning was done almost entirely by children and the elderly, seldom even by adult women. An adult male laborer could not, or would not, work for that kind of return" (1990, 84–86).[37] Huang explains that because there was no demand for women and children's work outside the home, families could increase their commercial output by adding more labor to this low-return work (2002, 513). Even if it had been possible to hire women and children by "overcoming cultural and logistical constraints," enterprises that hired laborers could not compete with cheap family labor (Huang 1990, 85).[38] The extremely low labor costs of home production by women and children are seen as one reason China was late to adopt labor-saving productive technologies (Huang 2002, 516).[39]

Pomeranz (2002) counters Huang's calculations by claiming that women's earnings from textile work were exceedingly high.[40] Seizing on a misplaced decimal point in Huang's analysis (1990), Pomeranz claims that women's weaving (not spinning) incomes were over ten times larger than Huang's calculations (and thus very high).[41] Huang admits the error but maintains his point of view. He counters that his arguments are not based on "price data" but on what he calls "conditions of production' such as farm size, labor input, crop mixes, animal and fertilizer use, techniques, yields, and the like" (2003, 157). In turn, Huang criticizes Pomeranz for miscalculating the relative amounts of time that it took a woman to spin and weave a bolt of cloth,[42] and he decides to "refrain from attempting any exact quantitative estimate, given the many imponderables involved (especially the composition of household labor)" (157). One of those imponderables is girls' labor.

The notorious bottleneck in preindustrial cloth production was spinning yarn. The shortage of yarn clearly affected the amount of time a weaver could devote to her cloth making.

> Concentrating on weaving generally required having kin who would provide yarn. . . . The market did not generally replace the family (or extended family) in organizing this part of the division of labor. Thus, it is somewhat misleading to think of the value of "a woman's labor" outside her particular family structure: teenage girls or an elderly mother-in-law, for instance, might be economically quite valuable insofar as they could supply yarn for their thirty-five-year-old mother/daughter-in-law to weave, but they became liabilities overnight if the family suddenly lost its weaver. (Pomeranz 2005, 247)

Despite the acknowledgment that not all the girls and women working within a household were as productive as the skilled weaver, Pomeranz does not raise questions about age hierarchies and power relations among women within the household. Focused on market prices that assume a somewhat free market in commodities, including labor, he ignores the almost serflike quality of labor by junior females.

Pomeranz is also puzzled about the monetary returns from spinning and, like Huang, doubts claims "that spinning was a consistently viable way for adult women to support themselves" (2005, 248).[43] But at the same time Pomeranz wonders why little yarn was sold:

> Since a woman could make much more money by freeing herself from spinning and doing more weaving, even if she had to pay well above the apparent going rate for yarn, why didn't the price of yarn rise and the amount sold increase? Surely some families—such as those of widowers with teenage daughters—could produce yarn but not weave it and needed extra income. Explaining why such households did not sell yarn is particularly difficult. (248)

Pomeranz's puzzlement is a result of his tendency to posit a more or less well-established market economy. Although he allows for the embeddedness of female labor in the nonmarket setting of the household, as he attempts to value that labor, he accords the market much greater strength than does Philip Huang's version.

Pomeranz suggests that shifting women into textile production was associated with economic growth and rising incomes rather than, as Huang argues, increased labor just to maintain basic subsistence. For Pomeranz, women's domestic textile work was "partly a matter of more families feeling that they could 'afford' to keep women sequestered." He concludes that "economic growth was associated with better lives, greater skill levels, a sharper gender division of labor and a mixed picture for sequestration (more women working away from home, but also more working indoors instead of in the fields, and probably more footbinding)" (2005, 242). This is one of the few references to footbinding, but like the women's and gender-studies historians discussed in the preceding section, footbinding is not explored in regard to the way girls worked to produce the *tubu* (handmade cotton cloth) worn by most Chinese. Overall, Pomeranz's view of the value of weaving women's labor is expressed as follows:

> [Women] who engaged proportionately in all parts of the process of turning raw cotton into cloth would earn about enough per day to provide rice for a bit over four adult-person days. To the extent that an adult woman could delegate spinning, cleaning, and other tasks to others and concentrate on weaving, she could make much more, since weaving paid over thirty times as much as those tasks. (2005, 247)[44]

Although based on mid-eighteenth-century conditions in Jiangnan, this view illustrates his more general position that the productivity of women weavers was high.

In calculating women's labor productivity, Pomeranz also mentions the labor of children or, more specifically, girls. He charges that Huang "indiscriminately compared adult male, female, and child labor as if we would expect them to be equally productive" (2003a, 167). To correct what he assumes is a flaw, Pomeranz decides to "discount" the labor of girls "by roughly two-thirds" (2002, 548).[45] Pomeranz clearly lacks data on the ages at which girls began to spin full time and their output per day or when women become "elderly" and ceased to be capable spinners or weavers.[46] Skill at light labor such as spinning or weaving does not necessarily decline with age as, for example, does the strength needed for plowing or digging irrigation channels.[47] Our data show that girls could spin at an early age, and for the ordinary homespun cotton yarn used to make *tubu*,[48] it is doubtful that there was much difference in spinning output by age. We do not accept the assumption that any of the labor-days of children or older women should be discounted.

Pomeranz claims to be conservative in granting women productivity equal to that of men but then radically discounts the larger part (two-thirds) of the textile labor that he attributes to children (and the elderly). By considering how much more a woman could weave if she bound her daughter's feet and induced her to start spinning at age seven, we realize that most calculations regarding textile work probably grossly underestimate how much work was done by young girls or even older women.[49] This is a prime example of how numerical calculations often appear authoritative even when they are not based on any actual evidence.

Both Pomeranz and Li Bozhong believe that the market economy worked efficiently so that women rationally moved out of farming, where they were allegedly not very productive, and into textiles, where they could earn more. Li (1998) asks whether this change was induced by population growth and shrinking farm size. He claims that with half as much land a couple could produce more if the woman worked full time in textiles while her husband worked full time in the fields. To Li this division of labor and spreading of risk mean increased productivity. Based on estimated labor-days for women and estimated prices for handwoven bolts of cloth, he determines that weaving women could earn more than male agricultural laborers (on an annual basis). Li comes down on the side of women being drawn out of the fields rather than driven out by the scarcity of land. But when we consider the labor of seven- and eight-year-old girls whose feet have been bent and broken, sitting daily to produce their quota of yarn, can we really be so sure that women and girls were "drawn" and not "driven" to the spinning wheel and loom?

Lacking even very limited information about how rural women worked within their households, we must be skeptical when economic historians make assumptions and calculate how many days a woman could work per year and how much she could produce. These assumptions and estimates often ignore matters essential to the successful reproduction of households. They do not consider whether women's workdays were piled on top of other obligations, whether there was coercion involved, or whether women were able to sell the cloth themselves and control the income. They simply assume an "average" rural woman could work—uninterrupted by pregnancy, childbirth, breast feeding, or child care—at the calculated rate for the calculated return.

Huang has criticized Pomeranz for his imaginative estimates of women's access to improved technology, "capped off . . . with the implausible construction of a supposedly typical woman spinner-weaver who earned several times the wage of a male agricultural worker" (2002, 521). In contrast to Huang, Pomeranz and others make highly specific assumptions about female labor capabilities and pile estimate on estimate to make grand claims about economic progress in imperial China. Indeed, we believe that the uncertainties about female labor render most of the detailed estimates wishful thinking. Without reliable data on how many women and girls were working or the types of looms and spinning wheels they used, these claims fall into speculative exercises that are highly skewed by the assumptions made.

The heuristic exercises and debates of economic historians have helped formulate questions about female roles in China's development, but answers to these questions will benefit greatly from considering the kinds of evidence we present. Until factory-spun yarn reached China's markets, the higher productivity of the mother or mother-in-law who wove rested on the intensification of girls' labor facilitated by footbinding.

Whether approaching history from gender or economic perspectives, China historians have largely missed the connections between female hand labor and footbinding.[50] Our research aims to restore female labor to China's economic history through a closer examination of the work women and girls did when they had bound feet—not only in the inner quarters of wealthy palaces but in the millions of rural mud-walled courtyards. These women were responsible for clothing their families and producing cloth that was collected and traded across the empire and beyond. Enlisting the young hands of their daughters and daughters-in-law enabled them to produce not only textiles but a myriad of other hand products such as quilts, mats, sacks, straw hats, cloth shoes, and straw sandals that are no longer sought or valued by contemporary consumers accustomed to industrial goods.[51] Our intent is to allow the last generations of footbound women to describe their work as young girls. We use this precious "living archive" before it inevitably passes away. In Chapter 2, we explain where we traveled to meet these women, why we chose these locales, and how we interacted with them.

CHAPTER TWO

Seeking Answers
Research Methods and Fieldwork

In Chapter 1, we explain why mothers had an incentive to bind their daughters' feet and restrict their mobility; they needed the hand labor of young daughters to increase family income. Here, we discuss how we gathered data to test the power of this explanation. Such data were not easy to acquire. Further, this spatially extensive project confronted the enormous variability of China's rural society from region to region. We introduce the methodology and complexity of a research undertaking that—because of this variability—is unfortunately rare in social analysis.

Our primary hypothesis is that in China's preindustrial era, female commercial handcraft labor was closely related to high frequencies of footbinding. We asked: Did rural mothers in fact bind their young daughters' feet to obtain their assistance in household hand labor? Was footbinding useful as a way to make girls persevere at hand labor when household handcrafts were important to family income? If so, it should have persisted longer in areas where female commercial handcrafts survived. In areas where industrial goods began to compete successfully with handmade goods, we would expect footbinding to be abandoned earlier. When girls' hand labor ceased to provide significant returns, the incentive to bind their feet would erode. While political and cultural changes, including education, have long been credited with ending the practice of footbinding, we maintain that economic pressures played a decisive role that has been almost entirely ignored.

A grand plan is one thing; execution is another. This chapter outlines and explains how we conducted research. While earlier local research supported our hypothesis in particular settings, we wanted to see how well it worked on a larger scale. Skeptics, accustomed to the idea that footbinding was primarily driven by the quest for beauty and a husband, could easily dismiss our results as local exceptionalism, not generalizable throughout China. Accordingly, we set out to test our hypothesis that girls' hand labor and footbinding were linked by interviewing elderly women in a large sample of provinces and locations that stretched across the country.

Exploring these hypotheses required gathering data from rural women themselves. Rural women, largely illiterate, are the part of China's population that has been most neglected and rendered mute by many generations of China scholars. When rural women were included at all, with rare exceptions others spoke for them. Western missionaries, Chinese reformers, and revolutionaries saw rural women as oppressed in multiple ways but rarely examined the details of their laboring lives. Stereotypes took hold and remained difficult to dislodge. It was commonplace to portray women as passive victims of a patriarchal system. Yet when China scholars collected oral histories from women of the Republican period, a different, much more dynamic picture emerged (Pruitt 1945; Hershatter 2011; Gao Xiaoxian 2006). Our study builds on those of many contemporary scholars who have tried to rescue women's working lives from invisibility and obscurity. Chinese women were *there*, they reproduced, and many experienced domination—but they did much more than that.

After China's opening to foreigners in the 1980s, many visitors were surprised to see that, in rural areas and sometimes in cities, elderly women with bound feet still survived and went about their business. In 1988, at a major Chengdu temple festival attended by crowds of footbound worshippers, Hill Gates recognized a rapidly disappearing opportunity to learn more about this debilitating custom from living women. In 1991 and 1992 she launched a large-scale project with the help of the Sichuan branch of the All China Women's Federation; women then in their eighties and seventies had been born in the 1910s and 1920s. Her questionnaire pioneered a method of interviewing that revealed the kinds of work that village elders had performed as girls and young women and documented their experience of footbinding in the early twentieth century. This research established a quantitative base of almost five thousand women demonstrating that the majority of ordinary village girls had been bound and had done many kinds of handwork that actively contributed to their households' economies (Gates 2015).[1]

Laurel Bossen, conducting anthropological field research in a village in Yunnan Province, used Gates's questionnaire to compare the demise of footbinding in her focal village with that in other research sites. She found important differences in the kinds of work women did and the tenacity of footbinding in Yunnan, where girls in some villages were still being bound in the 1950s (Bossen 2002, 2008).

Both of us were disheartened that elderly women who had experienced footbinding were rapidly dying off. We both knew from our travels around China that footbinding among rural women had been extremely wide-spread, but beyond Sichuan and Yunnan we had little formal data to docu-ment and analyze the relationship of footbinding to female work.

Concerned that the opportunity to interview women from the prerevo-lutionary era was passing, we decided to conduct rapid surveys of elderly village women in other provinces. As the twenty-first century opened, we undertook a large, multi-province sample of interviews with surviving women;[2] our goal was to delve deeper into the relationship between rural women's labor and footbinding and extend our research beyond the sites we had already examined. We aimed to collect quantitative data to document both the varied forms of female hand labor and the extent of footbinding in rural areas across China's broad territory. Between 2006 and 2010, we conducted surveys in northern and southwestern provinces. We searched for rural women aged sixty and older, making particular efforts to find women in their seventies and eighties. Being footbound was not a criterion. Only by including the bound and the unbound would our sample reveal the ratios of those statuses in different cohorts of women. While surveys form a crucial component of this research, as anthropologists we also emphasized combining open-ended interviews, discussions, and direct observations of local conditions with the surveys of hundreds of elderly women. In addition we drew on a wide range of other local sources, from elderly male traders to local historians and colleagues.

SELECTION OF RESEARCH SITES

By the late nineteenth century, Shanghai was a rapidly growing port city already heavily transformed by modern industry, transportation, and trade. Up and down the Middle and Lower Yangzi River and its tributaries, junks and steamboat traffic carrying foreign and domestic commerce converged on Shanghai. Other coastal regions of southeastern and northeastern China also developed early hubs of foreign trade, much of it passing through Hong Kong, Guangzhou, Fuzhou, Qingdao, and Tianjin.[3] By the early Republican period, the Yangzi delta was already deeply influenced by the influx of foreign and domestically produced industrial textiles and other products. As we contemplated our project at the turn of the twenty-first century, we realized that these coastal areas and their major river systems so richly studied by earlier generations of China scholars offered few opportunities to find surviving rural women who had engaged in domestic handcrafts, particularly spinning and weaving, in an earlier era of footbinding.

Bypassing this busy but exceptional core, we chose sixteen village sites in interior regions beyond China's Middle and Lower Yangzi River basins and the southeastern and southern coasts. There, we had a reasonable chance of finding surviving elderly women who grew up when footbinding was still widely practiced and when most consumer goods were handmade. Our sites, shown in Map 2.1, extend across eight northern, northwestern, and southwestern provinces where nineteenth-century transportation was limited and arduous.[4]

North China is dominated by the densely populated, broad, flat North China Plain with its silted Yellow River and yellow soil. Farther inland, the northwestern region's loess plateau borders the plain as well as the Taihang Mountains, Inner Mongolia, and the Gobi Desert. We analyze the North China Plain and Northwest China in Chapters 3 and 4 and present findings from Southwest China, a warmer, mountainous area bordering Tibet and Southeast Asia, in Chapter 5. For comparative purposes we also draw on Gates's earlier surveys in populous Sichuan Province,[5] which has a large fertile basin at the upper reaches of the Yangzi. Together these provinces cover a vast expanse of China's territory and population. Until the early twentieth century they were largely outside China's industrial heartland, with rural markets not yet inundated by industrially produced textiles and other goods. We interviewed women who grew up when these interior regions suddenly confronted the rising force of industrial competition. In this broad expanse of China's hinterland, rural women's labor and footbinding practices were largely uncharted.

In choosing village sites in each province, we sought diversity, hoping to capture the circumstances that generated varied work for girls and women. Difference was not hard to find. Locality itself had nurtured considerable

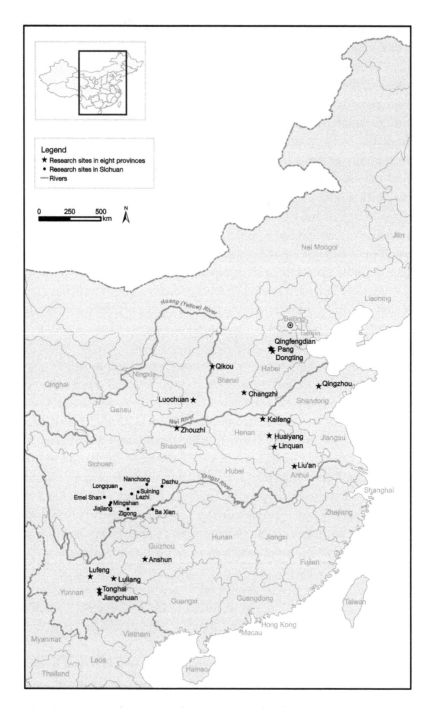

Map 2.1. Research sites in eight provinces and Sichuan

difference among villages, reflecting centuries of environmental and historical accidents. Some communities are densely populated and concentrated into tight clusters, while others are dispersed settlements. They have developed differently according to local resources and specialties, access to urban markets, and diverse political overlords. We describe these variables in our discussions of individual sites. Our selection of villages was also influenced by the social networks that enabled us to conduct fieldwork. Those networks differed for each province. That is, we did not choose villages principally because they had histories of handwork or footbinding but because they were places where we could mobilize the help of Chinese associates who would vouch for us to the local officials and facilitate our access.

We also drew on earlier economic, sociological, ethnographic, and historical studies when they could complement our research. Local sources for the Republican period or late nineteenth century sometimes offered valuable background material regarding the pace of change, although they rarely had much to say about women. Secondary sources about local changes in the economy, technology, transport, and trade in the late nineteenth and early twentieth centuries contributed important background information and guided our choice of some sites. Such sources useful for the 1920s and 1930s include massive surveys of rural China by John L. Buck ([1937] 1964), rural studies by Li Jinghan (1933) and Sidney Gamble (1954) in Hebei, and studies by Fei Hsiao-tung and Chang Chih-I (1948) in Yunnan. We drew as well on local gazetteers for supplementary information and on a growing body of fine historical studies by Chinese scholars.

Transportation convenience was also a factor in site selection; it deterred us from exploring extremely remote locations. Fortunately, transportation in China has improved so enormously in recent years that some villages once quite off the beaten path are now easily reached by good roads and even becoming semi-urban. Our village selection, while not random, allowed us to examine the labor-footbinding relation in a wide variety of settings and seems unlikely to have produced a systematic bias.

VILLAGE SURVEYS AND INTERVIEWS

Survey research and fieldwork in China nearly always provoke official concern over China's image. Our topic, girls' and women's labor and footbinding in the prerevolutionary period, was in many ways noncontroversial;

any blemishes we might uncover would not reflect badly on the Communist government, which assumed power in 1949. National pride, however, is easily offended by outsiders who so often denigrate China and its culture. For that reason, even the long-abolished custom of footbinding can be a sensitive topic, no matter what the finding. With nervous officials, we walked on eggshells, emphasizing our interest in the work contributions of girls and women to family and society.

Our questionnaires and interviews were designed to collect information on labor that was not politically or culturally sensitive and that could be easily supplied by the women we interviewed. From this information, systematically collected from a large number of women, we seek general patterns in the activities of girls and young, unmarried women and young wives. Using the survey approach Gates developed for Sichuan in the 1990s, we adapted and expanded the questionnaires to include more information on kinswomen and on local economic conditions.[6] We then refined and pretested our questions. The standard questionnaire asked relatively objective questions about each woman's background, marriage, and the various forms of work performed at the natal and marital homes. For women who were capable of describing their early lives, a second questionnaire asked about village conditions and their senior kinswomen (mothers and grandmothers). A third questionnaire guided interviews with elderly village men who had engaged in trade in the Republican period. At first, we feared that our standard questionnaires were too long because they often entrained lengthy conversations with women about their childhood experiences and labor. We became more efficient as we learned about women's lives in each setting. In sites we visited later, we reorganized and expanded our questionnaire to include brief questions about footbinding in the mothers' and grandmothers' generations for each woman, extending the historical record of footbinding back in time.

Our detailed questionnaires took an hour or more to complete. They included each woman's personal history: birth year, birth place, age at marriage, and marital residence.[7] We divided questions regarding labor into pre- and post-marriage sections: as an unmarried girl; from when she began to work under her mother's supervision (roughly ages five to sixteen); and as a new bride, typically in her husband's house under the supervision of her mother-in-law. A woman born in 1925 and married in 1940, for example, would describe work that she did at her natal home in the 1930s. This method of bracketing the time and place of a girl's labor is extremely helpful when memories are not tied to a calendar. As a rule, elderly rural women without formal education have relatively few temporal anchors with which to fix events, but they all know their birth animal in the Chinese zodiac, which can be used to calculate their birth year.[8] In addition, they know their age at marriage, at the death of a parent when they were children, and the birth years (using zodiac animals) and ages of their own children. Most women could also specify their own age when footbinding began.[9]

For our surveys, we necessarily worked in teams, Chinese style. We were aided by scores of interested local colleagues, graduate students, village research assistants, and Chinese friends.[10] Because most of our interviews were with women, most members of each interview team were women. It was extremely helpful to include local assistants as guides and interpreters because the elderly women usually had no formal education and often spoke dialects that were not merely provincial but often very localized. Such dialects are difficult to understand and to learn to speak for students or urban residents from other parts of the province. Despite an abundance of goodwill, talent, and energy, our assistants' abilities as interviewers were uneven.[11] Some were better at recording verbatim explanations. They not only verified unusual terms in the local dialect but also asked about local units of measure from the past that young people no longer learn or use. Interviewers with rural backgrounds found it easier than students raised in the city to relate to village women. These individual differences influenced the depth of qualitative information from interviews. At each site, we climbed a learning curve, struggling to learn about the local economy and how to ask about different kinds of work. Younger assistants from the village as well as university students were often surprised and touched by elderly women's narratives of childhood labor and hardships when parents died young or the family faced famine.[12] Anthropologists recognize the importance of interviewing and listening carefully to people to understand their interpretations of their culture and behavior. At the same time, the person who describes or explains local practices and beliefs does not necessarily understand the larger context or wish to defend or explain the complex underlying motives of behavior. This is particularly true for sensitive topics such as sexuality and gender or income and wealth.

Using a questionnaire to initiate most interviews, we also leapt at opportunities to expand discussions on relevant topics. Our target was to speak with one hundred elderly women per site for two separate regions in each province.[13] We then obtained information from villagers and officials on all the elderly women residents and tried to get a distribution of women from different age cohorts. If the initial village or village group did not have enough surviving elderly women, we continued to the closest neighboring village, interviewing *all* surviving elderly women capable of hearing clearly and speaking.

Our village samples ended up slightly smaller or larger for various reasons. Conditions at each site posed unique challenges. In some areas, homes were quite dispersed, making it hard to locate many women of advanced age. Sometimes we walked for an hour or more along dirt or mud paths only to find that our proposed subject was off visiting relatives in the city. Sometimes a village housed too few old women, pushing us to travel to nearby administrative units to fulfill our quota. In peri-urban areas, older villages were being submerged in urban development, and former village residents no longer lived in discrete neighborhoods. Because of the difficulties of finding enough women in the oldest age groups, we increased our sample size in some of our final field trips. Bossen expanded small samples from her earlier, mid-1990s sites to reach the target of one hundred. Basic details on the village samples are presented later in the chapter in Tables 2.1 and 2.2.

We sought a distribution of elderly women born in different time periods to pinpoint the moment when footbinding began to decline. Initially, we had thought that footbinding had died out in most regions for women born in the 1930s, but we discovered that even women born in the 1940s sometimes had their feet bound, although they were usually "let out" in the 1950s. At each site, we aimed to survey a reasonable number of women born in each decade from the 1920s or earlier through 1950. The largest cohorts in each site were generally women born in the 1930s. It was difficult to find enough women born in the 1920s or earlier who were healthy enough to be interviewed. If a woman felt weak, was hard of hearing, or responded with confusion, we gently ended the interview. Most women answered our questions with ease and clarity.

Doubtless, our surveys reflect some selection bias toward survivors. By age sixty or seventy, many women of our interviewees' birth cohorts had already died from varied causes, influencing our samples. Elderly women with bound feet seem no more likely that those whose feet had never been bound to have survived the catastrophic Great Leap Forward famine of 1958–1961, when tens of millions died.[14] Indeed, at that time, if footbinding was more prevalent among the elite, they were more likely targets for class struggle during the Maoist years, whether classified and punished as "landlords" in the 1950s or as counterrevolutionaries in the Cultural Revolution. Yet poor village women and widows who supported themselves from handcraft textile work also had bound feet. The footbound were less capable of shifting to the heavy physical work demanded of women during the collective period, particularly during the Great Leap Forward famine. They probably suffered higher mortality.[15] If so, it would mean that fewer women with very deformed feet survived into the twenty-first century. The fact that our study encountered such high proportions of surviving women in widely dispersed rural areas who, as children, had experienced temporary or permanent footbinding indicates that we have not exaggerated the extent of the practice.

Elderly villagers were often pleased (and surprised) to have foreign visitors and were very gracious. Our foreignness was enormously entertaining to them, and their curiosity about us was sometimes as great as ours about them. We rarely encountered resistance from our subjects to discussing their work experience. Rather, they responded with pride as they described it, rummaging through old, wooden trunks to show us their surviving handwork: handmade clothing, stacks of beautiful quilts, handwoven bedsheets, embroidery, cloth shoes, and other crafts. When we showed interest in their tools, some women went to discarded piles of lumber in storage rooms or the corner of the courtyard and, pulling out dusty pieces of wood, showed how they once were assembled into working looms. They spoke with personal expertise about their handmade textiles, once so essential to villagers, so vital to their dignity, and so full of memories. These pieces of cloth held the histories of their handwork, their marriage and family bonds, their hardships, and their celebrations. As anthropologists we especially value the firsthand quantitative and qualitative data we obtained through village surveys and our in-depth interviews. We feel both fortunate and grateful that these elderly villagers were willing to take the time to speak with us and to convey their rich, local knowledge.

Natal Villages

The elderly women at each site almost all married into the village where we interviewed them. For a married woman there is an important difference between natal village (where she grew up) and marital village (where her husband grew up). Chinese marriages predominantly follow the pattern of patrilocal postmarital residence and patrilineal property rights: women move to their husband's family home at marriage, and men stay put.[16] That most wives come from other villages puts women at a serious disadvantage in terms of property rights, local kin support, and gender solidarity. As we pursued our interest in the labor that village women learned and performed as young girls before marriage, we asked about the location and conditions in their natal villages.

We also asked almost identical questions of each interviewee about conditions in and the work she did in her marital village in the years immediately after marriage. These postmarital data are not the focus in the present study because the natal family almost always conducted the footbinding, but they do provide us with reasonably complete knowledge about the work of young, newlywed women in the villages that became our sites. Marital homes were generally within walking distance of natal homes, within a ten- to fifteen-kilometer radius. The village origins of women we interviewed were thus not strictly delimited in space. Men's families usually did not search far away for brides.[17] As a result, women's multiple accounts of child labor at natal homes richly and fully describe conditions surrounding the interview village. The diverse origins of the wives mean that the economic activities they learned as children could be more varied than those of their marital village, depending on the extent to which particular villages in a region developed specialties such as weaving baskets, growing and spinning cotton, or making straw shoes. In each setting, mothers taught their daughters certain skills, and mothers-in-law prized daughters-in-law who came well trained in local handcrafts.

Women's Daily Work

Modern social science partners economics with demography to study male and female employment patterns; formal and informal employment; and proportions of adult men, women, and dependents and to anticipate the burdens of supporting children and the aged. But these categories are often not the uniform, comparable units they are assumed to be. Our effort to peer inside the household worksite and ask about the work girls performed reveals a labor force considerably larger than one estimated by defining the working age as sixteen or older. As Bray observed,

The significance of women's work has been masked by the enduring importance of household production in China—an indisputable fact, invariably re-
marked upon, but one which has not been sufficiently probed. The household
can remain the basic unit of production over centuries, yet within this "unit"
the composition, the division of labour, the control of skills and the claims to
managerial or earning power may change drastically. (2013, 130)

Taking account of girls' labor casts a new light on the early development of
the textile industry and industriousness in China.

When we asked rural women about their work, they often responded
that they did housework (*jiawu*), a conventionally vague, modest answer
that conceals more than it reveals. They sometimes told of *gan huor*, doing
agricultural work. We soon learned that *gongzuo* (labor) was a phrase at-
tached to manual work in official employment—a term from Communist
times and not relevant to their own early lives. Women raised to work in
village households before the spread of formal education were not schooled
in listing their skills or calculating the market value of their labor.[18] They
had no experience of explaining to outsiders the many kinds of tasks they
performed since most women around them learned and performed similar tasks. Under Communism, with its emphasis on workers in factories
and peasants in fields, rural women's heavy domestic labor obligations did
not bring the recognition, prestige, and benefits of farm or factory labor,
let alone government jobs in cities. Women who did not work in fields or
factories were led to think that the many different types of labor they did
at home—weaving cloth; making quilts, jackets, and shoes; or processing
food for family and for sale—did not count as work.

At the very least, women underestimated the worth of their own work.
Gender ideology muddles women's knowledge of their own worth and the
worth of their products because it is both "only housework" yet is something that they know is essential to family subsistence. We met women who
were proud of their well-made cloth, or healthy pigs, or a well-tended field.
But this is not the message society offered them.

Women responded positively to our explanations that their own past
experience of labor and their knowledge of different types of work were
significant and should not be forgotten. Concretely, we asked each woman
about many different kinds of crops, products, and types of labor that she
contributed. From previous research we were already familiar with northern and southern farming systems and many variants. However, at each site

local women taught us about their training, work lives, and local customs; they explained local terms and technologies and helped us improve our ways of asking about female labor. We asked if they had earned incomes through sale (*mai*), wages (*gongzi*), or exchange (*huan*) from different activities. We also asked about their family's ownership of tools such as weaving looms and the ages at which they learned to spin and weave. It initially took effort for them to recall and explain the everyday activities of their childhoods more than half a century earlier; yet they gradually opened up with explanations once they were prompted with specific and systematic questions. As Jacob Eyferth observed,

> One of the great advantages of discussing the concrete details of daily work . . . is that it allowed me to treat my informants as skilled actors competent in all areas of their daily lives. Much social science research defines its field of inquiry in ways that makes the outside expert appear more knowledgeable than the local informant. Shifting the emphasis to a field in which the informants were highly skilled allowed me to partially redress that imbalance. (2009, 19)

Our experience was similar; we were very impressed by the many women who patiently taught us about the past as they lived it.

Footbinding

Footbinding has been treated as a sensitive topic by China scholars, perhaps due to the publicity given to Howard Levy's (1966) study asserting that it was primarily an erotic practice catering to male foot fetishism (discussed in Gates 2015). Some officials may not have thought it a proper topic for research or had been offended by journalists seeking sensation. However, we did not encounter such attitudes among the elderly women themselves who had been bound or whose family members were bound. They understood that footbinding was painful and debilitating, but they also understood that it was once a mark of status. Elderly women did not hesitate to answer questions about whether they had been bound or not and frequently volunteered to show us their bound feet, their handmade shoes, and then even their naked feet to show us their actual shape. If the bound foot was truly an erotic object, we believe they would have responded to foreign strangers with the same modesty with which they treated sexual matters.

Our survey asked women if they had ever been bound, at what age, and if so, whether they had been unbound or remained bound. We also asked various questions surrounding the whole procedure, including their own explanations for the practice and its disappearance. We encouraged them to tell us about the experience, and it was not uncommon for them to remove their shoes and socks or bindings to reveal a wide range of deformations, from broken arches or toes bent under the ball of the foot, to toes broken, twisted, and bent at odd angles—far from conformity to ideal. Not all footbinders were skilled, leaving some women with feet that were quite mangled and misshapen. Differences in binding ranged from the stereotypical "three-inch golden lotus" to the half-sloped *ban po jiao*, also called *huanggua jiao* (cucumber foot) in some regions. They were all included as bound feet. It is nearly impossible to classify the many variations with any consistency, and measurements of feet once bound and later let out would be meaningless. We found it useful to divide women into those who were "ever bound," even if for a short while, and those who were "never bound." Because these women lived through a period of transition, many had their feet bound and later let out or bound and unbound more than once, responding to changing demands. The degree of permanent damage to their feet was highly variable depending on how tightly they had been bound initially and how long they experienced binding. Even a single experience of binding, however, left vivid memories of its painfulness.

In addition to recording the footbinding experience of each woman interviewed, we asked questions about the footbinding of their immediate kinswomen—grandmothers (maternal and paternal), mothers, and sisters—that allowed us to estimate the prevalence of footbinding in earlier periods and the timing of its decline. The senior generations of kinswomen whose bound feet were witnessed by and obvious to their juniors (now elderly women) were mainly those whose feet were rigorously and permanently bound and encased in special shoes; the women we interviewed might not have known of footbinding among elders who had been allowed to unbind before their foot shape had changed. By estimating senior generations to have been born twenty-five years earlier for mothers and fifty years earlier for grandmothers, we extended our sample to include women born in the nineteenth century. Elder and younger sisters were estimated to be either five years older or younger than the woman interviewed.

We warn that we do not expect to reduce girls' labor or footbinding to a simple formula in which one or two variables explain every individual case. Yet by close scrutiny of their dynamics we can address the grand-scale and local-level changes in female handcraft labor that contributed to the termination of this painful practice. We evaluate this argument for the whole arc of our sites in Chapter 6. Chapter by chapter, we present glimpses of specific rural Chinese communities across a vast territory held together by state and market forces.

SITE IDENTIFICATION

The site names used throughout this study are in North China, Northwest China, and Southwest China (Tables 2.1 and 2.2). To preserve the confidentiality of people interviewed but still give readers an idea of the locations, we use administrative names of larger units (cities or counties) to designate villages located within their administrative borders. Ding County is an exception; the published literature makes it important to distinguish particu-

TABLE 2.1
Research sites in North, Northwest, and Southwest China

Province	County/city: site	Location	Rough distance from village sites to provincial capitals and cities
NORTH CHINA			
Hebei	Ding County: Qingfengdian	NCP	400 km SW of Beijing
	Ding County: Pang	NCP	400 km SW of Beijing
Shandong	Qingzhou	M	95 km E of Jinan
Henan	Kaifeng	NCP	20 km S of Kaifeng City; 80 km E of Zhengzhou
	Huaiyang	M	27 km E of Zhoukou; 210 km S of Zhengzhou
Anhui	Linquan	NCP	60 km W of Fuyang; 275 km NW of Hefei
	Liu'an	NCP	30 km NW of Liu'an City; 70 km W of Hefei
NORTHWEST CHINA			
Shanxi	Changzhi	NCP	SE Shanxi, 15 km N of Changzhi City; 250 km S of Taiyuan
	Lin County: Qikou	M	NW Shanxi, Yellow River border with Shaanxi, 230 km W of Taiyuan
Shaanxi	Zhouzhi	NCP	90 km W of Xi'an
	Luochuan	M	200 km N of Xi'an; 100 km S of Yan'an
SOUTHWEST CHINA			
Yunnan	Lufeng	V	100 km W of Kunming
	Luliang	V	100 km E of Kunming
	Tonghai	V	100 km S of Kunming
	Jiangchuan	V	80 km SE of Kunming
Guizhou	Anshun	V	90 km SW of Guiyang; 420 km E of Kunming

NOTE: NCP = North China Plain, M = margins of North China Plain, V = valleys in the Southwest

TABLE 2.2
Village survey characteristics

Province	County/city: site	Survey years	N	Birth year range	No schooling (%)	Illiteracy rate (%)
NORTH CHINA						
Hebei	Ding County: Qingfengdian	2008	138	1916–1944	62	64
	Ding County: Pang	2008	63	1921–1939	76	78
Shandong	Qingzhou	2007	137	1918–1940	85	82
Henan	Kaifeng	2007	100	1916–1951	77	75
	Huaiyang	2007	100	1913–1950	82	84
Anhui	Linquan	2007	100	1916–1950	88	85
	Liu'an	2007	101	1915–1950	91	87
NORTHWEST CHINA						
Shaanxi	Zhouzhi	2007	102	1914–1956	74	68
	Luochuan	2007	104	1915–1950	75	76
Shanxi	Changzhi	2006	97	1914–1948	70	75
	Lin	2006	99	1916–1943	73	77
SOUTHWEST CHINA						
Yunnan	Lufeng A	1996	56	1915–1939	79	81
	Lufeng B	2010	50	1921–1950	65	67
	Luliang A*	1996	49	1913–1941	100	100
	Luliang B	2010	114	1918–1950	94	95
	Jiangchuan	2010	212	1918–1950	85	84
	Tonghai	2008, 2010	121	1912–1950	83	75
Guizhou	Anshun	2009	200	1916–1941	89	91

NOTE: These interviews include 1,943 women. Lufeng samples were two distinct samples from the same village at different times. Luliang samples were two different villages in the same county at different times.

*Because of differences in the 1996 interview format, Luliang A is not used in calculations involving handwork.

lar areas within the county. When sites belong to a rural district under city rather than county jurisdiction, we use the city name (e.g., Kaifeng, Liu'an, Changzhi, Qingzhou) to identify the general location within the province. We also use the township name (e.g., Qikou) or a village pseudonym to highlight particular historical or local situations.

The eleven northern sites can be loosely grouped as seven on the North China Plain's flat alluvial land: Qingfengdian and Pang (Hebei), Kaifeng (Henan), Linquan and Liu'an (Anhui), Zhouzhi (Shaanxi), and Changzhi (Shanxi). The remaining four—Huaiyang (Henan), Qingzhou (Shandong), Lin (Shanxi), and Luochuan (Shaanxi)—are more peripheral to the plain. They enjoy the advantages and disadvantages either of more varied environments, with lakes or low mountains, or a loess plateau that is colder, more rugged, and drier than the plain proper. The five southwestern sites are located in different valleys of the two mountainous provinces, Yunnan and Guizhou. The aggregated twenty sites from Gates's Sichuan survey are drawn from ten different counties or cities, largely circumscribed by the high mountains that delimit the Sichuan Basin.

CHAPTER THREE

North China Plain

This chapter and Chapter 4 provide evidence for the persistence of footbind-ing and describe girls' and women's work for each of the eleven northern and northwestern sites located on or near the North China Plain. For these sites, we explore local conditions for women's handcrafts and the changes in technology and transport that affected their ability to contribute to fam-ily income when they were young girls. Footbinding was pervasive in rural farming populations, not just imposed on girls raised in elite families, and aligned in persuasive ways with patterns of young female labor. Document-ing the prevalence and disappearance of footbinding in each location allows us to consider whether, case by case, the patterns we observe are consistent with our hypothesis.

Our surveys in northern villages (Figure 3.1) give the rates of footbind-ing among women we interviewed and their senior kinswomen, showing that footbinding constrained girlhood and womanhood across this region. (Data tables for figures are in Appendix A.) The rate of rural footbinding declined slowly from the 1860s to 1920s but remained stubbornly above 80 percent, beginning its steep decline only in the early twentieth century.

What kinds of economic and political conditions historically shaped the lives of the women in this region? The North China Plain is the vast, deforested drainage basin of the Yellow River, where early rulers built their first states. Millennia of heavy use degraded its resources, while human action—governance, warfare, construction—maintained in it a persistent social unity. In Hebei, Shandong, Henan, and Anhui Provinces we surveyed seven sites,[1] learning from elderly inhabitants what kind of home their cor-ner of the region had once made. Listed and mapped in Chapter 2, the sites

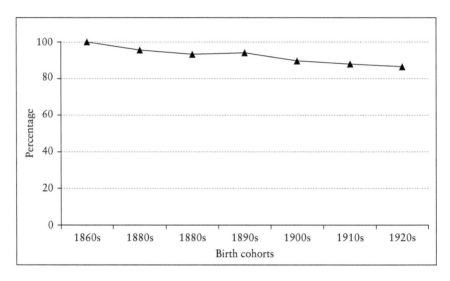

Figure 3.1. Percentage footbound in northern and northwestern provinces by birth cohort, 1860s–1920s

NOTE: Based on ascending generations in six provinces (Anhui, Hebei, Henan, Shaanxi, Shandong, and Shanxi) and eleven sites. N = 2,045. The ascending generations are the grandmothers (interviewee's father's and mother's mother, husband's father's and mother's mother), as well as the interviewee's mother and mother-in-law if these were people she actually knew.

encompass varied terrain with different local environments, histories of modern transport, and experiences of post-1911 political and economic change. For each site, we briefly summarize gendered work and changes in local patterns of footbinding. The timing of the abandonment of footbinding throughout the area accords well with our hypothesis that it was driven by loss of handcraft work for girls.

The relationships between people in North China's low, flat core and its varied highlands were anciently those of mutual interdependence: the plains provided grains and fibers; the hills and heights, minerals and animal and forest products. Transport by pack animals, human carriage, and simple vehicles was costly. Within the plain itself, similar environments encouraged similar production and thus discouraged elaborate market relations. This natural setting supported China's earliest empires. In the Tang dynasty (618–905) when goods from the Yangzi River and farther south became the mainstay of Chinese prosperity, rulers cut the Grand Canal across the plain. Eventually, it ran 1,794 kilometers from Beijing in the north to Hangzhou in the south, assuring reliable commercial and tributary transport over its length (Van Slyke 1988). The political significance of the north increased when China's last dynasty, the ethnically Manchu Qing government, made Beijing its capital. Apart from the generally east-west Yellow River and the north-south Grand Canal, the vast region we examine here was transected by long-distance imperial roads built to transport tax commodities and soldiers. Cargoes such as export silk and tea, whose price could cover expensive carriage, traveled along them as well. Built across alluvium and loess soils, these and lesser roads were quickly nibbled into gullies by mule, camel, and wheelbarrow and drowned in mud by rain and snow. The cheap goods rural folk produced, even when surplus to their needs, did not travel far unless requisitioned as tribute or taxation.

The mid-sixteenth-century arrival of cotton as a commercial crop in Hebei and Shandong was a major development in North China. It spread throughout the plain to supply the great cotton handcraft industries of the lower Yangzi region. It became a more lucrative crop than food grains, doubling or tripling the value of the yield per unit of land (P. Huang 1985, 108).[2] Initially, few northerners made cotton cloth for export beyond their own area because the dry climate caused the threads to snap (111–114, 118).[3] By the mid-eighteenth century, Ding City in Hebei, one of our research sites, was a regional center of cotton wholesaling, a place where speculators and merchants lined up to buy cotton for Southeast China producers. In return, cotton cloth was shipped back north. Gradually, northerners learned how to dig damp cellars for cotton spinning and began to weave their own cotton cloth for export. Families who grew no cotton bought it from peddlers (Li Jinghan 1933, 704, table 296). By the late nineteenth century, much home weaving used homespun yarn wefts on warps of factory yarn (695), increasingly supplied by rail from China's coastal mills. Despite commercialization, throughout the preindustrial development of northern cotton, growing it remained largely based in the household, with family rather than hired labor central to the immense trade.[4] Philip Huang rightly warned, however, that "cash-cropping could cut both ways" (1985, 108). It brought higher returns than grain but less certainty that the family would have noodles in the bowl.

Nature made life hard in North China. Its artery, the Yellow River, shifted course by hundreds of kilometers in 1897, a natural catastrophe for millions. The growth of the population from an estimated seven million in

1393 to fifty million by 1800 and seventy-six to eighty million in the two provinces of Hebei and Shandong by the 1930s overwhelmed people, land, and water (P. Huang 1985, 324). Illness in new and old forms was driven by poverty and social turbulence. Historians agree that the late nineteenth and early twentieth centuries were grim for most Chinese. The variability of rainfall and frequency of natural disaster in North China were unparalleled in densely populated world regions (L. Li 2007, 24). Regional environmental decline was "historically unprecedented" (307). Repeated and horrific famines such as those of 1876–1879, 1888–1889, and the 1920s eroded human bonds. The north as a whole suffered between nine and thirteen million deaths (284). By 1930, life expectancy for rural Chinese newborns hovered around twenty-five years.[5]

From the 1850s through the 1940s, villagers endured nearly continuous wars and rebellions from the Taiping and Nian Rebellions that killed tens of millions to the Boxer Rebellion and county insurgencies. Twentieth-century politics, like those of previous centuries, found ideal battlegrounds on the North China Plain. At the end of the empire, warlords fought each other; and after unification efforts in 1927, they fought or made brittle peace with the Nationalist Party (the Guomindang, GMD). In 1935, after the Long March brought Mao's Communists to a safe redoubt in northern Shaanxi, Communist soldiers and locally recruited guerrilla partisans spread through the highlands of Shanxi, Hebei, and Shandong, deposing or co-opting the last of the local warlords. Communist troops joined in loose alliance with GMD forces to oppose the 1937 Japanese invasion, remaining behind Japanese lines when the GMD was forced south. Communist and Nationalist guerrilla forces sustained resistance across large areas of the North China Plain and its highlands throughout the war.[6] Neither peace nor stable government existed in the region from the late nineteenth century until the national reunification under the Communists in 1949.

In the late nineteenth century, foreign commercial interests and Chinese rulers' efforts to defend themselves against such pressures initiated an era of transport transformation. By 1895, an "iron road" 1,213 kilometers long connected Beijing with the huge, inland port of Hankou on the Yangzi. This Jinghan line, extending straight south across the North China Plain, began to affect the region's old economy, greatly facilitating the export of grain and raw cotton along its course. By 1907 a flurry of east-west railroad construction had produced further segments of the Longhai line, facilitating trade across the plain. Finally, by 1934, it stretched from Xi'an to the coast, connecting the four quadrants of the plain as never before. Coal drew railroad building early to Shanxi, with a line following the former trade route from Russia straight south to the Yellow River at Cizhou. Other lines connected Beijing with Tianjin and Shanhaiguan on the coast and with coal fields and the northeast and linked the capital of Shandong, Jinan, to the port of Qingdao, enriching one of our sites, Qingzhou. Tianjin, western Shandong, and Nanjing had a linking line by 1912. The steamship revolution that was transforming transport and commerce in China's central and southern sections had little value on the plain, where low-draft local craft dealt best with shallow and seasonal waterways. Although the level topography aided road building, lack of construction materials hampered it. Roads usable by bus and automobile began to be built in the 1910s and 1920s; the paucity of motor roads is shown by the praise given to the Shanxi warlord Yan Xishan in 1923 for building more than 215 kilometers of roads (Franck 1923, 259–260) in a province of about ten million people (Lu and Teng 2006).

Generally speaking, changes stimulated by global commerce and Western industry radiated and percolated from the eastern coast to China's western interior, but they followed no simple linear path. Hebei is our starting point for the north because it surrounds China's imperial capital city, Beijing, a magnet for northern and foreign commerce that had a strong political influence on surrounding areas and thus early rail lines. South of Hebei, the western half of Shandong is an integral part of the North China Plain. Our Shandong site, Qingzhou, is peripheral to the plain, mountainous but influenced early by railroad. To the south, neighboring Henan and Anhui are completely inland provinces with diverse local economies. In Northwest China we examine two sites each from Shanxi and Shaanxi, two of which lie on the western reaches of the plain and two on the Loess Plateau. Because of their various distances from the Pacific coast trade and industry, these interior sites present distinctive economic and political backgrounds and different paths toward modern economic integration.

Our sites illustrate the reach of footbinding and the kinds of rural economies and labor conditions in which it once flourished. They should not be seen as "typical," representative of their province as a whole or even their counties. China's village realities are too diverse for that. Rather, each site can be seen as a natural experiment, an opportunity to see how particular configurations of local conditions shaped the division of labor, the commercial context, and the reliance on young girls' labor in the household economy. Each site also allows us to estimate when and how modern changes in transport, technology, and trade filtered or flooded into its region. Whether our interviews come from a single village or a set of villages in a single county, we are interested in local features and evidence of temporal change. The period we examine, largely from 1900 to 1940, encompasses momentous economic change punctuated by social and political disruptions, military occupation, and wartime mobilizations, especially after 1937. These events could accelerate, freeze, or reverse rural economic transformations to various degrees depending on the locality. The late nineteenth- and early twentieth-century turmoil created hardships that our informants experienced directly or knew from the living memories of their kin. They spoke to us of fleeing famine and warfare and having witnessed starvation. These events gave context to the family decisions that shaped their lives.

HEBEI PROVINCE

The North China Plain in Hebei wraps around Beijing and the port city of Tianjin. In Hebei, low mountains to the north and west stand between the plains and the steppe and desert beyond. South-central Hebei is a region both illustrative of the North China Plain in our period and historically a starting place for change there. Classical old-empire territory, dense with villages growing grains and cotton, it has been a frequent battleground. The Taiping rebels swept as far north as middle Hebei in 1853, causing a decade of disruption. By 1900, foreign and especially Christian presences had made sufficient inroads in Shandong and Hebei to set off the antiforeign Boxer Rebellion. Rebel Boxers built recruiting and training centers in our Hebei research area, Ding County. Boxer struggles against regional Christians in turn attracted foreign troops bent on Boxer suppression (Gamble 1954, 437–439).

After 1895, life in Ding City and nearby Ding County towns and villages was greatly altered by the construction of the Jinghan railway line. The most obvious change was the ease with which soldiers could be brought into the heart of this countryside. Throughout the post-Boxer period, peace was fragile across the region, with meaningful government control rationed to key infrastructure such as the Jinghan railway. In 1920, warlords Zhang

Zuolin and Yan Xishan began fighting for control of Beijing. "Whenever there was fighting . . . , levies were made on the countryside for carts, animals, manpower and food" (Gamble 1954, 451)—shakedowns by uniformed racketeers. Their conflicts remained unresolved until 1931, when Ding was bombed by the GMD. After the arrival of Japanese troops in 1937, Ding changed hands seven times until the Japanese gained a firm hold on its rail connections. Thereafter in Ding County as throughout North China, though the Japanese held the cities and railroads, village resistance fermented in the countryside, drawing raids if not occupation.

Against this turbulent political background, the Jinghan railway also promoted extraordinary economic change along its length, directly affecting millions of village girls and women. This is particularly well documented for Ding County.

Ding County: A Research Monument Revisited

In the early 1930s, Ding County had an area of 1,240 square kilometers, with 453 villages and a population of 408,000 (Gamble 1954, 4). It also has a special place in our understanding of Hebei handcraft production and footbinding. Sidney Gamble's study of Ding Xian (Ding County) has encouraged a widely held view that new ideas and education permeated North China villages and led to the end of footbinding around the time of the Republican revolution. Our data show that these claims are exaggerated even for Ding Xian, where Gamble's and Li Jinghan's fieldwork was conducted.

Ding City (now Dingzhou), the county and prefectural seat,[7] had been an important center of raw cotton export and regional government for hundreds of years. In the early twentieth century the county's cotton handcraft industry was a significant specialization in the city, with over sixty thousand female workers spinning and weaving locally grown cotton (Gamble 1954, 288). Perhaps because of its reputation for scholarship and its suitability as a model for future expansion of new government policies, parts of Ding City and its peri-urban villages were chosen for an early Republican experiment in educational and social development, the Mass Education Movement.[8] Fortunately, the experiment was documented in great detail by the Chinese and American sociologists Li Jinghan and Sidney Gamble in a field study lasting from 1926 to 1932 (Li Jinghan 1929, 1933; Gamble 1954).[9] Zhang Shiwen ([1936] 1991), one of their collaborators, focused on handcraft and other nonfarm production.

Girls' and Women's Work in Ding County

Like most research into Chinese family life, political economy, and their
intersections, Li Jinghan, Sidney Gamble, and Zhang Shiwen's publications
offer little direct information about girls' work as opposed to female work
in general. What there is focuses on the experimental area, Dongting, a section of Ding City itself where many more girls attended school, generally
between the ages of 7 and 12, than girls living beyond it (Li Jinghan 1933,
198, table 79). This took them out of the labor force in their youngest work-
capable years, after which most left school and some began to spin. More
schooled, Dongting girls began to spin at ages 12 to 13. In contrast, Qingfengdian and Pang village girls who were born up to and including 1930
learned to spin earlier, on average at 11 and 8.6 years, respectively.[10] Li
Jinghan's descriptions of spinning and weaving, in some ways meticulous,
do not differentiate between women in various stages of life, disregarding
how the female necessity of managing both reproduction and production
makes for complex work lives.

Many of the changes that affected girls in Ding County were involved
with cotton. The 1895 Jinghan railway not only expanded the regional
market for raw cotton on the North China Plain; it brought in factory yarn
as well. This yarn was soon used for warps on cloth that was still referred
to as *tubu*, because it was handwoven with hand-spun wefts (Li Jinghan
1933, 696; Gamble 1954, 303). Machine spinning was vastly more efficient
than hand spinning, causing prices for hand-spun yarn to drop in order to
compete.[11]

> The result was a product so cheap that it sometimes sold at close to the cost
> of raw cotton. In these circumstances, spinning hardly paid as a sideline
> activity. In Dingxian [Ding County], for example, the net annual income of
> spinners had fallen to a mere 3.26 yuan a year by the 1920s, compared with
> 22.15 yuan for hand weavers. (P. Huang 1985, 132, citing Chao Kang 1977,
> 179–183, 185)[12]

Nevertheless, hand-spun cotton yarn remained useful, particularly for
households that grew cotton (Figure 3.2). With the breaking of the production bottleneck that slow hand spinning had formerly created, hand-loomed
cloth expanded. The introduction of improved "pull looms" in the 1910s
and the transition to iron-gear looms (*tielunji*) operated by foot pedals in
the 1920s also increased weavers' productivity. Low-cost machine yarn and
better looms allowed weavers to increase their output, particularly when

Figure 3.2.   Woman spinning cotton in Ding County, 1931–1932. One bound foot is visible.

SOURCE: Sidney D. Gamble Photographs, David M. Rubenstein Rare Book and Manuscript Library, Duke University

they had good access to distribution networks, as Ding weavers now did. By the 1930s, iron-gear looms accounted for 49 percent of the total 2,648 looms in one district but produced 77 percent of the output (Gamble 1954, 302). From 1921 to 1930, "over 10,600,000 pieces of *chuang* cloth [made with machine-spun warps] worth over $11,000,000" were shipped from Ding County with "over 70 percent" going to Chahar (Inner Mongolia) and the rest going to Shanxi and farther northwest (308). Thus, while incomes from hand spinning in Ding County fell, handloom weavers were at that time able to compete for inland markets. Additional demand for cloth came from clothing required by the many soldiers who tramped through the north in the 1920s and 1930s, men at the end of what were usually very long and often corrupt supply lines.

Qingfengdian. During the girlhoods of our oldest informants, Qingfengdian villagers produced, ginned, and exported raw cotton through the local railroad station. Spinning cotton from home plots or local markets was part of the duties of 86 percent of the women interviewed there; nearly 70 percent sold at least part of their yarn. Half wove cotton into cloth or into grain bags on special small looms, with 28 percent weaving cloth for sale on typical cloth-weaving looms in their natal homes. Almost one-fifth of Qingfengdian girls also spun hemp thread to use for stitching the family's shoe soles (only 3 percent sold the thread). Households depended almost entirely on these home-based labors for bedding, clothes, and shoes.

Pang Village. The combination of cotton spinning, weaving, and reed mat making as girls' work in Pang Village created a complex pattern in which traditional hand spinning and cloth weaving were each differently affected by technological change and the families' ability to invest in new equipment. Most Pang women (81 percent) reported that as girls they had spun cotton yarn for use, including 75 percent who also sold it—heavy homespun cotton yarn was used in hand weaving as wefts with machine-spun warps and was also needed to sew neat edges on mats (Gamble 1954, 93). Another girls' handcraft was twisting hemp into yarn or thin twine: 25 percent made twine, including 5 percent who also sold it. Hemp twine was essential to every family for stitching shoe soles. Almost half of the families had cloth looms, corresponding to 46 percent who wove for home use, including 30 percent who also wove for sale.[13]

Like some communities in the Li/Gamble/Zhang study (although not included among them), our second Ding County site, Pang Village, was (and still is) home to many makers of reed mats. The reeds were purchased from a wetland area, woven up, and then shipped out regularly in huge bundles from Qingfengdian. With hemp or cotton wefts, reeds made a smooth covering for the warmed brick or adobe bed platforms (*kang*) on which most people in the North China Plain sat and slept. Mats did not last as long as quilts, especially when babies slept and wet on them, and were replaced every few years. Men and women, boys and girls wove mats, varying in productivity depending on what other duties required their efforts. Of the Pang Village women interviewed, 22 percent had made mats before marriage, all for sale. In these interviews, they described a range of experiences and work abilities:

• "One day, one mat" (from four women, one saying that she began at age fourteen or fifteen, one adding that the rate required quick work, and another saying that it was a single-person mat).

- "In one day, I wove two six-foot [single-person] mats; I could weave mats at age seven."
- "I began at seven or eight years. . . . I wove to sell but also wove for others [who supplied the material] for twenty cents apiece."
- "I was one of four girls, and we all wove mats. I wove mats by day, cloth by night."
- "At a five-day market I sold five or six mats for money that bought my food until the next market."

For those who depended on mat weaving for their next meal, these spontaneous comments reflect the indelible memories of a childhood work routine. Mat-making areas were not uncommon in Hebei and elsewhere. The waterlogged parts of Hebei's Yongqing County grew little cotton; women there generally did not spin or weave but in some villages wove mats from reeds, a crucial part of household income (L. Li 2007, 108). Mat-weaving handwork, which we encounter again in this and the following chapter, was less affected by industrial changes in the early twentieth century than spinning and weaving.

The early twentieth century was a period of rapid transition in hand-weaving technologies in Ding County. Unfortunately, we do not know what proportion of looms in our village sites were the traditional "clumsy" looms, improved pulling looms, or iron-gear looms—three types identified by Gamble (1954, 301). Households that continued to use the traditional wooden clumsy loom were at a significant disadvantage in producing for the market. The iron-gear loom was larger than and four times as fast as the traditional wooden loom (Chao 1977, 184). The investment in more expensive iron-gear looms using foot pedals was often accompanied by a shift from female to male weavers, as was the case in Gaoyang (Grove 2006). Some Pang women mentioned that adult men in their families wove. Big looms were easier to use than small looms but also dependent on a larger body size than that of a small woman or girl.

Textile mills were soon proliferating on the North China Plain near abundant sources of cotton. In 1913, a mill was built in Anyang, near Baoding, and in 1925, Shijiazhuang and Zhengzhou, both to the south on the Jinghan line, had mills (Lai 1967, 87, 89, figs. 2, 8). By the late 1920s and early 1930s, garments of foreign or fully machine-made factory cloth were becoming precious additions to wardrobes for the better-off residents in Ding County (Li Jinghan 1933; Gamble 1954, 101, 123).

Footbinding in Ding County

Evidence about footbinding from the Ding County project has been much cited, usually in Sidney Gamble's words: "The amount of footbinding among women of different ages showed how, even in country villages, a social custom that was able to defy the edicts of early Manchu emperors disappeared in 25 years" (1954, 7).[14] In a sample of 515 families taken in 1929, footbinding had been "universal" at 99 percent among women over forty, born before 1892. These researchers found no new bindings on girls younger than thirteen, those born in and after 1916 (Gamble 1954, 48, 60, table 9; Li Jinghan 1933, 281, table 149). Gamble concluded, "If these figures are typical we can say that foot-binding came to an end in Ting Hsien [Ding County] in 1919" (1954, 48).

Li attributed the end of binding to the magistracy of Sun Faxü, who served from 1914 to 1916, mandating both the cessation of new bindings and the unbinding of girls under sixteen. Scofflaws were to be fined, with the result that no new footbindings would have been done in Ding County after Sun's orders had been implemented (Li Jinghan 1933, 280). Had Magistrate Sun actually enforced his mandate by the end of his tenure in 1916, girls sixteen years old and younger would all have been unbound or left with natural feet; no girl born in or after 1900 should have been listed as footbound. Figure 3.3, using the Li/Gamble data for Dongting, shows that many girls who were born from 1905 to 1914 had been bound and remained so in the research period. This was clearly a time of steep decline in footbinding for Dongting, but there was also resistance.

Figure 3.3 also shows the footbinding status of women interviewed in Qingfengdian and Pang Village and of their elder kinswomen.[15] It shows that Dongting girls were more likely than those in our village sites to abandon footbinding early. Even before government control returned in 1913, footbinding had decreased in Dongting by almost one-fifth. This left four-fifths of Dongting women born from 1900 to 1909 reported as bound when the survey was taken in 1929. By the time new footbinding in Dongting had dropped to zero for those born in the 1920s, 38 percent of our Qingfengdian and Pang Village subjects who had been born in the 1920s cohort were still newly bound. Dongting District (a section of Ding City) data show a smooth curve representing change that began among a minority (born 1900–1904 and, assuming a binding age of around seven, bound around 1907–1911), spread rapidly through the bulk of the population born by

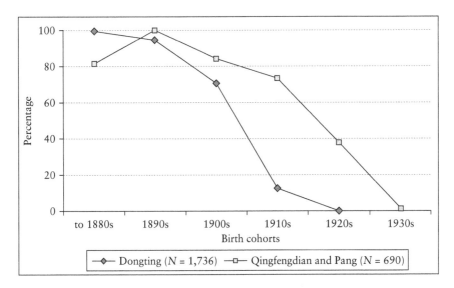

Figure 3.3. Percentage footbound, born before 1940, Ding County, Hebei

SOURCE: Data for Dongting is adapted from Gamble 1954, 60, table 9. Qingfengdian and Pang data are from authors' surveys.

NOTE: In Ding County, footbinding declined earlier in the Dongting experimental district than in two other villages, Qingfengdian and Pang, which did not receive special attention from reformers.

the early 1910s (binding years around 1917–1921), and tailed off slowly as the last holdouts accepted this change in their lives. Qingfengdian and Pang Village girls were on a slower path than those in the coastal cities of Guangzhou, Shanghai, Beijing, or even Dongting. Footbinding persisted longer and did not begin its steep decline until the 1915–1924 birth cohorts, who would have been bound from 1922 to 1931. Why do the sites differ, and what can the difference reveal about factors that influenced change?

Compared with the Li and Gamble surveys, our retrospective data support two main observations. Abandonment of footbinding was beginning before the county was firmly under governance; and in villages beyond Ding's center, footbinding was abandoned much more slowly than in the Dongting site that Li Jinghan and Gamble used as evidence for change. Anti-footbinding influences were particularly strong in Dongting, an "experimental district" in Ding County chosen by the Mass Education Movement in 1926 for heavily managed social change.[16] The Dongting footbinding sample included some who lived in the city proper (Li Jinghan 1933, 694), and half lived in a small town hosting the Mass Education Movement of-fices, with relatively prosperous owner-operator farm households (Gamble 1954, 24–26).[17] These families were more likely to send daughters to el-ementary school, where natural feet may have been required.[18]

Neither official control nor the Mass Education Movement arrived early enough to account for the initial decline in Dongting girls' rate of footbinding. However, the influx of machine-spun thread from Tianjin be-fore the turn of the century may have weakened the need to keep young girls at the spinning wheel, especially in more urban and prosperous Dongting. Also, if educational effort decreased Dongting's burden of footbinding in its middle phase, it had less effect in Qingfengdian and Pang Village, where roughly 70 percent of the women in our sample had never attended school and remained illiterate (see Table A.2 in Appendix A).[19] Both village samples lay outside the experimental district, across the Tang River, each about thirty kilometers north of Ding City proper. They depended on the Qingfengdian railway station, not Ding City itself, and were more rural and handcraft oriented, a point underlined by the fact that Zhang Shiwen ([1936] 1991) chose their district for his study of home industry. It thus seems possible that the influx of imported machine-made yarn from the late nineteenth century and the adoption of new flying-shuttle and iron-gear looms that used machine thread in the 1920s reduced the pressure on young girls to sit spinning yarn and thereby loosened the commitment to footbinding (Figure 3.4).[20]

The case of footbinding in Ding County is valuable because our data can be compared to those from a large, well-done survey carried out when footbinding was in decline. The comparison of the two data sets offers a rare chance to question the typical, ideological reasons given for the aban-donment of footbinding: political action and education. At the same time, the wealth of data on economic and technological change in the early Ding County surveys offers significant support for the view that footbinding de-clined in part because young girls' labor in spinning was no longer as valu-able or helpful to the family.

SHANDONG PROVINCE

The western and southern counties of Shandong, the easternmost and only coastal province in our research set, are continuous with those of Hebei,

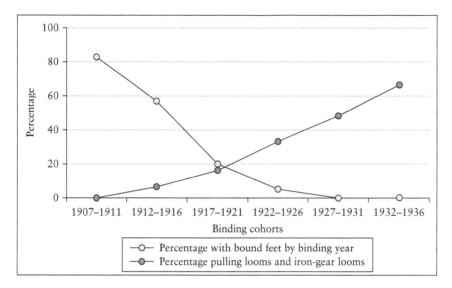

Figure 3.4. Percentage of improved looms and percentage footbound by binding cohort, Ding County

SOURCE: Data adapted from Gamble 1954, 60, 314, tables 9 and 96

NOTE: The total data set includes 1,736 women; 704 women born before 1900 had a foot-binding rate above 94 percent and are not shown here. See Bossen 2002, 47. The adoption and increased use of more productive looms from 1907 to 1936 corresponds to a rapid decline in new footbinding of Ding County girls in the same period. Binding is assumed to begin at age seven, meaning that seven years were added to the range of birth years given in Gamble 1954. Although Gamble believed binding began at age three, the vast majority of our interviews suggest a range of age five to ten is more likely. See also Croll 1995, 20–24, and Gates 2015.

Henan, and Anhui.[21] Over centuries of imperial rule, the flat, bleak landscape was scraped bare of forest and wetland in favor of millet, wheat, and cotton. Interminable flat fields and brown dirt villages were subject to the whims of rivers diked so high that farmland lay below the riverbed. In 1897, the vast Yellow River changed its banks from the southern to the northern border of Shandong, exacerbating a time of famine, drought, pestilence, and misery across the North China Plain.

Cotton entered Shandong in the Yuan dynasty and by the Qing had become essential to rural life in regions where it grew well, notably southwestern Shandong (Tang Zhiqing 2004, 218–221; P. Huang 1985, 112). Women old and young (*funü laoxiao*) "saw neither dawn nor sunset" and provided a substantial share of a household's income with their spinning and weaving

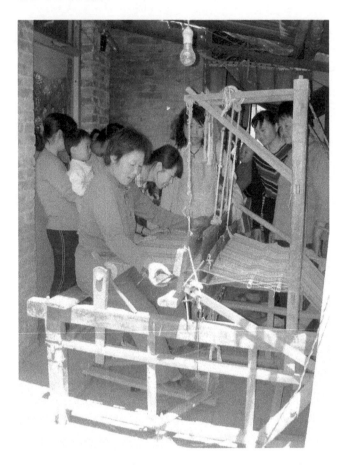

Figure 3.5. Woman demonstrating weaving on a wooden
treadle loom in Shandong

(Figure 3.5). The province sent cotton goods as far as Shanxi (Tang Zhiqing 2004, 450). While people in plains Shandong farmed cotton, villagers
in our mountainous site, Qingzhou, turned to other crops better suited to
their environment. Shandong's central hilly core had some forest cover and
adequate water from rain and high ground: a more complex environment
than the flat grain-growing region. Wild silk, historically a local specialty,
was encouraged by the state in the 1840s, along with tobacco (249, 455;
Esherick 1987, 10–12).

East-west transport between coast and hills was hampered by the fast
fall of local rivers and a topography that did not lend itself to road building.

The Grand Canal, for centuries a major north-south conduit linking the Yellow and Yangzi Rivers, passed through western Shandong, with barges carrying tribute grain and fine textiles from Hangzhou to Beijing. In the mid-nineteenth century, problems with silting, the changing course of the Yellow River, and the Taiping Rebellion left the canal in disrepair. Consequently, employment in canal towns dwindled while banditry in western Shandong grew. As canal traffic dried up, steamships expanded the possibilities for coastal shipping to ports such as Qingdao, Yantai, and Tianjin. Between 1899 and 1904, against great resistance expressed in the Boxer Rebellion against foreign influence, the Germans built a railway from the port of Qingdao in southeastern Shandong to Jinan. By 1912, the north-south Jinpu line from Tianjin to Nanjing linked Jinan to the wider rail network growing from a Beijing hub.

The 1911 revolution resulted in a major decentralization of Chinese rule, with Shandong managed extensively by British and German authorities. After World War I the Treaty of Versailles transferred Qingdao from German to Japanese control. Japan was eager for rice, silk cocoons, and, especially, raw cotton from Shandong (Tang Zhiqing 2004, 448). From 1927 to the early 1930s, Shandong experienced sporadic fighting between anti-GMD (northern) and GMD (southern) troops. Because Qingzhou stood on the railway, our nearby sites were frequently in contention.

Shandong had already begun to feel the impact of foreign imports after the opening of treaty ports at Tianjin in 1861 and Yantai (formerly Chefoo/Zhifu) on the northern shore of the Shandong peninsula in 1862. The port of Zhenjiang, where the Yangzi meets the Grand Canal, also reopened to North China trade after the Taiping rebels were defeated at Nanjing in 1865. Foreign cotton textiles reached Shandong "first in the form of piece goods, then increasingly in the 1880s and dramatically in the 1890s in the form of cotton yarn" (Esherick 1988, 69). In 1882, Yantai imported roughly 1.5 million pounds of cotton yarn. By 1899, the year of the Boxer Rebellion, Yantai's cotton imports had surpassed 20.7 million pounds. Factory-yarn imports similarly increased in Tianjin and Zhenjiang.[22] Meanwhile, textile employment declined rapidly in coastal Shandong from the 1860s to the late 1880s. In 1866, the Yantai commissioner of customs praised the quality of native Shandong textiles that were widely used within the province. According to Joseph Esherick, two decades later, in 1887, the Yantai commissioner reported that imported cotton yarn was "seriously interfering with the local industry of spinning which affords a means of support to many poor women." A year later the commissioner reported that "the reeling of Native Cotton Yarn in this province is almost at a standstill" (China Maritime Customs 1887, 41, and 1888, 43, quoted in Esherick 1988, 70).

In 1901, Arthur H. Smith, an American missionary living in En County in northwestern Shandong, wrote of steamships bringing cotton goods to China along the coast:

> One reads in the reports to the directors of steamship companies of the improved trade with China in cotton goods, and the bright outlook all along the coast from Canton to Tientsin [Tianjin] and Newchwang [Niuzhuang] in this line of commerce, but no one reads of the effect of this trade . . . upon innumerable millions of Chinese on the great cotton-growing plains of China. They have hitherto been just able to make a scanty living by weaving cloth fifteen inches wide, one bolt of which requires two days of hard work, realizing at the market only enough to enable the family to purchase the barest necessities of life, and to provide more cotton for the unintermittent weaving, which sometimes goes on by relays all day and most of the night.
>
> In some villages every family has one or more looms, and much of the work is done in underground cellars where the click of the shuttle is heard month in and month out from the middle of the first moon till the closing days of the twelfth. But now the looms are idle and the weaving-cellars are falling into ruin. (Smith 1901, 90–91, quoted in Esherick 1988, 71)

Through firsthand observation of northwestern Shandong, Smith unambiguously attributed the immiseration of north China's villagers to the new cotton mills:

> The phenomenal activity of the mills in Bombay, in Japan, and even in Shanghai itself, has inundated the cotton districts of China with yarns so much more even, stronger, and withal cheaper than the home-made kind, that the spinning-wheels no longer revolve, and the tiny rill of income for the young, the old, the feeble, and the helpless is permanently dried up. (Smith 1901, 90–91, quoted in Esherick 1987, 71)

As a result, "the factors for the wholesale dealers no longer make their appearance" (Smith 1901, 90–91, quoted in Esherick 1988, 72).[23] Esherick concludes that the impact of factory yarn was not necessarily the displacement of homespun in cotton-growing areas but the diminished opportunities to sell homespun yarn to cotton merchants.[24] "These regions were losing their external markets—most of them to the north and west—which were now served directly by imports through Tianjin" (Esherick 1988, 72).

Competition between factory and handcraft textiles ratcheted up in the early twentieth century. Shandong cotton production doubled from 1914 to 1936 in response to growing demand for raw cotton from foreign and domestic cotton mills. While sales of hand-spun cotton declined, other handcrafts such as straw braid and hairnets grew. Shandong historian Tang Zhiqing concludes that German and Japanese capitalism broke the structural barriers of Shandong's small family economy (2004, 433–436). In the 1920s and 1930s, increases in marketed cotton goods and other handcraft commodities may have improved general living standards (435–450), but the impact on handcraft cotton spinners and weavers depended on access to new technology, factory work, or alternative crafts. Without these, they were likely to be unemployed. Anthropologist Martin Yang described the changes affecting girls in his home village in Shandong:

> Recently they [the weavers] have been forced to compete with factory-made cloth which comes into the country daily in increasing quantities. . . . Many families have given up the traditional spinning of yarn from raw cotton and now they buy the factory-made cotton yarns in the market town and weave it into cloth at home. . . . Their elders console themselves by listening to the sound of the old loom, . . . taking comfort in the thought that the old traditions still exist and that the world still has not gone to the devil. They are much concerned, however, about a new problem created by the situation— how to keep their daughters occupied during the long spring, now that they do not have to spin. (1945, 26–27)[25]

Qingzhou County: Silk and Persimmons in the Hills

Historically an important center of government and commerce on the North Slope of Shandong's hilly spine, the Qingzhou area had an ancient specialty in silk.[26] The road to Qingzhou City encouraged the scattering of villages along its route until the railroad was built from Jinan in the west to the Qingdao port on the eastern coast in 1904, connecting Qingzhou to a much greater marketing area. Villagers near Qingzhou trekked to the city, where they sold local products to Japanese traders for shipment to Japan. As the Japanese seized control of Shandong (1937–1938), they were eager to hold Qingzhou for its railway station, so its inhabitants found themselves on a dangerous interface.

Our interview sample comes from seven closely spaced mountain communities between twenty and forty kilometers from Qingzhou City and strung along a new well-surfaced road. Historically, the region had only footpaths, lacking the advantage of the imperial road to their north. Local food crops included wheat, corn, millet, sorghum, beans, and sweet potatoes.

Girls' and Women's Work in Qingzhou

Raising silk cocoons was the main source of income for Qingzhou girls and women in our sample. Just over half (52 percent) of the Qingzhou women reported raising silkworms as girls before marriage, and one-third (36 percent) produced them for sale or wages.[27] Cotton products were less important here than on the plain in southwestern Shandong. Although over one-third of the families grew cotton, less than 10 percent sold some of it. Roughly 40 percent of natal families had a spinning wheel and spun cotton,[28] but less than 10 percent had a loom or wove cotton.[29] Most girls did not spin or weave cotton for sale or wages. Qingzhou girls also engaged in seasonal picking, slicing, preserving, and packing persimmons and hawthorn berries for sale to merchants. Like raising silkworms and spinning cotton, processing dried fruit employed the hands of young girls.

While village girls of Qingzhou earned income from hand labor, their families purchased handmade cloth from other villages. In the early twentieth century, the influx of machine-spun yarn from Tianjin enabled specialized weaving villages to develop in other parts of the North China Plain (including Ding County and Gaoyang in Hebei) and to increase the output of handwoven cloth for rural markets by adopting improved looms (Chao 1977, 197–199).[30] By 1899, the coastal areas of Tianjin and Shanghai were producing factory cloth, some of which was sold in Qingzhou,[31] and by 1925 Shandong's cities, Jinan and Qingdao, had begun factory production of cotton cloth (Lai 1967, 89, 123). In the 1930s and 1940s, village traders who sold silk cocoons and dried fruit from this area carried *tubu* and factory cloth from other regions back to our survey villages.

Footbinding in Qingzhou

Roughly three-quarters (74 percent) of the women who were born before 1930 were footbound (Figure 3.6), while their mothers' and grandmothers' rates of binding ranged from 80 to 100 percent.[32] Women born before 1930 had a lower average age of binding (eleven years) than those born in 1930 or later (twelve years). The relatively late age of binding suggests that girls' work was not predominantly sedentary, such as raising silkworms and

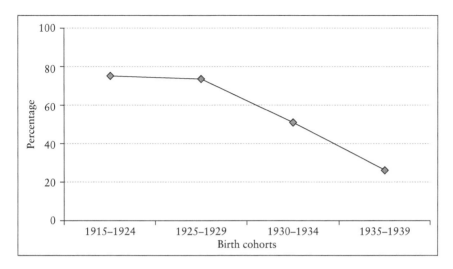

Figure 3.6. Percentage footbound by birth cohort, Qingzhou, Shandong
NOTE: *N* = 136.

processing persimmons, which required more walking about than spinning or weaving. Several Qingzhou women expressed the idea that footbinding meant that they would not be asked to do heavy, outdoor labor. The relatively late age of binding and its gradual decline are consistent with the relative importance of raising silkworms over cotton spinning and weaving. When handwork in cotton textiles encountered competition, the presence of other forms of domestic handwork such as raising silkworms or preserving and packing persimmons meant that girls' labor did not have to be transferred to fieldwork or work outside the home.

As Tang Zhiqing (2004) notes, the impact of machine-made cotton textiles depended on access to new technology, factory work, or alternative handcraft incomes. Our Qingzhou sites showed no evidence that villagers had looms with improved efficiency. If some girls found factory work, it would have drawn them out of the villages (and our sample). For rural women and girls the influx of machine-spun yarn and cheaper cotton cloth supplies could well have displaced one of their previous sources of income, even if mitigated somewhat by raising and selling silkworms and dried fruit. Because imports of machine-spun yarn reached Shandong in the late nineteenth century before our oldest age groups were born (in the 1920s), we could not determine whether hand spinning for income or exchange in kind was at one time more widespread. If such a shift occurred, then the high rate of binding for our oldest cohorts would be consistent with our theory. At the same time, much of the hand labor for raising silkworms and drying and packing fruit is also consistent with the limited mobility of footbinding.

HENAN PROVINCE

Our study enters the classical North China Plain environment in the Henan research sites. South of Hebei and mainly south of the Yellow River, the broad expanse of the plain in northern Henan and Anhui Provinces has seen an astonishing history of floods, droughts, famines, and violence. In Henan the Yellow River bed is sometimes higher than the surrounding plains, resulting in swampy wetlands as well as dry agricultural areas. Here most farms grew wheat, millet, sorghum, beans, and peanuts. Describing the low standard of living characteristic of North China in the Qing period, historian Lillian Li notes different local specialties among counties that had dry or swampy land. In dry areas where farmers grew cotton, women specialized in spinning and weaving. In swampy, waterlogged areas little or no cotton was grown, but reeds were harvested that women wove into mats and curtains.[33] In both settings, women's handcrafts earned a critical part of household income (L. Li 2007, 106–108). Our Henan sites are examples of both types of environment and the corresponding craft specialization by women.[34]

Kaifeng County: A Cotton-Growing Village near the Yellow River

The city of Kaifeng, an ancient capital of China during the Song dynasty, is located about fifteen kilometers south of the Yellow River. Kaifeng City was historically linked with other regions by its major waterways: east-west by the Yellow River and north-south by the Grand Canal. By 1910, the earliest completed section of the east-west Longhai railway in Henan passed through Kaifeng to reach Luoyang in western Henan. When the Longhai railway intersected with the north-south Jinghan railway at Zhengzhou, long-distance trade possibilities in North China rapidly multiplied (Wou 1994, 15–17, map 1). Zhengzhou, as a rail hub sixty kilometers west of Kaifeng, consequently drew more commerce than Kaifeng and assumed the leading position in the region. Despite an explosion of new transportation potential along the railways and improved roads, in the 1930s and 1940s transportation within the rural areas remained rudimentary. Our village site in Kaifeng County is located about fifteen kilometers south of Kaifeng City. Two traders recall walking the distance (in about three hours) to Kaifeng City with a carrying pole or pushing a wheelbarrow along dirt roads. They mainly exchanged grain or peanuts for money; there was little local trade in cloth.

Girls' and Women's Work in Kaifeng

As in most of northern Henan, Kaifeng villagers grew cotton, spun it, and wove their own *tubu* (Figure 3.7). Villagers did not buy factory-made yarn or cloth. "They were poor and could not afford it," explained one trader. *Tubu* could be bought or sold in the local market, but there was little demand because most households included women who produced it themselves. Villagers were largely self-sufficient (*ziji zizu*) in clothing. Another trader recalled that some women participated in local markets, but both agreed that women did not engage in long-distance trade because they had bound feet and "could not walk [that well or that far]." Both men affirmed that there were no textile factories nearby. However, by 1920 the new large-scale Yufeng Cotton Mill established in Zhengzhou could easily send large quantities of yarn and cloth by train to Kaifeng. A report from 1929 shows the Yufeng mill had fifty-three thousand spindles, two hundred looms, and nearly four thousand workers (Pearse 1929). Those factory spindles had to have an impact on Henan's village hand spinners. The indirect effect was to reduce urban demand for hand-spun yarn and handwoven textiles much as previously described for Shandong, where cloth dealers "no longer made their appearance" (Smith 1901, 90).

Interviews with village women in our Kaifeng County site demonstrate female specialization in textiles and capture the gradual decline of this form of handwork. In their natal villages, roughly one-third of the women grew cotton, three-quarters spun it, and more than half wove it into cloth. One-third of the households owned their own loom, which some shared with neighbors. Households that did not grow cotton obtained it in local exchange with other cotton-growing households or peddlers.[35] Comparing before- and after-marriage work to detect change over time showed a slight decline in cotton growing, weaving, and loom ownership but a much larger decline in spinning cotton.[36] Spinning dropped from roughly three-quarters to one-half, in response to the substitution of factory yarn

Figure 3.7.   Weaver in Henan, 1989. Village weavers like this woman have become rare.

for homespun yarn. Although spinning declined by the end of the 1940s, some women continued spinning and weaving for family use well after the establishment of a Communist government in 1949 because of scarcity of goods. Others stopped when cloth coupons were introduced (during the Great Leap Forward, 1958–1961).[37] The persistence of home weaving is not surprising given the scarcity of cloth due to constant disruptions to trade as roads and railroads were dismantled or bombed during the war years, blocking textiles from the east and raw cotton from the west.

Huaiyang County: A Lakeside Marshland Village

Huaiyang County is located south of Zhengzhou and the Yellow River and east of Zhoukou City. This is the southeastern quadrant of Henan formed by the intersection of the Longhai and Jinghan railways. Huaiyang is ninety kilometers east of the Jinghan station at Luohe. The completion of these railways in the early twentieth century undoubtedly expanded trade and redirected some of the local commerce. Our research site, Weixi Village, at the edge of a large lake had relatively little agricultural land. Villagers grew wheat, millet, sorghum, beans, and sweet potatoes as staples. Unlike most villages in the region, Weixi controlled valuable water and wetland resources. With rights to portions of the lake, villagers depended on fish and the marshland grasses, cattails, reeds, and willow branches that made excellent materials for weaving mats. Villagers wove reeds to make sleeping mats, bags, and nets (as they did in Pang Village in Ding County). Hence we call this site Weixi (Reed Mat) Village.

Girls' and Women's Work in Huaiyang

Women in Weixi did not weave cotton cloth even though about a third of them grew cotton for family use at both their natal and marital households.[38] Only 9 percent wove cotton before marriage, and just one woman wove after marriage. Correspondingly, only 20 percent of their natal families had a loom, and only 3 percent of their marital families in Weixi Village had one. Half the women had spun cotton or hemp as girls at their natal homes,[39] and 40 percent wove reed mats or made cattail bags. Often, several family members worked together to make a mat. Cotton or hemp thread was used as warp and edging for some of the woven mats and bags. This explains why so many girls spun cotton, even though they did not weave cloth. Almost a third (30 percent) of the women reported that they sold mats, bags, or other handmade products. When they were young girls, they worked on mats with other family members who took care of sales.[40]

Elderly Weixi traders recall that they used boats or trudged over dirt roads with carrying poles to reach local markets. Whether by boat or on foot it took three or four hours to reach the larger markets such as Dancheng to the east or Zhoukou to the west; a round-trip took two days. After selling their local products, they brought back salt, flour, and bolts of cloth to meet their needs for clothing. Weixi villagers bought locally handwoven *tubu* from the surrounding villages. Factory cloth produced in distant places like Shanghai was available in the county town, and we can assume that after 1920 the output of the Yufeng Cotton Mill in Zhengzhou also reached Zhoukou City and possibly Huaiyang's town markets. Villagers, but not townspeople, almost exclusively bought sturdy, local, handmade *tubu*.

Footbinding in Kaifeng

Elderly men of rural Kaifeng said that the village women of the Republican period all had bound feet. Our data confirm that before 1930 footbinding was nearly universal, although some women later had their feet unbound. The average binding age was roughly eight and a half years old, with the majority bound between ages five and eleven. One woman explicitly linked binding and spinning: "After footbinding I did not leave the house; I spun cotton and wove cloth at home."[41] Beginning with the cohorts born in the 1920s and expected to bind in the 1930s, our interviews paint a picture of rapid decline in footbinding.[42] Thirteen women recalled Feng Yuxiang, a Christian warlord who became governor of Henan in 1922 and opposed footbinding.[43] Footbinding rates were still high for those born in the late 1920s, but a sudden drop occurred for those born 1930–1934. These girls reached binding age during the Great Depression, which was followed by the Japanese invasion and occupation of North China. Our village site was under Japanese control, yet women did not credit Japanese regulations with the end of footbinding. Two women noted that when the Japanese invaded, women with "small feet" could not run to escape. For those born from 1935 to 1939 the rate of new binding fell below half.

Footbinding in Huaiyang

Footbinding was also standard among the oldest women in our Huaiyang sample (Figure 3.8). In Huaiyang, the average binding age of seven years was younger than in Kaifeng, but the decline of binding started later than in other villages on the North China Plain. For women born in the early 1930s, a decline is hardly perceptible (Figure 3.9). In the late 1930s, under a Japanese puppet government in Zhoukou, young girls were still having their feet bound. For those born in the late 1930s, whose binding would have begun in the mid-1940s, footbinding ceased rapidly.[44]

A combination of pressures acted on Kaifeng villagers during this period: changing markets, economic depression, warfare, and new governments (including the Christian warlord and military governor of Henan, Feng Yuxiang). If we focus on changes in girls' and women's work, high rates of hand spinning and weaving for Kaifeng regional markets are consistent with high rates of footbinding, but in the 1930s these hand skills met increased competition from machine-made textiles transported by rail from

Figure 3.8. Bare foot, poorly bound. This foot, of a woman in Huaiyang, Henan Province, has the big toe twisted sideways and small toes folded sideways or embedded in the sole to reduce length. Such binding was not ideal and hence not only painful but shameful.

Zhengzhou. In contrast, Huaiyang County villagers making reed mats and bags had little or no competition from machine-made products. Families could continue to train their daughters for sedentary domestic handcrafts, such as making reed mats and bags for the market. Continued reliance on girls' and women's handwork is consistent with a somewhat later decline of footbinding efforts there.

ANHUI PROVINCE

Considered a backwater by denizens of China's coast, Anhui is one of China's poorer provinces. Two major rivers, the Huai and the Yangzi, cross Anhui from west to east, while the Yellow River passes just to its north. Northern Anhui, also called Huaibei, is north of the Huai River. Central Anhui lies between the Huai and Yangzi Rivers, and southern Anhui is south of the

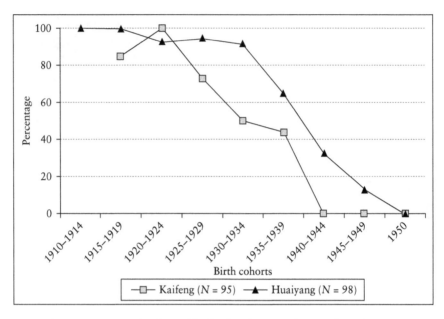

Figure 3.9. Percentage footbound by birth cohort, Kaifeng and Huaiyang Counties, Henan

NOTE: $N = 193$. In Kaifeng County, close to Kaifeng and Zhengzhou cities, the Yellow River, and the new railroad, footbinding declined about ten years earlier than in Huaiyang County. The 1910–1914 cohort in Huaiyang has only one case.

Yangzi. Writers on Anhui stress the variability of its terrain and culture and pay special attention to the southern sector along the Yangzi and its merchant class (L. Johnson 1993a; Walker 1999). Its powerful families and lineages capitalized on the silk and cotton textiles that flowed both up- and downriver, allying themselves culturally with similar parts of Zhejiang and Jiangsu Provinces, "the Jiangnan," rather than with their poorer fellow provincials to the north. We chose counties in the less prosperous and less well-documented northern and central sectors. Our two village sites are on different sides of the Huai River, which is often used as a dividing line between China's wheat-growing northern and rice-growing southern regions. Linquan County, north of the Huai, depended mainly on wheat. Liu'an County to the south grew more rice.[45] Both counties grew cotton.

In northern Anhui, frequent floods, lack of governance, rampant banditry, and warfare had stymied trade and development throughout the late Qing and Republican periods (Perry 1980, 35; FYXZ 1994, 197, 95).

Although ancient roads connected towns, overland transport was slow and costly. Water transport by small craft was widely used when the rivers ran deep enough.[46] Following the late nineteenth-century opening of treaty ports, steamships increased China's volume of trade. Early twentieth-century railroad construction further increased the capacity for bulky trade goods such as textiles to reach small towns. By the 1930s, four railroad lines across or near Anhui increased interregional trade, favoring some regions while marginalizing others (Perry 1980, 33–34).[47]

Anhui historians argue that after the Yangzi treaty port at Wuhu opened in 1877, competition with foreign yarn and cloth devastated rural hand spinners and weavers. Handcraft producers' incomes deteriorated not just in cities but also in remote areas of Anhui such as Liu'an County. There, villages once had many looms and weavers, but after foreign cloth entered western Anhui, many renowned weavers no longer wove (Cheng 1989, 121–124). Factory textiles moved along the Yangzi by steamship and then overland by animal-drawn carts and human porters to inland towns. North Anhui villagers were farther from Jiangnan's textile factories, but by the late nineteenth century indirect effects were felt across the province. Southern Anhui's Yangzi River port at Anqing is only 175 kilometers from Liu'an County. Because numerous smaller rivers were open to boat traffic, traders could reach many towns that served Anhui farming villages.

In city and town markets, competition with factory goods brought hardship to hinterland households that depended on farming and handcrafts. In the early twentieth century, Anhui's rural regions that had formerly supplied Anhui's markets were abandoning handweaving (Cheng 1989, 121–122). The lost income from sales of handmade textiles exacerbated the rural poverty and deepened Anhui's reputation as an impoverished backwater compared to the flourishing textile centers of Jiangnan. Despite official urging "to resume cotton cultivation and to raise silkworms" and "to encourage the development of a spinning industry," villagers did not respond; handcraft production was not "a lucrative profession" (Perry 1980, 36–37).[48]

Linquan County: An Old North China Plain Village

Our village site in Linquan County resembles most traditional North China Plain villages with dusty, flat land, mud-brick walls, and houses clustered under the shade of old trees. The main crops in Linquan, like those of northern Anhui farms generally, were wheat, soybeans, sorghum, and cotton. In our village site, over 80 percent of the farmers grew wheat, but only 3 percent grew rice. Because the village is located just outside the expanding county seat, village traders needed less than an hour to walk to the city market, carrying goods or pushing carts.[49] In the Republican period, local commerce mainly involved trading grain for salt, silk, and clothing.[50] Linquan County itself was served by three navigable rivers. The main river, the Quan, flowed southeast toward the Huai. By the 1930s, road-construction projects had opened the county seat to automobile traffic, but village roads were still suitable only for rickshaws and hand carts (MGLQXZ [1936] 1998, 284–285, 291). In 2011, wide, paved roads on the outskirts of the county seat passed close to our site, but the old village, facing imminent demolition to make way for new apartment buildings, was still unpaved.

Girls' and Women's Work in Linquan

In her ethnography of a northern Anhui village, anthropologist Han Min generalized that in the Republican era women in the Huaibei Plain "only stayed home, sewing, spinning, weaving, and cooking" for their families (2001, 71, 160).[51] In our Linquan village, women and girls spun cotton and wove cloth for family needs (clothing, shoes, sheets, quilts), yet more than 80 percent had weeded and picked cotton crops as girls before marriage. Because families grew their own cotton, most girls (70 percent) were spinning cotton at age thirteen, often starting at age seven. Girls usually learned to weave by age sixteen, when they were physically big enough to operate a loom. Half of the women's natal families had looms, but only 30 percent of the girls learned to weave before marriage.[52] We estimate that approximately three-quarters of girls who spun or wove routinely produced income in kind through exchanges.[53] As in much of northern China, given the reputation for banditry, men did most of the marketing.

Villagers sold raw cotton, but in the 1930s and 1940s sales of homespun yarn in the county market were limited.[54] Local weavers could buy machine-spun yarn produced in Shanghai, Tianjin, and Nanjing. Town merchants also sold factory cloth imported from big cities, Japan, and other foreign countries. Unlike townsfolk, villagers bought very little cloth and saved money by using their own cotton and hand labor. In Fuyang, roughly sixty kilometers from Linquan, an entrepreneur set up a small weaving factory as early as 1908 (Wang and Shi 1991, 339, 363; FYXZ 1994).[55] Two weaving factories opened in 1928 with thirty looms that produced one thousand meters of white cloth per day using cotton yarn from Shanghai. These looms were twice as fast as the looms used by village women (FYXZ 1994, 148).[56] Many small factory start-ups in Anhui failed in the early years, but as competition drove prices down, innumerable women skilled in spinning and weaving stopped producing for the market.

Liu'an County: Dispersed Hamlets amid Rice Fields

In west-central Anhui south of the Huai River, Liu'an County descends from the northern flank of the Dabie Mountains to the plains. Liu'an had three useful rivers that were prone to flooding but shrank to narrow, shallow passages in the dry season. The Pi River, flowing north to join the Huai, was historically an important trade route linking rural areas to the outside world. During the Qing dynasty, Liu'an County merchants depended on these rivers to import commodities.[57] In the Republican period, "hundreds of boats" were always moored near Liu'an, with especially heavy traffic during the Sino-Japanese War (LAXZ 1993, 235, 294). In 1927, construction of improved roads and bridges opened Liu'an to automobile traffic; a section from Hefei opened in 1932 and soon was traveled by commercial buses. Most roads were damaged during the Sino-Japanese War and not repaired until 1945 (217).

Our research area north of Liu'an City and about twenty kilometers east of the Pi River occupies rolling terrain dotted with small groups of houses and ponds connected by rutted dirt roads. Although we were able to travel by bus from Liu'an City to the village in about fifty minutes, once there, we usually reached dispersed homes on foot. Liu'an is the only village among our north-central sites with irrigated rice as the major grain crop. Villagers also grew wheat, beans, and peanuts. Since many villagers double-cropped their land—irrigated rice followed by winter wheat—and grew cotton, the farms needed more field labor throughout the year than simple single-crop wheat farms.

Girls' and Women's Work in Liu'an

In the Republican period, over 60 percent of the women weeded, picked, and spun cotton as girls at their natal homes. More than a quarter sold or exchanged some of the yarn for other goods.[58] Few women (10 percent) wove cotton cloth before or after marriage. Nonetheless, 24 percent of their natal households and 20 percent of their marital households owned a loom. In a few families, women spun and men wove. Some families grew cotton and hired someone to weave cloth for them. Hired weavers may have used improved looms, as men tended to weave when more efficient looms were adopted (Grove 2006, 20). We asked many times to see old looms, but in Liu'an none survived. The old looms and spinning wheels have vanished, thrown away or burned during the late 1950s Great Leap Forward campaign to smelt iron at home.[59] We could not find traders old enough to have engaged in trade themselves before 1949, but one reported that his father sold yarn and brought back cloth from Hefei, the provincial capital.

In 1922 in Liu'an's county seat five different household workshops began to make white and checked local cloth on wooden looms, each loom producing nearly thirty meters a day. This rate suggests they used improved wooden looms with faster shuttles. In 1933 five suburban households set up larger factories; one used iron-gear looms to make checked cloth. Another factory opened in 1937 with one iron-gear loom and thirty wooden looms, recruiting hundreds of workers to produce white cloth. After 1937, war with Japan stimulated production.[60] In the 1940s, a factory with two hundred knitting machines made socks and towels, and a cloth factory opened with sixteen wooden and six mixed wood-iron looms (LAXZ 1993, 187). Gazetteers report new businesses producing and selling textiles as signs of progress in the 1920s and 1930s. Despite the local visibility of these businesses, the larger transformation involves the massive growth of eastern coast textile factories and the extension of railroads and shipping into the interior.

While village girls still learned to spin, fewer learned to weave. In both sites the proportion of households with looms was higher than the proportion of women weavers, suggesting that home weaving was in decline. Looms were capital equipment that could be used by more than one person in a household or shared among households, so having a loom does not directly correspond to levels of engagement in weaving. Yet in Liu'an only 7 percent of the women wove after marriage.[61] With Liu'an's relative proximity to Yangzi River cities (175 kilometers to Anqing), cloth from Jiangnan textile centers may have supplied the regional textile markets. Also, growing rice and cotton, both labor-intensive crops, may have drawn Liu'an women into fieldwork when homemade yarn and cloth gave way to factory textiles.

Footbinding in Anhui

In the late nineteenth century, footbinding in our northern and central An-hui sites was nearly universal and stayed above 80 percent for women born up to 1920 but tumbled for women born in the 1930s (Figure 3.10). This is well illustrated by the experience of one woman born in 1933: "My mother bound my feet when I was around ten years old. At around age ten I started to spin cotton. Each time she bound my feet, it hurt until I cried. She bound my feet for around six months and then released them. I still had to labor, including harvesting wheat in the fields."[62] Binding and starting to spin coincided at age ten, but family demands for field labor led to cessation of footbinding.

Although half of the Linquan women interviewed experienced binding or attempts at binding that lasted for several months, most were not bound permanently.[63] On average, girls were bound at age eight. In the 1930s

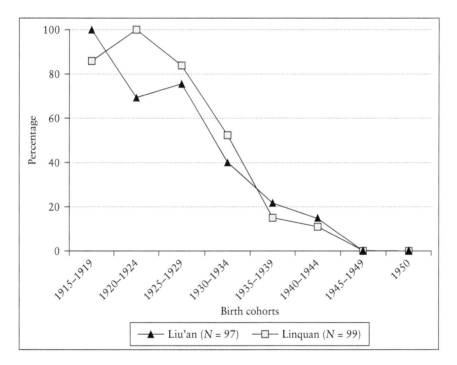

Figure 3.10. Percentage footbound by birth cohort, Linquan and Liu'an Counties, Anhui

NOTE: $N = 196$.

and 1940s many girls were allowed to unbind. Over half of those who unbound were bound for two years or less. Women who had bound feet at the time of marriage (12 percent) were all born before 1930 and stayed permanently bound. Some Linquan women explained that they had only "half-bound," feet whereas their mothers or grandmothers were bound to the tighter standard.

In Liu'an, the rate of binding dropped below 80 percent for women born in the 1920s, suggesting that the practice of footbinding was starting to decrease. As in Linquan, many girls were either allowed to unbind after a short time or were bound only enough to create the half-bound shape (without breaking the arch). Binding began early, with seven as the average age.[64] Of forty-four Liu'an women who were "ever bound," forty-two (95 percent) later unbound. Most unbinding took place in the late 1920s, 1930s, and early 1940s before Communist victory.

High rates of footbinding in northern and central Anhui persisted in the late nineteenth century, while handwork in spinning and weaving was still unchallenged. At first, as merchants introduced foreign and factory-made yarn and cloth to town markets, rural producers were still able to compete. By the 1930s, many large factories and improved channels for selling factory yarn and cloth made in China meant that there was little to gain from making a village girl sit and spin all day and into the night. Footbinding became less useful to mothers. Notably, some women said their fathers opposed binding because they needed the daughter's help in the fields. The rural labor force was changing.

Village girls born in the 1930s faced a world in which new motor roads and railroads brought factory-made products to town markets to compete with village women's handmade yarn and *tubu*. As demand for homespun yarn shriveled, the political turmoil of the 1930s and 1940s disrupted rural livelihoods. After the Japanese invaded eastern China, Nationalist, Communist, and Japanese forces fought across Anhui for seven years, followed by civil war. The recurring violence of competing armies demanding labor, food, and clothes created many difficulties for villagers. Warfare disrupted trade and sometimes stimulated demand for local goods, particularly for the armies, but also accelerated changes in transportation and industry that displaced villagers' handmade textiles and integrated their economies into wider systems. The tradition of binding girls' feet and spinning yarn to increase income was no longer tenable. The declining economic value of home spinning and weaving goes hand in hand with the decline of footbinding.

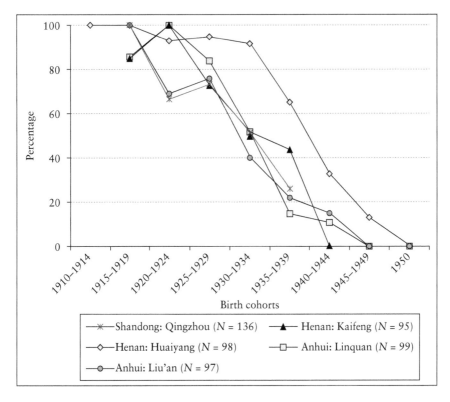

Figure 3.11.   Percentage footbound by birth cohort, northern sites in Shandong, Henan, and Anhui

NOTE: $N = 525$. Qingzhou, Kaifeng, Linquan, and Liu'an show a similar rapid decline in new footbinding for girls born 1930 or later, while in Huaiyang, a mat-making village, the steep decline began five years later.

Figure 3.11 shows similar patterns of decline for the sites in Shandong and Anhui and the Kaifeng site in Henan, where women had once specialized in cloth production. They contrast with Huaiyang, where mat weaving was less affected by mechanization and footbinding lasted a few years longer.

THE NORTHERN EXPERIENCE

The northern villages and provinces we surveyed present intriguing patterns. In Hebei's Ding County sites, we find divergence between the rapid drop in footbinding for those born in the early 1910s in Dongting, the central experimental zone, and the later decline in footbinding in the 1920s birth cohorts in the two other Ding County sites. Footbinding in Pang, the site with mat weaving, persisted a bit longer. In Shandong's Qingzhou, the main decline in footbinding occurred among those born in the 1930s. In Henan and Anhui, we find a similar decline for those born in the 1930s for three of four sites, with a delay evident in Henan's Huaiyang, where making reed mats was the main handcraft. To a large extent, the increasing displacement of hand-spun yarn by factory yarn, followed by competition in cloth markets coming from weaving centers with improved looms and power textile mills, led to a reduction in village girls' hand labor and coincides with the decline in footbinding. Village mat weavers faced less competition from industrial sources, and correspondingly, footbinding was more persistent.

CHAPTER FOUR

Northwest China

Shanxi Province and the northern section of Shaanxi Province face each other across the Yellow River as it flows south, Shanxi to the east and Shaanxi to the west.[1] The river then bends sharply on its long, east-flowing route to the sea. But while Shanxi is hilly throughout, southern Shaanxi is a westward extension of the great North China Plain, with ancient Xi'an as its center. Together, the two provinces have been a bulwark between the Han core and the many steppe-adapted Central Asian peoples. Sections of the Great Wall cross the northern edges of both provinces.

SHANXI PROVINCE

Shanxi's landscape is a rumpled quilt of low mountains catching enough rain to water the small valleys that harbor most of the population. Farmers grew wheat, millet, maize, opium, and tobacco and practiced handcrafts that included papermaking and home production of cotton textiles. Given the rugged terrain, only one-fifth of the Shanxi's land was arable. By the mid-eighteenth century, because of the growing importance of trade and nonagricultural occupations, "mountainous Shanxi had lost the ability to feed its burgeoning population." Grain-poor Shanxi had come to depend on wheat and rice imports from Shaanxi sent down the Wei River to the Yellow River and upstream on the Fen River and, to a lesser extent, from areas to the north, including southern Inner Mongolia (Edgerton-Tarpley 2008, 22, 29, 30).

Shanxi historically had important silk and cotton centers in Taiyuan, the capital, in the Fen River valley and in Changzhi, located on the Lu'an plain in Shanxi's southeastern quadrant. During the mid-eighteenth century, Qing commercial and military interests in China's west increased demand for locally made cottons. Long, cold winters meant that local demand for padded clothing and bedding was high. Although an imperial road ran from Beijing to Taiyuan and then to Xi'an, Shanxi's rugged terrain limited its river transport system and local road networks (Drake 1897, 9–10). Transport difficulties impeded the development of dense commercial networks in Shanxi. Paradoxically, the province was famous for its great merchants, holders of state-granted monopoly rights to sell salt and, from the mid-Qing, to export tea from the central and southeastern provinces to Mongolia and Russia (Avery 2003, 54–68). Merchants benefited from the state-improved route through its central valley that linked them to the Yellow River (Zhang Zhengming 2001, 62–63). In the 1930s, caravans passing through southeastern Shanxi carried "silks and cloths and tobacco" southward from Beijing and the northern territories and returned north (upriver) from Shanxi's southernmost entrepôt on the Yellow River carrying "coal and iron goods, chinaware and cotton wool humped up from the Yellow River by the mule-trains" (Burgess 1957, 105).

Before the drought-induced famine of 1876–1879, Shanxi was a relatively prosperous province. Despite its limited farmland and unreliable water supplies, Shanxi was "rich in natural mineral resources including coal, iron ore, salt, tin, copper, marble and agates" (Edgerton-Tarpley 2008, 22). The province's wealth in coal and iron had long made it a target for distant attention and by the nineteenth century contributed to its "thriving trade networks, evidenced by the abundance of foreign goods in Shanxi's market towns" (20). In 1866 the missionary Alexander Williamson took note of trade goods that included Manchester cottons, Russian woolen goods—"quantities of Russian cloth" due to "a most extensive trade through Mongolia" (Williamson, quoted in Edgerton-Topley 2008, 20). Despite Shanxi's relative wealth and prosperity, the difficulties of grain transport and a weakened Qing state left it vulnerable to the "Incredible Famine" that swept away over a third of the population through starvation, famine-related diseases, and flight from famine (Edgerton-Topley 2008, 1). The massive depopulation, economic disruption, and nineteenth-century shift of trade from China's northwest to southeast meant that Shanxi never recovered its former prosperity. During the Republican period it was "one of China's poorest provinces" (15–22, 24).

Following the Boxer Rebellion and its suppression in 1900, foreign interests imposed reparations on Chinese authorities for Boxer destruction and with the proceeds founded a Western-style university in Taiyuan. By 1907, higher education was spreading through urban Shanxi, and a Beijing-to-Taiyuan railway had been completed (Richards 1916, 299–307). The governing warlord, Yan Xishan, gave Shanxi an unusual degree of political stability for roughly three decades prior to the Japanese invasion (Bonavia 1995, 127; Gillin 1960).[2] Although Yan resembled other warlords of the time, he was both more effective and, to some degree, progressive, enacting many reforms from 1911 to 1930 (Chi Hsi-sheng 1969, 72–73; 1976). He had a road built north as far as the Great Wall and purchased motor buses, bringing his government's stable to forty vehicles (Franck 1923, 259–260). Between 1933 and 1937 he completed most of the Tongpu railway across the province from Datong in the northeast to Puzhou in Shanxi's southwestern corner (Chen Minglu 2011, 33). Yan campaigned to have farmers grow more cotton, erected cotton mills, and subsidized cottage industries such as manufacture of stockings, mats, straw hats, and willow products (Gillin 1960, 303).

Yan Xishan also paid unusual attention to women's issues, giving Shanxi a special place in the abandonment of footbinding (Gillin 1960, 295; Ko 2005, 50–64). In addition to establishing schools and encouraging girls' education, he took a firm line against footbinding with a province-wide campaign to eradicate it (1917–1922). Inspectors could fine women who bound their daughters or refused to unbind themselves (Franck 1923; Gillin 1960, 295; Harrison 2005, 131; Ko 2005, 53–64).

From 1937 to 1945, the Japanese occupied Shanxi largely because of its coal reserves (Bonavia 1995, 127). They controlled the capital, Taiyuan, and the northern coal city Datong. Efforts to control smaller urban centers and their rural hinterlands were less successful. The Red Army and Communist Party had a strong base in northern Shaanxi, across the Yellow River on Shanxi's western border, near our site in Lin County. From there, they developed an effective underground, recruiting Shanxi men for the army and Shanxi women to make up in textile production by hand for deficits from the wartime severing of trade.

Changzhi County: Peri-urban Villages Lacking Local Cotton

Located on a small plain, Changzhi City has long been the administrative center of a small valley southwest of the Taihang Mountains in the southeastern part of Shanxi. Almost encircled by higher ground, Changzhi County is relatively well supplied with water both from small streams and modest amounts of rain. With its own patch of rich loess, it has been one of Shanxi's most agriculturally productive regions, growing North China's typical staples: wheat, corn, barley, millet, and, notably, hemp (Zhang and Sun 2005, 356). It also preserved remnants of what was once a famous silk industry. Yet it lacked transport advantages. The rugged Taihang Mountains separated Changzhi by about sixty kilometers of hard travel eastward to the Hebei flatlands. Another difficult trail northward linked it with the imperial road that ran through the Fen River valley. Its main river, the Zhuo Jiang, is not navigable. Most trade and migration moved eastward into some of the poorest counties in Hebei or southward along a mule track to the Yellow River. Only in 1929 (under Yan Xishan) was the mule path from the Yellow River to Changzhi replaced by a rough road adequate for automobile traffic, including occasional bus service (Karlbeck 1957, 69). In 2006 our survey covered thirteen villages in two townships in the suburbs of Changzhi, about eleven kilometers east of the city center, in order to find enough elderly women for our sample.

Because each village site has somewhat different resources and market access, our sample villages contain varied patterns of economic activity.[3] Overall, the villagers' main grain crops were wheat, corn, and beans. Some of the villagers grew hemp or raised silkworms to obtain textile fibers, but less than a handful grew cotton. The closest areas that specialized in growing cotton were located to the east in Henan and Hebei and in the southwestern part of Shanxi (Buck 1937, 64, map 27). Most villagers had to purchase raw cotton brought over the mountains from areas much like Ding County for their clothing and quilts. Women said they could buy cotton at village or temple markets.

Girls' and Women's Work in Changzhi

Before marriage, girls spun and wove cotton to clothe their families, but not many sold surplus cloth. Of the women surveyed, 58 percent had spun cotton (12 percent for sale) when they were young girls. A woman born in 1930 reported that spinning a *jin* (sixteen *liang*) of cotton could be sold for a few *mao*. "I gave the yarn to my father to take to neighboring villages to sell. From age eleven I started to earn money for the family."[4] Another, born in 1934, told of exchanging her hand-spun yarn for "rough cloth" (*cubu*), and a woman born in 1935 sold her finished yarn to a weaving workshop. One might spin all summer to make enough yarn for a set of clothes and a pair of shoes. As in many parts of China, spinners could produce three to five Chinese ounces (*liang*) of yarn a day. In Changzhi's peri-urban villages, roughly two to three days of spinning earned a *jin* of raw cotton. As sixteen *liang* of yarn could be made from one *jin* of raw cotton,[5] a day's spinning earned the raw material for one to two additional days' work. Each *liang* brought "ten cents," one *mao qian*,[6] as did a pair of footbinding cloths. Some girls combined half a day of spinning with half a day of embroidery.

In our sample 19 percent of the women wove cotton cloth before marriage, closely corresponding with the 18 percent whose natal homes owned looms, but only 4 percent reported selling cloth. Long Bow Village (Zhangzhuang), studied by William Hinton in 1948, is located on the outskirts of Changzhi within fifteen kilometers of our village sites.[7] Then, Long Bow villagers all wore homespun cotton clothing and cloth shoes, except the gentry, who on special occasions wore silks and satins imported "from the South" (Hinton 1966, 24). Hinton told of old Lady Wang, with bound feet and hands always busy at spinning, winding, and weaving, who was "one of the few women who still knew how to weave at a time when that ancient art had suffered almost total extinction due to the cheap imported and coastal manufactured textiles" (292, 428).

In some Changzhi villages women and girls worked with other fibers: 22 percent had made hemp twine, including 8 percent who sold it. One woman recalled that she was just six or seven when she began to learn to twist hemp rope, while another was doing so at eight.[8] Another craft was reeling silk, accounting for 12 percent, and 5 percent had raised silkworms for sale or exchange. Taken together, the Changzhi villages present a picture of women performing varied handcrafts, many beginning to work with their hands on a regular basis from a tender age.

Lin County, Qikou Town: A Strategic River Port

Our Lin County site at Qikou sits beside the Yellow River at Shanxi's western border. With little arable land on its high, gullied plain, Qikou grew as a ferry port on the north-south stretch of the Yellow River, a crossing place for east-west trade with Shaanxi. The Qing dynasty's encouragement of trade to China's far west brought merchants who rafted wheat and vegetable oil downriver from northern Shaanxi in reed baskets. Camel and mule caravans carried goods across the river through Shaanxi to Mongolia and points beyond (Gao Chunping 2006, 180–182). In the late Qing, Qikou ranked among the top five commercial towns of North China (177). Between 1916 and 1919, 361 local shopkeepers and transport merchants subscribed to the rebuilding of the local Black Dragon King temple;[9] almost 700 more peddlers made the town their base. The richest Qikou magnates built stone cave complexes strong enough to secure them against bandits and handsome enough to allow gracious entertainment of fellow merchants and their trains of men and animals. By the 1930s, some shops sold Japanese and German textiles. Qikou merchants had few dealings in local products (Karlbeck 1957, 67).

In 1929, Orvar Karlbeck, a Swedish treasure hunter, passed through Qikou just as Yan Xishan was having a road built there from the main, Fen River valley, road. It was still so incomplete that travelers reached the town on foot along the dry bed of the Qiushui River. Karlbeck crossed north of Qikou in ferry boats like "gigantic troughs—large enough to carry about ten mules in addition to loads and human passengers" (1957, 65).

> The name Chik'ou [Qikou] may be translated as "the entry to the Gobi Desert," and this seemed apt, as the country further upstream looked like a desert. . . . Yet the town itself was quite unlike a desert town, and south of it I could see green fields. It was a long, narrow place, built on the very banks of the river that seemed to be simply "liquid mud." (Karlbeck 1957, 65–67)

Yan Xishan's power was evident in Qikou. As early as 1915 and 1917, respectively, Yan brought telegraph lines and a post office to the town, twenty years before such amenities were bestowed on the county seat, Lin Xian (Karlbeck 1957, 182). As an important entrepôt and river crossing point, Qikou was militarily strategic. In 1938, the Japanese bombed Qikou flat, leaving only sixty-one of an original four hundred businesses operative (Gao Chunping 2006). Previously Yan's construction of both a railway and a motor vehicle road down the central Fen River valley had undermined Qikou's significance as a commercial town. Today, farming villages cluster near its center, a few fisher families among them. Irrigation and shallow wells supply staple crops, but apart from a small stream of tourists, the little port languishes.

Girls' and Women's Work in Qikou

Women's handcrafts in this region were both important and acknowledged in the literature on the Communist base area. In our Qikou survey, 93 percent of the women spun cotton before marriage, 49 percent doing so for sale. Almost 60 percent of natal households had owned a loom, with 55 percent of informants weaving in girlhood, 25 percent weaving for sale. Hemp spinning was also important: 50 percent of the girls spun it, 25 percent doing so for sale.

A commemorative plaque above the Qiushui Cloth Shop in Qikou emphasizes the importance of cotton textiles in this region but also implies cotton was scarce prior to 1920. According to this plaque, in 1920 Li Xiang-ting from Lijiashan Village of Qikou "took the lead in growing cotton," and later it became widespread. In 1941, all rural families were planting cotton, and every household was spinning and weaving. Shops for purchasing ginned cotton, cotton thread, and hand-loomed cotton "emerged as the times required." The Qiushui Cloth Shop is mentioned as part of the Chinese Communist Party (CCP) Shanxi-Suiyuan border region, which purchased cotton, yarn, and cloth from peasant families. These products were then "transported to many parts of the country by camels, to meet the demands of the army and the areas without cotton."[10] This record points to a deliberate promotion of cotton and handcraft production in the early twentieth century following an earlier period when traders brought cotton and cloth to Qikou from other regions.

The intensity of women's handcrafts in this area must be considered in the context of Communist base areas and their influence on Shanxi women's wartime textile production.[11] Oral histories from elders who lived through the Communist takeover of the region are replete with descriptions of villagers organized into shoemaking and textile teams, women and girls predominating. Cadres were not shy about describing the difficulties of getting participation from these already busy women (Zhang and Sun 2005, 41, 79, 82–90).[12] Figures 4.1 and 4.2 illustrate the use of the spinning wheel by a contemporary woman of Qikou and by a young girl spinner in the 1940s.

Footbinding in Changzhi County and Qikou Town

Our two Shanxi sites differ in the timing of abandonment of footbinding. In Changzhi, the late decline in footbinding is consistent with our hypothesis

Figure 4.1. Woman demonstrating use of simple spinning wheel in classic seated position in Lin County, Shanxi

Figure 4.2. A seven-year-old girl spinning cotton yarn in Yan'an, Shaanxi, 1942

regarding girls' handwork. In contrast, Lin County data from Qikou show a relatively early decline in footbinding; Qikou does not fit the prediction that associates intense hand labor by girls and women with the practice of binding. We do not expect that each and every site and individual will conform to our hypothesis or that we can explain each and every exception. Nonetheless, we try to understand the particulars of each site.

In Changzhi County, the high proportion of girls born before 1930 who experienced binding is consistent with the large proportion who engaged in some form of handcraft, whether spinning and weaving cotton, making hemp twine, or reeling silk. Despite the publicity given to Yan's reforms, the decline of footbinding in Changzhi was not particularly early (Figure 4.3). The slight dip in the footbound percentage for those born 1920–1924, during his tenure, is not significant given the small number of individuals (four) in that cohort. The rate of binding was high for the larger

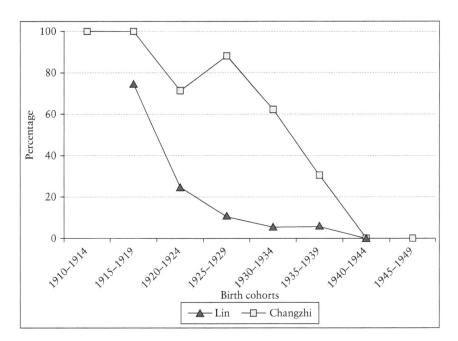

Figure 4.3.   Percentage footbound by birth cohort, Lin and Changzhi Counties, Shanxi

NOTE: *N* = 189. In Qikou, Lin County, footbinding declined rapidly for girls born in the early 1920s, while in the Changzhi County sites, comparable decline occurred in the late 1930s.

1925–1929 birth cohort, only to begin its final decline for those born 1930 or later, when road and railroad transport projects neared completion. In 1948, in nearby Long Bow Village (occupied by the Japanese from 1937 to 1945), Hinton observed women's bound feet with the "bones stunted so that they formed a crushed stump," making their walking movement stiff, "as if on stilts." [13] He also noted the unevenness of change. "Foot binding came to an end almost everywhere in the period between the two world wars but even in 1945 young girls with crippled feet could still be found in the mountain counties of Shansi [Shanxi]" (Hinton 1966, 24).

In Lin County, the percentage of women who experienced footbinding dropped relatively early in Qikou, yet spinning and weaving were widespread (Figure 4.3). For those born in the 1920s (who would have reached binding age by the early 1930s) binding had already declined to less than 15 percent and stayed low until it stopped completely for those born in 1940. Why did footbinding in Qikou decline so much earlier than in the villages of Changzhi?

As a busy river port and commercial town through the nineteenth and early twentieth centuries, Qikou differs from the more isolated inland village economies of Lin County. Among the important considerations is Qikou's greater degree of urbanization due to the many resident merchants and long-distance traders who gathered there. Other possible influences include strong enforcement of Yan Xishan's anti-footbinding reforms and early decline of handwork as a result of changing transportation and foreign textile competition as early as the late nineteenth century. These influences were then obscured by the revival of cotton growing promoted in the 1920s and the heavy pressure to revive hand spinning and weaving cotton cloth in response to the economic needs of local Communist bases during the Anti-Japanese War.

The effectiveness of Yan Xishan's ban on Shanxi footbinding in general is debatable (Ko 2005, 50–64). In the 1920s, foreigners resident in Taiyuan opined that his "laws against opium and bound feet would be better enforced . . . if the officials under him were really in favor of such reforms. . . . Bound feet are most persistent in rural districts . . . [but] little girls with bound feet may be seen near and even in Taiyuan" (Franck 1923, 259–261). In the mid-1930s, Gladys Aylward, a missionary–turned–foot inspector, visited villages one hundred kilometers south of Changzhi, unbinding feet, but there are no reports of follow-up visits by Aylward to see if girls' feet remained unbound (Aylward 1970; Burgess 1957). Two early 1930s census reports from Shanxi show contradictory evidence regarding the decline of binding; one gives an optimistic report of its decline between 1928 and 1934, while another in 1932–1933 counted "almost one million women aged thirty and under who had bound feet" (Ko 2005, 62).[14]

Our Changzhi evidence supports the view that Yan Xishan's early efforts to eradicate footbinding did not produce a definitive change there. Government efforts to halt footbinding may have been stronger in Qikou, where one elderly woman born in 1916 recalled that about forty female inspectors arrived riding on donkeys and pulled off women's binding cloths. Over 90 percent of the Qikou women said that, as girls, they had heard of government bans on footbinding (in contrast to 75 percent in Changzhi). Two Qikou women specifically mentioned Yan Xishan, while several others mention seeing or hearing of footbinding inspectors. We are uncertain, however, whether these visits were organized through Yan's efforts or the later Communist campaign.[15]

Qikou's early footbinding decline may relate to its position as a strategic ferry crossing on the Yellow River. A gateway for long-distance trade, Qikou probably had early access to imported cotton cloth from eastern China. The commemorative plaque mentioned previously suggests that before 1920, Qikou grew little cotton or had poor access to it. By the early twentieth century, improvements in northern overland transport between Beijing and Baotou (Inner Mongolia) may have ousted locally handwoven cloth from northwestern export markets and opened Qikou itself to cloth imported from eastern China's expanding textile mills and workshops. The Beijing-Baotou railway (begun in 1905 and completed in 1923) was one of many transportation changes that lowered transport costs from China's eastern coast to northwestern markets in Inner Mongolia, Shaanxi, and Gansu. These changes may have led Qikou townswomen to limit textile work, diminishing their incentive to bind their daughters' feet.

By 1938, when Japanese occupation blocked trade (including textiles) from the east, the demand for locally produced Shanxi cotton cloth in Communist base areas surged. Local women were recruited to make up the deficit. The establishment of Shanxi women's textile teams in areas under Communist influence changed the domestic economy of handcrafts. An extraordinary body of oral histories of elderly men and women who lived through the Japanese period was collected by Shanxi historians Zhang

Chengde and Sun Liping (2005). Respondents who had been party activists emphasize the efforts they made to turn women's time from domestic to public work. Zhang and Sun's three thousand oral histories rarely refer to footbinding. During the Japanese and Civil War years, the CCP could ill afford to risk the goodwill of the populace on whom they were entirely dependent for food, clothing, and silence in the face of Japanese threats.[16]

Those impressed into women's war work often expressed pride but also noted the difficulties of meeting the many demands on them. These textile teams supplied ten million pieces of military clothing that, without their work, would have required the import of twenty million *zhang* (3.3 meters) of *tubu*. Shanxi women's teams also plaited straw sandals by the millions (Zhang Guoxiang 2005, 271–272, 292). Most of the output of these textile teams came from the Communist Eighth Route Army's main Shanxi base in the Taihang Mountains, which separated Shanxi's central valley from the plains of Hebei to the east. Women's textile teams were also organized in areas around our two Shanxi research sites in Changzhi and Lin Counties.[17] Handwoven *tubu* produced in Lin County could be exported through Qikou to Yan'an, the Communist base area in northern Shaanxi.[18] Women interviewed in both research sites remembered the Eighth Route Army as a vivid presence in their girlhoods, as did many old men and women interviewed by Zhang and Sun (2005) about the Anti-Japanese War.

Textile teams, formed from groups of women, were often given spinning wheels and looms. In Qikou the influence of Communist organizers is commemorated in large posters and pictures displayed on building walls and in homes. Although we saw little evidence of anti-footbinding reforms, the very act of spinning or weaving *together* as part of a group in a public space would have replaced the private discipline and discretion of mothers to discipline daughters with the public discipline and incentives of the women's textile teams.

When the Communists promoted textile production, they aspired to re-create industrial and improved production technologies but lacked the means. Many efforts were made, with the limited wooden materials available, to build more productive spinning wheels and looms for use by cooperative workshops as well as in homes. As a result of cloth scarcity and high military demand, incentives to learn spinning and weaving were revived during the war, while in the general context of moving women's labor outside the home, the incentives to bind girls' feet for domestic work were further undermined. Higher authorities would ensure labor discipline. These special circumstances may explain why Qikou's early decline in footbinding was not reversed when spinning and weaving were revived.

Shaanxi Province is divided by topography into dramatically distinct parts. The sparsely populated northern region, Shaanbei, is an arid, corrugated upland typical of China's Loess Plateau where compacted and eroded layers of windswept dust from Central Asia have been carved into a maze of gullies, rifts, and chasms. In contrast, Shaanxi's central plain, Guanzhong,[19] is a densely populated, relatively flat area with fertile, well-watered farmland. It stretches past the western limits of the North China Plain along the Wei River valley, a belt across the middle of Shaanxi. Fed from alluvial land, enriched by river trade, and linked by imperial roads to Beijing and Sichuan, Guanzhong formed the heartland of China's oldest empires. The walled capital city, Xi'an (once Chang'an), in Guanzhong was the eastern terminus of the Silk Road. Shaanxi's southern region is dominated by the towering Qin mountain range that divides Shaanxi from Sichuan. (In the days before smog, you could see the mountains from Xi'an.) Our research sites in Shaanxi are in the Guanzhong and Shaanbei regions. The first site is in Zhouzhi County on the plains just south of the Wei River, around 85 kilometers west of Xi'an. The second, Luochuan County, about 200 kilometers north of Xi'an at an elevation of 975 meters, has a notably shorter growing season and a colder, harsher climate in winter. Rugged loess terrain separates Luochuan from the Yellow River 125 kilometers to the east.

Throughout the nineteenth century, riverboats, human porters, and pack animals plodding over narrow dirt trails remained the main modes of conveyance. The two major rivers of Shaanxi are the Wei and the Yellow. Flowing east, the Wei passes Zhouzhi and Xi'an to join the Yellow River at Tongguan, the junction of Shaanxi, Shanxi, and Henan Provinces. In the eighteenth and nineteenth centuries, large vessels on the Wei shipped Shaanxi rice and wheat eastward to Shanxi (Edgerton-Tarpley 2008, 30). By 1931 the Longhai railway had reached Tongguan at the eastern border of Shaanxi and was extended westward (1934–1938) along the Wei valley, connecting Xi'an and Zhouzhi. In 1931 Shaanxi had but one improved dirt road following the old Silk Road from Tongguan to Gansu, but over the next decade road building with asphalt or gravel for trade and military transport greatly expanded.

In northern Shaanxi, the Yellow River flows south along its eastern border with Shanxi to Tongguan and then turns east on its long course to the sea. Snaking through the rugged Loess Plateau of Shaanbei, punctuated by the large Hukou waterfall and the often violent current through gorges, the river was not suited to large craft or steamships (Edgerton-Tarpley 2008, 30; Clapp 1922, 10–12), but camels and riverboats made the trip with goods from Mongolia and farther east.[20] Shaanbei traders, including those of Luochuan County, made their way through terrain "cut up in all directions by enormous rifts" (Teichman 1918, 344), relying on pack mules, horse carts, and carrying poles. A motor road from Xi'an was completed in 1936.[21]

Zhouzhi County: Cotton by the Wei River

In the early twentieth century, Zhouzhi farmers grew a wide variety of food, fiber, and other crops on their partly irrigated land. Staple grains included wheat, corn, beans, and rice, which were consumed locally and exported to other parts of China (Bossen et al. 2011). Zhouzhi's excellent cotton, the most important commercial crop, was easily shipped down the Wei and Yellow Rivers to supply neighboring provinces and the coastal textile industries. From 1925 to 1932, cotton competed with the opium that the warlord required for tax payments. These years coincided with a devastating drought and famine (1928–1934) that killed millions in Shaanxi (ZZXZ 1993). Although opium remains a sensitive subject, almost one-fifth of Zhouzhi village women said that their natal families had grown and sold opium. Harvesting opium by scraping the pods of the opium poppy involved light hand labor, which in some parts of China was performed by girls (Gates 2015, 139–140; Hershatter 2007).[22]

Girls' and Women's Work in Zhouzhi

Zhouzhi women's experiences emphasized the importance of cotton, which they picked, processed, used, and sold.[23] More than 80 percent of our sample households grew cotton, and more than 50 percent of the girls also contributed labor to the crop. In addition, 90 percent of them spun it, 20 percent spinning for sale or exchange. Of the women interviewed 75 percent wove cotton as well, although only 15 percent said they wove for sale, wages, or

Figure 4.4. Woman and discarded wooden loom in her courtyard in Zhouzhi, Shaanxi. In many households, the old looms were abandoned long ago. Because her feet are bound, this woman needs the support of a cane.

exchange of other goods (Figure 4.4). That more than half their families owned looms in their girlhoods and after marriage is consistent with the general importance of cloth weaving in Guanzhong (Bossen et al. 2011; Vermeer 1988, 334–345; CXZZXZ 1925). Households with access to homegrown cotton, a female labor force skilled in hand labor, and good transportation to markets with a demand for cloth had a strong incentive to spin and weave.

Although factories came late to Shaanxi itself, access to machine yarns via the Yellow River and Longhai railway after 1909 began to reduce the need for spinning all the thread used in weaving. In 1936, the Dahua Textile Factory was built in Xi'an, the first in the province, with twenty-five thousand spindles and nine hundred workers (Lai 1967, 123; Zhang and Shi 1997, 192; Vermeer 1988, 345), and by 1937 the provincial government was promoting improved looms and training schools. These changing market conditions led to a drop in demand for local handmade yarn and cloth, a drop that was temporarily reversed when war with Japan disrupted the import of finished textiles from the east (Bossen et al. 2011; Vermeer 1988).

As women recalled what they earned as girls when hired to spin or spinning for market exchange, the many variables involved proved intractable for determining price changes. A woman born in 1931 reported that a *jin* of spun thread that would have taken two or three days' labor earned a *sheng* (about one liter) of corn kernels. A woman born in 1926 reported that as a girl she received a *jin* of raw cotton for spinning a *jin* of yarn, while another, born in 1936, earned only half as much. Others told of earning two or three *yuan* for a *jin* of spun thread. The many factors involved in these exchanges—the inflow of factory yarn; variations in local units of measurement and individual capabilities; local and seasonal price fluctuations for cotton, yarn, and different types of grain; and different monetary units—combine to make judgments about returns for work exceptionally difficult. In addition, Zhouzhi women engaged in forms of handcraft other than cotton textiles. Roughly a quarter (27 percent) reeled silk, although only 11 percent reported selling the thread. Twisting hemp into twine was rarely mentioned, but some Zhouzhi women plaited straw hats for sale.

Historian Gail Hershatter has conducted in-depth interviews with elderly women who grew up in Shaanxi's Guanzhong region where cotton crops and cotton textile work were common. Her accounts of girls' labor in the early twentieth century are similar to our findings in Zhouzhi:

> When Shan Xiuzhen turned eight [in the 1920s], her mother set up a spinning wheel for her. Like many other young girls, she was then required to spin cotton daily, her mother's unceasing labor a model and a goad. *My natal mother was very strict with me. I was afraid of her. She did needlework at night. You couldn't stop spinning until she stopped working. I spun for others, not for myself. You were not allowed to run away.*
>
> Young girls were given quotas by their mothers. . . . They remember spinning as part of what made their mothers' lives and their own childhoods "pitiful": working at night, too poor to light an oil lamp, threading the spindle by the light of the glowing tip of an incense stick. (Hershatter 2011, 45–46)

Luochuan County: Cave Homes in Rugged Terrain

Luochuan lies in the southern part of Shaanbei, where transport routes were treacherous. Shaanbei's rich, loess soil is flat overall but deeply gullied by rivers, cart wheels, and donkey hooves. This region is arid with few trees, but the steep slopes and narrow paths are slippery when wet. Cold winters limit the growing season to four or five months in the year. The main crops for our site were wheat, corn, sorghum, buckwheat, millet, and beans. In this area with low population density, long distances "separated hamlets from each other and from markets" (Keating 1997, 31). Internal caravan roads moved goods slowly through the region to the north beyond the Great Wall to Mongolia. From the north, traders brought sheep's wool, pelts, felt, and donkey hides south to Xi'an in exchange for superior raw cotton, cotton wadding, or cotton cloth from Guanzhong (Huang Zhenglin 2006, 140; Keating 1994b, 138).

Most Luochuan villagers live in earthen "cave homes" (*yaodong*), arched tunnels carved out of the loess soil. Despite the association of caves with prehistory and hardship, these homes are cool in summer and warm in winter. In Luochuan they are generally very tidy inside, with smooth, whitewashed walls and orderly arrangements of cooking, sleeping, work-ing, and storage areas and solid doors. South-facing windows catch sun-shine, and courtyards are enclosed by walls. Because of the short growing season, Shaanbei women and girls devoted considerable energy to hand-crafts, making products from many fibers, each requiring distinct skills (Huang Zhenglin 2006, 444). Among them, spinning and weaving cotton predominated, but women and girls also made various products from hemp (yarn, twine, or paper) and silk (yarn, wadding), often for sale (140, 443).

From 1936 to 1949 a large part of Shaanbei belonged to the Shaan-Gan-Ning Border Region under Communist rule. The Communist presence there, based in the city of Yan'an and extending northward beyond Yulin, has left large, disorderly, and politically inflected bodies of information about this region that rarely illuminate our quest for the work of girls. Moreover, our site was just south of the Communist-controlled area, so generalizations based on writings about the Shaan-Gan-Ning region can be misleading.

Girls' and Women's Work in Luochuan

Acquiring sufficient clothing in this area of bitterly cold winters was vital. Most women worked with cotton to make clothing, padded jackets and pants, quilts, warm bedding, and cloth shoes. Cotton was not grown in or near Luochuan, so villagers had to buy it from other regions.[24] According to local traders, they could buy raw cotton in Chengcheng and Heyang Counties, roughly 150 kilometers overland to the southeast. Cotton cloth may also have been sold there, but villagers did not buy it. Most village girls (72 percent) worked at spinning raw cotton into yarn. All of the Luochuan woman we interviewed said their families did not buy machine-made thread for their weaving. Two-thirds (66 percent) of their natal households had looms for cotton weaving. As teenage girls, nearly 40 percent of the women interviewed had woven yarn into cloth, thus helping their mothers clothe the family. The average marriage age for girls was quite young, just over fourteen years for girls married before 1940.[25] Only a few women (3 percent) reported selling cloth, and very few used machine-made cloth before 1945.

Over a third of our Luochuan sample had reeled silk as girls. Twelve had also raised silkworms, but few sold silk floss. Home-reeled silk could be used for sewing sturdy cotton garments or dyed for embroidery. A few women reported that they had woven silk as girls. Although often associated with elite clothing, silk could also be made into rough, hard-wearing, and absorbent fabric or used as wadding for the winter jackets and pants worn by villagers.[26] Some women also made their own hemp thread or twine, which they used to stitch together layers of cloth to make shoe soles and shoes.[27] Roughly 80 percent of the women had stitched clothes and shoes as girls (there were no sewing machines). Virtually all married women stitched cloth shoes for their families and sometimes for sale. Women also made baskets from sorghum stalks, as well as pillows and waistbands.[28]

An unusual hand skill of Luochuan women was using scissors to cut out fine paper designs for which the area has become famous. In the past, these paper cuttings were made as gifts, not for sale.[29] Many older women are still highly skilled in cutting complex designs and pictures out of colored paper, which they place on the south-facing windows to decorate their cave homes, while copies of their work are sold as folk art, gift cards, and calendars in today's urban Shaanxi gift shops. Alongside these varied forms of hand labor, Luochuan women had daily courtyard chores that included pushing the heavy millstone used to grind flour from coarse grains.

Luochuan women and girls practiced many varieties of skilled hand labor but produced little surplus and had few opportunities to sell. Unlike the northeastern part of Shaanbei bordering the Yellow River (Keating 1994b), the southern part had a low incidence of commercial handcraft production. This dispersed population, lacking easy river, railway, or road connections, had few possibilities for commerce. Finally, women themselves rarely went to markets because of the difficult roads between settlements and the dangers of banditry (Keating 1994b, 129; Teichman 1918). With little commerce, Luochuan women had to be self-sufficient, making most of what they needed at home.

As larger and more mechanized textile industries began to supply markets in northern Shaanbei, such as Suide City, and to the south in Guanzhong, the cost of getting Luochuan's homemade cloth to market centers gave women almost no chance to compete for sales.[30] Disruptions of cloth supplies and military demand for cloth during the war years temporarily revived demand for village women's spinning and weaving in Shaanbei. Much has been written about the spinning and weaving cooperatives in Yan'an's border region in both Shaanxi and Shanxi (see the Lin County section), yet their impact on girls' labor remains difficult to assess. Access to cotton and the skills that turned it into clothes and bedding became military treasures. During the Anti-Japanese War, government efforts by both Nationalists and Communists to introduce better spinning wheels and looms as well as specialized workshops turned the tide, shifting away from girls' and women's home-based handwork (Bossen et al. 2011; Keating 1994a, 1034; LCXZ 1994; Schran 1976).

Footbinding in Zhouzhi and Luochuan

When did efforts to initiate new bindings on young girls' feet stop in rural Shaanxi? Our interviews show that in Luochuan, footbinding stopped for those born by 1935, but in Zhouzhi it slowed or stopped falling temporarily for those born 1935–1939 (Figure 4.5).[31] In terms of household labor decisions, this difference was probably related to villagers' access to raw cotton. The cotton-growing Zhouzhi villagers would have sufficient cotton supplies to respond to heavy demand for cloth and shoes for the military until the war with Japan ended in 1945. It was expensive for Luochuan villagers to buy cotton or cloth, so they mainly purchased the cotton they needed for their own clothing. Once the war with Japan ended, textile factories could resume production and distribution, putting downward pressure on the prices for homespun yarn. The strategy of requiring young girls to have bound feet and stay home and spin, weave, and perform needlework was massively challenged for the 1940–1944 birth cohort. As the Anti-Japanese War and Civil War ended, both cloth production and young women textile workers were about to leave the family courtyard.

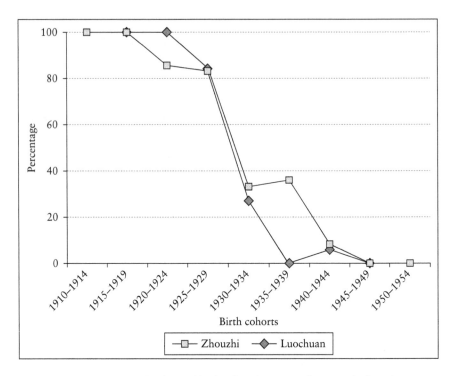

Figure 4.5. Percentage footbound by birth cohort, Luochuan and Zhouzhi
Counties, Shaanxi

NOTE: *N* = 205. In Shaanxi, footbinding steeply declined in both sites for girls born in the
late 1920s, yet about one-third of the Zhouzhi girls born in the late 1930s (binding age in
the 1940s) had their feet bound. In Luochuan, footbinding had basically stopped.

THE NORTHWEST EXPERIENCE

In the northwest, footbinding in Qikou, the Yellow River crossing in Lin
County, stopped for those born in the 1920s, unusually early for those born
in such a remote, inland setting. Most likely this was due to a combination of three factors: the scarcity of local cotton; concentrated commercial activity, including transport of eastern cloth to northwestern areas in
Shaanxi and Gansu; and possibly early warlord and Communist policies.
The villages neighboring Changzhi City, in contrast, gave up binding only
in the 1930s. With diverse handcraft possibilities besides cotton textiles,
footbinding persisted a bit longer. In Shaanxi, both northern Luochuan and
central Guanzhong Counties experienced their dramatic drop in footbind-

ing for those born in the early 1930s, with cotton-growing Zhouzhi stalling a bit during the war years. Competition brought by the new transport and textile technologies spurred changes in the value of girls' hand labor.

As we see in Chapter 3 and in this chapter, the varieties of girls' and women's hand labor across North and Northwest China reveal an important amount of economic activity by girls that has been commonly overlooked. This was particularly true during the period when textiles, the dominant handcraft sector and China's dominant export, experienced a major cataclysm in the form of machine-made competition. Although the women and girls employed in domestic textile production were never formally counted, their work accounted for a huge part of China's nonagricultural production. No wonder cries and laments came from distant parts of the empire and republic as their work became obsolete and devalued. The areas—mostly coastal—that were first able to seize on and embrace the new industrial technologies enjoyed not only higher production but also higher consumption. The rural areas of the interior from north to northwest, with very few exceptions, lacked such "first-adopter" opportunities.

Considering the pervasiveness of handwork in the lives of rural women and the wide geographic spread of footbinding across the North China Plain and beyond, it is truly remarkable that an entrenched custom that so transformed and constrained the bodies of Chinese girls could be abruptly abandoned in the early twentieth century. Yet this rapid abandonment took place. We have not only traced the decline of footbinding in different places over time but also examined the varieties of work that girls and women could do with bound feet. In most cases, transportation improvements and the expanding trade in machine-made yarn and cloth led to a decline in the possibilities for girls and women to earn handcraft income at home, a shift accompanied by a decline in footbinding. While mechanized yarn and cloth production in the textile industries visibly created employment for young, unmarried women in the large coastal cities, it invisibly eroded the income-earning opportunities of a vastly larger labor force of home-based rural girls and women.

In Chapter 5, we move away from the North China Plain to China's southwestern provinces to further examine the links between girls' and women's handwork and bound feet.

CHAPTER FIVE

Southwest China

How did the patterns of intensive hand labor and footbinding associated with the old centers of Han civilization reach and ultimately recede in the remote southwest? An exceptionally rough topography limited both ancient long-distance trade and the unrelenting Han colonization that dispersed indigenous ethnic groups. These processes shaped a distinctive social order in Yunnan and Guizhou. In the nineteenth century, the difficulties of developing modern transport in the mountainous southwest delayed villagers' encounters with industrial products. Changes in women's lives resulting from such transport emerged still later, in the early twentieth century. The foreign trade and industrial technologies transforming China's eastern coast in the late nineteenth century took longer to reach the southwest.

Southwest China differs from the north and northwest in that cotton did not grow well in most of the region. We consider the effect that the lack of locally grown cotton had on Han women's customary specialization in textile production and hence on the incentives to bind girls' feet. As in Chapters 3 and 4, we explore the relation between hand labor and footbinding in different village contexts, looking specifically at the prevalence of footbinding with respect to different patterns of female hand labor and farmwork. How common was the practice of footbinding among Han women in this remote part of China? Did villages with different patterns of female hand labor and farmwork exhibit different footbinding practices? This chapter concentrates on our findings from Yunnan and Guizhou. To augment our examination of Southwest China, we include a brief section on neighboring Sichuan Province, drawing on a separate, detailed study of labor and footbinding conducted by Gates (2015). Although large enough to warrant a separate study, Sichuan is often grouped with Yunnan and Guizhou as part of China's southwest. Including a summary of the Sichuan findings here presents a unique opportunity to examine and compare patterns of labor and footbinding on a very large scale.

YUNNAN AND GUIZHOU

The provinces of Yunnan and Guizhou, similar in environment and economic history and often grouped as Yun-Gui (Skinner 1977), form China's southwestern frontier. Guizhou lies at Yunnan's northeastern boundary, and both provinces face Sichuan as a northern neighbor. Yunnan borders Southeast Asia (Burma, Thailand, Laos, and Vietnam) and Tibet to the south and west, while Guizhou abuts Guangxi to the south and Hunan to the east. Most Yun-Gui terrain is rugged, karst or mountainous, with highland valleys cultivated by settled farmers. The great Yangzi, Mekong, Red, Salween, and Irrawaddy Rivers that pass through Yunnan are mostly not navigable within the province.[1] Central and eastern Yunnan contains several large lakes and fertile plains. Southern Yunnan descends into tropical lowlands. Water transport was largely limited to lakes located in valley basins. Lacking fertile valleys and plains, Guizhou was sparsely settled. Mountainous terrain made for high transportation costs in both provinces. In the late nineteenth century, it took more than forty days on foot to travel the six hundred kilometers between Guiyang and Kunming, the capitals of Guizhou and Yunnan (Hosie 1890; Oakes 1998, 88–89). Until the twentieth century, most trade went overland by caravans of pack animals and human carriers. Despite the difficulty of overland transport, the southwest had contact with other regions, notably India, Central Asia, and Southeast Asia. Historian Bin Yang stresses the importance of the "Southwest Silk Road," or southern overland trade route (2009, 23).[2] Although culturally and politically incorporated into China, Southwest China had long been a cultural crossroads.

Imperial Expansion and Gendered Work

The Chinese Empire incorporated Yunnan and Guizhou through a lengthy process of conquest and colonization, leaving few records of women's lives. Both provinces still have relatively high proportions of non-Han populations, or ethnic minorities, though Han Chinese account for more than

60 percent of the population in each province. After conquest by the Mongols in 1253 brought Yunnan under imperial control,[3] subsequent Ming and Qing dynasties sponsored migrations of families of Han soldiers, agricultural colonists, and prisoners to hold the frontier, supply the soldiers, requisition horses, and extract minerals such as copper, iron, tin, silver, and salt (Giersch 2001; Lee 1982; B. Yang 2009, 213).[4] Yunnan tea was highly prized in the rest of China. In the late Qing period (particularly 1821–1850), Yun-Gui opium became a major cash crop and an indirect source of tax revenue despite imperial prohibitions (Bello 2003, 1111, 1120). During the Qing, urbanization and the role of merchants increased (Lee 1982).

Under imperial command, Han migrants established a political organization and communication network that linked the settlements and towns into a common system of defense and control. By the early nineteenth century, Han Chinese controlled the heavily populated valleys and flatlands (*bazi*, or basins) with dense networks of military settlements and garrisons, reflected in the widespread use of military terms for place-names (B. Yang 2009, 39, 151; LFXZ 1997; LLXZ 1991). During the mid-nineteenth century, a weakened Qing state, defeated in the Opium Wars by Western powers, battled to retain control against major internal rebellions. The Taiping Rebellion in southern China as well as the so-called Muslim and Miao Rebellions in Yunnan and Guizhou, respectively, were long and devastating. The Muslim Rebellion (1856–1873) seriously challenged Qing control of Yunnan and western China.[5] This bloody conflict disrupted trade and left parts of Yunnan depopulated and in ruins by the time the Qing regained control.[6] Similarly, the rebellion in Guizhou (1854–1873) resulted in a huge loss of population, particularly among the Miao minority (Jenks 1994). As the 1911 Republican revolution loomed, shifting alliances of local leaders with Sun Yat-sen's Canton faction kept the two provinces militarized. This chaotic situation prevailed until the Japanese pushed the armies of Jiang Jieshi into China's southwest in 1937 and 1938, where they established their capital in Chongqing.

Up to the fourteenth century, Han immigrant soldiers often married local women and blended into aboriginal societies. During the Ming (1368–1644), Han women, who accompanied their soldier-colonist husbands, contributed to the maintenance and reproduction of the Han population and reduced the "absorption" of Han soldiers by indigenous cultures.[7] The indigenous ethnic minorities, scattered and interspersed across the province, had increasingly to accommodate the numerically and politically dominant Han.[8] As Han immigrants settled in the southwest, they adapted their knowledge of intensive grain and cloth production to the different local environments and reestablished their gendered systems of household production, particularly in the core agricultural and commercial regions.[9] They also dominated and displaced the indigenous farmers from the fertile valleys, forcing some ethnic groups to take refuge in the mountains and cultivate poorer lands. In contrast to most minority groups whose men and women both worked the fields, the Han often imported their standard, gendered household production system in which "men plow, women weave" (*nan geng, nu zhi*)—men working "outside" and women "inside" the home.[10] With this system, they also brought footbinding.

Transport and Trade in Cotton and Cloth

Although cotton did not grow well in Yunnan and Guizhou, parts of Southeast Asia and China grew more than they could process. Hence, merchants imported it not only as yarn and cloth but also as raw cotton for Han women to spin, weave, and use in quilt stuffing and padded clothing. Cotton was hauled in bulk by caravan from Burma, Siam, Laos, Tonkin (Vietnam), and Sichuan to meet both government and settler demands (Forbes 1987). "As the whole population is clothed in cotton material, the trade in this commodity is one of the largest and most necessary in the whole province" (Davies [1909] 1970, 318).[11]

After 1860, China was forced to open more treaty ports to Western powers, finally opening Chongqing in 1890. British and French explorers, keenly interested in expanding trade into Southwest China, conducted a number of expeditions to Yunnan and Guizhou to assess trade routes and potential markets for European products. They recorded the effects of the Yunnan and Guizhou rebellions, the movements of commodities across the provinces, the large and small markets, and the difficulties of travel (Colquhoun 1883; Davies [1909] 1970; Hosie 1890).

The significance of imported cotton in Yunnan's foreign trade is stressed by historian Andrew Forbes: "Cotton certainly reigned supreme as the chief and only really important import from northern Southeast Asia." Caravans transported raw cotton to Simao in southern Yunnan "for subsequent distribution throughout Yunnan" (Forbes 1987, 24). Tracing cotton's journey into northern Yunnan via the Sichuan route, Feuerwerker notes that in the nineteenth century, merchants shipped Jiangnan cotton up the Yangzi to meet Yunnan and Guizhou demand for cotton to spin and weave (1970, 340). Cotton was transported from Hubei to Sichuan by boat, and then porters and pack animals carried it into Yunnan. Cotton was also sent to Guizhou via Hunan, across Dongting Lake and along the Yuan River.[12]

> This was not, by contemporary standards, a petty trade either in size or in the distances traversed. As late as 1895, by which time radical changes in the structure of the handicraft cotton industry were already in train, more than 200,000 bales of raw cotton and 300,000 bales of piece goods were being imported annually into Szechwan [Sichuan] largely from Hupei [Hubei]. And some 3,200,000 pieces of cloth were reaching northern Yunnan each year from Shasi [Shashi, Hubei Province, a port on the upper Yangzi]. (Feuerwerker 1970, 340)

Thus, by the end of the nineteenth century, Yunnan and Guizhou imported both raw cotton and handcraft cotton goods. Factory-made yarn and cloth from Southeast Asia and eastern China also began to affect local textile production in Yunnan (Litton 1903). The new technologies of production in British India meant that the Yun-Gui had become "remote" only from a Chinese imperial point of view. In parts of Yunnan, links to the novel world of industry, though later than those of China's coast, were earlier and in some ways stronger than those in North China at the same period.

When industrial technologies outside the region lowered the costs of producing textiles and transporting them, Southwest China gradually shifted from importing raw cotton to importing factory-made yarn and cloth. Textile mills on China's eastern coast began to compete with home-based textile producers of Yunnan and Guizhou. In 1911 the completion of a railroad from the port of Haiphong, Vietnam, to Kunming lowered the cost of bulk shipments of cotton and cloth, as did new road construction. New industrial enterprises in Kunming were simultaneously transforming textile production, introducing imported textile machinery using electric power.

Despite increasing competition from Indian, Japanese, and European factory-spun yarn, "the trade in raw cotton from northern Southeast Asia apparently remained profitable until well into the 1930s" (Forbes 1987, 24). As late as 1935, caravans left Yunnan with their mules' bells "jingling along the track" with light loads, whereas caravans from Burma "were heavily laden with bales of cotton yarn and raw cotton to be woven into cloth by the country people in Yunnan" (Metford 1935, 146, quoted in Forbes 1987, 25).[13] As elsewhere, raw cotton remained important for quilts and padded clothing.

After Japan invaded and occupied eastern China in 1937, many of Republican China's industries and universities moved to inland provinces such as Sichuan and Yunnan. The relocation of government and industry accelerated change by bringing capital, skilled labor, and industrial technologies to the southwest. Thanks to this relocation, university scholars began to conduct detailed research on social and economic change in the southwest, providing vital information about sites that we later restudied.

RESEARCH SITES

We selected research sites in different counties in or near the fertile valleys of central Yunnan and Guizhou where Han settlers could practice intensive agriculture: four in Yunnan and one in Guizhou. The villages differ in environment and degree of proximity to mountains, trade routes, populous towns, and other ethnic groups. Several have developed distinctive specialties in response to varied microenvironments and changes in trade and transportation. Comparing villages that have different economic practices, some emphasizing women's handcraft labor and others requiring more work in the fields, illuminates the links between women's labor and footbinding.

Our village sites are located in five counties of this region. Yunnan's capital, Kunming, is located in the north-central part of the province. Taking Kunming as a center point, Tonghai County seat is roughly 100 kilometers to the south, Jiangchuan is about 80 kilometers to the southeast, Luliang is 100 kilometers to the east, Lufeng is about 100 kilometers to the west. Anshun, in Guizhou Province, is located about 420 kilometers to the east of Kunming and 88 kilometers west of Guiyang on the road connecting them (see Table 2.1).

Trade routes to these sites were undergoing change in the early twentieth century. Tonghai's county seat, resting in a mountain valley beside Lake Qilu, benefited from the major nineteenth-century north-south caravan route from Tonkin to Kunming, which linked Tonghai to wider commercial trade networks. In 1911 the French railway from Tonkin to Kunming began operation, passing to the east of Tonghai's town center. Jiangchuan County, north of Tonghai County,[14] has two large lakes for fishing and boat transport. The north-south caravan trade passed close to Jiangchuan, as did an east-west trade route to Yuxi City, the prefectural seat. A 1936 highway map of China (*Zhonghua Minguo gonglu luxian tu* 1936) shows a dirt motor road under construction from Tonghai to Hexi and a completed motor road from Hexi to Yuxi and then north to Kunming. Jiangchuan is located about twenty kilometers east of this improved road.[15] The Hanoi-to-Kunming railroad passed about the same distance to the west, on the other side of the lake. Historically, east-west caravan routes between Guizhou and Yunnan passed through Luliang County, our third site, but in the early twentieth century, Luliang was remote from Yunnan's new railway and road construction. Our fourth site, near the Lufeng county seat, was a convenient rest stop on the main east-west caravan route across western Yunnan, paved for motor traffic by the 1930s. Our fifth site, Anshun, a prefecture-level city and administrative region in Guizhou, straddled the major east-west caravan route and, by the 1930s, enjoyed long sections of paved road between the provincial capitals of Guizhou and Yunnan. Anshun was closer to the transportation developments in Guangdong and Hunan than the four counties in Yunnan; since the 1870s steamships had reduced costs of river transport from the coast to the interior. These new modes of transportation affected local trade by introducing products that competed with local goods. Each county encompassed diverse economic activities: some villages were known for particular specialties that reflected the local environment, resources, needs, and particular opportunities in a larger, dynamic system of transportation, technology, and trade.

What differentiated women's work in these villages? In the early twentieth century, when our research subjects were girls, their villages were integrated into market systems, and all the villages depended to some extent on trade. In some, women provided much of the field labor, while in others they specialized in domestic handcrafts for exchange. Skilled hand labor produced goods complementing agriculture, such as cotton textiles;[16] straw hats, mats, and shoes; plaited bamboo baskets and pot covers; twisted fiber ropes; woven saddle pads and fish nets; dyed cloth; brewed wine; and preserved food. Villages often became known for specific products because men's skills and knowledge were acquired among patrilocal kinsmen. But villages and regions could also become known for women's special products when wives who married in from nearby villages were already skilled in local crafts and able to train their young daughters in turn. Areas with less access to raw materials, transport, and markets sent men out to work in transport, mines, or construction, leaving more of the agricultural work to women.

The characteristics of our village interview samples are summarized in Table 2.2. The sampled women at each site were ethnically Han, with birth years ranging from 1912 to 1950. More than 80 percent had never attended school, and the illiteracy rate ranged from 67 to 100 percent.[17] In addition, most women married at a distance that averaged less than ten kilometers from their natal family; some women married within the same village, and a very small number married into families located far from their natal homes.

TONGHAI COUNTY: LAKESIDE CLOTH MARKETS

As I (Bossen) walked through Zhibu Village in 2006, the streets were deserted, so I peeked into a clan temple courtyard, finding a dozen ladies (the older ones with bound feet) chatting and beckoning me to enter and chat. I sat down on a bench and eventually asked if they had ever woven cloth. With great animation, all talking at once, they described their years of work at the loom, their bodies rocking, arms swinging, feet moving, and voices chanting rhythmic sounds as they spontaneously enacted the experience. They even corrected and competed with one another about proper weaving motions, as some apparently remembered working in slightly different ways or with different types of looms. Fascinated by the pantomime of weaving and the imprint that years of work had left on their bodily movement, I could readily see that weaving skills were like playing piano, typing, riding a bicycle, or sawing wood. They could get rusty, but the basic motions were part of what athletes call muscle memory. For these women, the skills involved the whole body, sedentary but intensely active, focused on the hands and arms of the weaver. When they were girls and young women, their excellent handwork brought them praise and admiration. Their bound feet belonged to this former world of work. In the 2000s, the old wooden looms were long gone, dismantled and discarded, but the last generation of elderly women who wove could instantly recall and replay the bodily motions.[18] This was once a weaving village par excellence.

By the late nineteenth and early twentieth centuries, cloth produced by the women of Tonghai and nearby Hexi Counties was famous and exported throughout Yunnan (Litton 1903, 3–4; Buck 1937, 2:35; Fei and Chang 1948).[19] Located at the edge of Lake Qilu, Tonghai was well connected to the caravan routes that carried goods between Tonkin and central Yunnan to Kunming. Tonghai and its central Yunnan neighbors produced cloth and other goods for sale. A simple rhyme widely known in Kunming in the mid-twentieth century linked town names and regional specialties:[20] *Tonghai jiangyou, Lufeng cu, Xinxing guniang, Hexi bu* (Tonghai soy sauce, Lufeng vinegar, Xinxing girls, Hexi cloth). Elderly people we interviewed recalled that Xinxing girls were desired as wives because they were hardworking and known for their weaving skills (Litton 1903, 4; THXZ 1992, 139). Xinxing and Hexi are both near Tonghai in Yuxi Prefecture. The town center of Tonghai was known for its soy sauce, but like Xinxing and Hexi, many villages surrounding Tonghai were known for handweaving on wooden looms with foot pedals and hand shuttles that made cloth about ten inches wide (XSZZ 1994, 66).[21] Tonghai villagers bought raw cotton in local cotton markets supplied by traders from southern Yunnan towns (Panxi, Quxi, Jianshui, Simao) and more distant sources (Tonkin and Burma).[22]

With Tonghai's considerable ethnic and economic diversity, not all its Han villagers made cloth, but it was a substantial source of income for a large number of them.[23] A local report observed that

> about 70 percent of all the county women spun yarn and wove cloth as their occupation. Male peddlers [*nanzi yunfan*] sold bolts of cloth. Over 20 percent of the men were long-distance traders who transported these goods throughout the province and beyond. In the villages, each household had on average at least one spinning wheel and one loom. Some had up to four or five looms. Looms were set up above and below the main hall of the residence. (THXZ 1992, 139)

By 1920, however, village women's income from hand labor at spinning was suffering serious competition from *yangsha* (foreign or factory-made yarn) imported from Shanghai, Burma, India, and other sources. Once women switched to factory-made yarn, the bottleneck of limited hand-spun yarn was broken, enabling weavers to work more continuously.[24] Local weaving technology evolved to make use of the expanded yarn supply. As a result, the production of *yangshabu*,[25] or handmade cloth using foreign yarn, greatly increased and fewer girls spent their days spinning (Litton 1903).

Next came modifications to weaving, both in the form of weaving technology and the organization of labor:

> In 1920, the first commercial textile factory was started by a skilled crafts-
> man from Sichuan who introduced a new type of loom with a pulled shuttle
> [*lasuo buji*], which was two to three times more efficient. After this, textile
> workshops using the new loom sprang up one after another. While most
> were probably small scale, there were several large ones, the largest being the
> Yuxi Technology Promotion Committee Textile Factory, which hired more
> than two hundred women to work on 120 looms. These workshops produced
> handwoven plain local cloth, woolen towels, door curtains, blankets, thread,
> and many types of colored cloth with patterns. (XSZZ 1994, 66–67)

Replacing hand spinning with purchased factory yarn, introducing
more efficient looms, establishing factory-like workshops, and switching to
imported dyes were not just technological transformations. Each changed
the ways that women worked, enabling well-located villages to increase the
quantity and quality of their handwoven *tubu* while decreasing the profits
from commercial handwork in other villages. Tonghai gazetteers stress the
positive aspects of industrial textile development in the town.[26]

In 1940, anthropologists Fei Hsiao-tung (Fei Xiaotong) and Chang
Chih-I (Zhang Zhiyi) (1948) conducted fieldwork in Yu Village, close to
the old trade route near Yuxi City (hence the name), and painted a different
picture of industrial development in the same region. In Yu Village women
still wove at home in 71 percent of the households.[27] Fei and Chang's description of the weaving economy shows relentless downward pressure on
village weavers' incomes:

> [Their weaving] cannot be sold to townsfolk but only the peasants; and,
> as better machine-woven cloth is coming in, the market for home-woven
> materials is shrinking. . . . The low profit from this industry is clear to the
> weavers. . . . People like to talk about the old days [around 1910] . . . before
> the importation of Western manufactured thread, when the weavers of the
> district produced their own cotton, spun their own thread, and made their
> own cloth, [and] they got much more income than they do at present. Since
> that time, things have been getting steadily worse. On the one hand, manu-
> factured thread has entirely taken the place of native thread, so that the
> spinning is entirely wiped out. . . . On the other hand, manufactured clothes
> [cloth] have reached the markets of the interior. They are better in quality
> and not much higher in price than the home woven. To compete with them
> the native cloth has to lower its price. . . . The weavers are squeezed on both

sides. The only thing they can adjust is their own wage. (Fei and Chang 1948, 241–243)

This in-the-moment description of the economic crisis facing female labor is remarkable for its attention to the plight of the weavers; we only wish these renowned anthropologists had also commented on the practice of footbinding among the girls and women who worked at the loom. But the ubiquity and persistence of footbinding in this weaving region have been documented by others who, conversely, largely ignored the economic activities of the women who were bound (Yang Yang 2001, 2004; Jackson 1997; Lim 2007).

Girls' and Women's Work in Zhibu Village, Tonghai

Zhibu Village had easy access to the county town and to a variety of markets in the valley.[28] Farming and making cloth were the two main occupations. Villagers grew rice, wheat, beans, tobacco, and corn. In addition, about one in twenty households had a small shop, and in nearly one-fourth of the households, men also worked as traders, porters, policemen, soldiers, or hired laborers, sometimes in Gejiu, a famous tin-mining town to the south. All but two of the women we interviewed were born in the county, their natal homes less than ten kilometers away, some within ten minutes' walking distance. Marriages with men who lived nearby were convenient to weaving households because most local brides already knew how to spin and weave competently when they entered their mother-in-law's house.

Spinning. Zhibu girls learned textile work at home. In our sample, 75 percent had spun cotton before marriage. Girls learned to spin at ages ranging from around five to fifteen, with age eight as the average. Most of the cotton thread they spun was then woven by the family for its own use and for sale. By the early twentieth century, imported factory-made thread had already replaced much of the homespun thread used by weavers. In the 1930s factory-made yarn was widely available, so homespun yarn would not have fetched good prices in local markets. As one woman born in 1917 put it, "If we really had nothing to eat, then we could sell it."[29]

Women who grew up spinning continued to spin at least some yarn after marriage, even when factory yarn was used for warps in their weaving. The timing of the decline of spinning is evident in changes in work done after marriage. Of the women born before 1930 ($N = 35$), 65 percent continued to spin after marriage, into the 1940s. This rate dropped to only

38 percent of those born 1930–1934, and to 23 percent of those born 1935–1939. In the group born in 1940 and after, the rate for spinning had fallen to just 5 percent (N = 22). Although most spinning provided yarn for use by family weavers, 27 percent of the women said they also sold yarn that they spun as girls living in their natal homes.

There is no easy way to measure how significant these incomes were before industrialization. The returns to girls who were spinning by hand were undoubtedly higher before they had to compete with machine spinning, as many economic historians have noted. Once machine-spun thread entered the local markets, there was every incentive to switch to weaving, which was more skilled work and required more capital (a loom was more costly and complicated than a spindle or spinning wheel). This meant, however, that girls who were too young to weave were less able to contribute to a salable product by spinning. This lost income may have hurt the family economy, reducing the incentive to bind young girls and keep them working at the spinning wheel.

Weaving. Women in households that spun usually wove as well. Loom ownership was very widespread in the girlhood homes of our sample; 87 percent of their natal families owned at least one loom, and 74 percent of the women wove cloth before marriage.[30] Some families had two or three looms. One woman explained, "We had two looms; Grandmother wove on one and Mother on the other."[31] Another said, "We had three looms: Mother wove on one, [my] older brother's wife used one, and I wove on the third."[32] Women from families that did not own looms or produce textiles explained that they grew up in the mountains and did farmwork, carried firewood to sell, or were simply too poor.[33] In one family specializing in prepared foods, there was no time for textile work.[34] Weaving required girls to be big enough to reach to the edges of the cloth while seated to push the shuttles across or reach the foot pedals of more complex looms. On average girls began to weave at age eleven, but this varied. Some women reported the age at which they could weave competently rather than the age at which they began to learn. When women gave both ages, starting to weave and weaving with skill, the learning process took at least one and often several years. The average age reported for weaving "well" was twelve.

Other handcrafts. Doing embroidery and cross-stitch, calendering cloth, and twisting pine needle bundles (to be sold as fuel) were some of the additional handcrafts reported by Zhibu Village women. Most also made their family members' clothes and cloth shoes. Some girls made hemp twine to stitch shoe soles made from pasted layers of cloth. Making cloth shoes for family members was such a standard part of women's housework that they often failed to mention it unless specifically asked. A few reported weaving mats, making straw hats, and making belts—forms of handwork that could occasionally earn extra income.

Textiles and income. Income from weaving was once the single most important source of income for Zhibu Village women. Girls who contributed to family income were usually not in charge of the market transactions, which were handled by their elders. Our effort to calculate outputs and incomes is hampered by the variety of products, sizes, and qualities produced by hand spinning and weaving and by the impossibility of knowing how much labor-time each woman gave to the tasks. Some women told of their mothers weaving every day of the year, from dawn to dusk; others described mothers weaving half the night after doing other work by day. The units for measuring yarn that weavers used were variable, referring to different types of spools, spindles, or bobbins. One woman remembered a *jin* of spun thread being exchanged for three of raw cotton. And of course, market prices fluctuated (Fei and Chang 1948). Cloth was usually exchanged for yarn, varying in value if cloth was hand-loomed or factory-made, top or poor quality. The value of supposedly formal units of exchange—copper, silver, or paper money—was subject in the 1930s and 1940s to rapid price fluctuations, which led eventually to hyperinflation and confusing multiple currencies as China switched from the silver standard to paper money. Hence, cash was an unreliable measure of value and purchasing power. We encouraged women to describe exchange equivalencies when they could.[35]

A further source of uncertainty was women's tendency to speak of "exchanging" (*huan*) their products rather than "selling" (*mai*) them. In many cases, this was the result of their engagement in putting-out systems, in which a broker supplied raw cotton in direct exchange for spun yarn. When their spun yarn brought in more raw cotton than they wanted to spin in the next round, they might receive grain in partial payment.

Footbinding in Tonghai

The late persistence of footbinding in villages near Tonghai has been widely publicized, particularly by the incongruity of a dance troupe composed exclusively of elderly village women who, elegantly dressed in traditional style, began performing in public in the early 2000s (Yang Yang 2001; Jackson 1997; Ko 2005; Lim 2007). Rather than conceal their condition (often viewed as a shameful reminder of China's past oppression of women), they theatrically converted the symbol of the bound foot into a symbol of elderly vitality and joie de vivre, with a touch of nostalgia for bygone customs as China catapulted into the industrial age.

Zhibu Village had many women surviving into the 2000s whose feet were still visibly bound (Figure 5.1).[36] Figure 5.2 shows by birth cohort the declining percentages of women who were ever bound. The sample includes those who were bound permanently as well as those who were bound for a short time before their feet were let out. Of women who were ever bound,

Figure 5.1.   Seated woman with bound feet in embroidered shoes in Tonghai, Yunnan

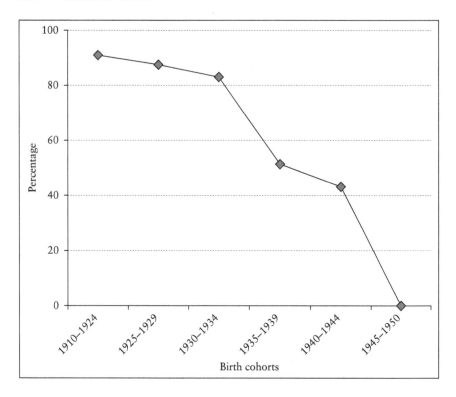

Figure 5.2.   Percentage footbound by birth cohort, Tonghai, Yunnan
NOTE: $N = 121$.

more than half (57 percent) said their feet had achieved a fixed shape
(*ding xing*).[37] Adding seven years (the average age of binding) to the birth
year gives an estimate of the year when footbinding decisions were made.
Binding began to decline from around 1930 when those born 1920–1924
reached binding age. The decline was initially gradual, but binding dropped
rapidly for those born 1935–1939, who would have attained binding age in
the 1940s before the Communist victory in 1949. Of Zhibu women born
before 1940 ($N = 100$), 73 percent had their feet bound.[38] Footbinding was
no longer attempted with girls who reached binding age in the 1950s.

The decline of footbinding accelerated after Japan invaded China in
1937 and Republican China's war industries moved west to Sichuan and
Yunnan. Nationalist campaigns against footbinding reached the county
towns and nearby villages like Zhibu. Eighty-one percent of the women
born before 1940 had heard of government anti-footbinding regulations

when they were growing up (they were not always clear about which government). One of the oldest women, born in 1917, reported that the government fine for footbinding was two buckets of oil or four suits of army clothes. Other women also reported fines to be paid in buckets of oil, suits of army clothes, or money if family members had bound feet. Government regulations against footbinding in many areas were ineffective; girls were temporarily unbound to avoid fines during a government campaign and afterward rebound to conform to local demands. In the 1950s, the new Communist government drastically altered the political economy by requiring women to work in the fields instead of weaving, by closing markets where cloth had been sold, and by directly opposing footbinding. In response to these new pressures, some Zhibu adult women then unbound their feet even after their feet had achieved a fixed shape.

If heavy household demands for female hand labor encouraged mothers to bind their daughters' feet, then Zhibu Village epitomized this relationship. The Han villages of Tonghai County and surrounding Yuxi Prefecture had once had a high concentration of rural spinners and weavers producing hand-loomed cloth. Figure 5.3 shows the percentage of Zhibu women in our sample who spun yarn or wove cloth at home before marriage. Eighty-seven percent of the 99 women born before 1940 spun or wove before marriage. Women born after 1940 abandoned textile work when new Communist government policies drastically changed the gender division of labor, with the state suppling factory cloth and prohibiting family-based enterprises. In Chapter 6 we consider at greater length the extent to which the declines in footbinding and female hand labor are related.

JIANGCHUAN COUNTY: CHANGING HANDCRAFT MARKETS

Jiangchuan's population is predominantly Han; ethnic minorities, almost all indigenous Yi, form less than 6 percent of the county population (JCXZ 1994, 105). The village women in our survey identified themselves as Han. As in Tonghai, local historians linked the spread of handcrafts in their county to Han immigration from eastern China:

> From the Ming dynasty, a large population immigrated [to Tonghai] from China's central plain; thereafter handcrafts arose in this region. In the Qing dynasty, spinning and weaving and iron, wood, pottery, etc., every kind

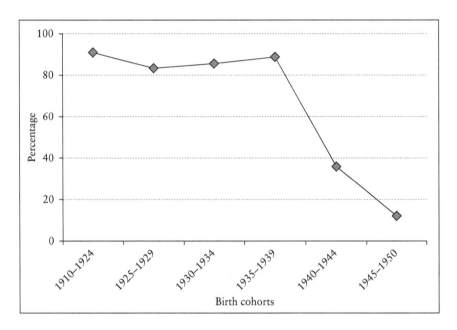

Figure 5.3.   Percentage of girls spinning or weaving by birth cohort, Tonghai, Yunnan

NOTE: $N = 121$.

of handwork spread all over [*bianbu*] to every village and town. (JCXZ 1994, 219)

Some of this may be Han chauvinism, although the Han surely promoted and improved cotton cloth technology in the region. Indigenous peoples of Yunnan and the Southeast Asian region have their own ancient traditions of textile work in a variety of fibers, including hemp, ramie, nettle, kudzu, wild silk, and cotton (Luo and Zhong 2000). In the Republican period cloth-weaving households in the county peaked at more than four thousand of an estimated ten thousand to twelve thousand total (JCXZ 1994, 219, 240).[39] With annual production estimated at about thirty-six thousand bolts, the main products, three types of blue cloth, were "sold to more than thirty neighboring prefectures and counties" (240).

The population of Jiangchuan County declined from a peak in 1931 of sixty-five thousand to fewer than fifty-two thousand by 1941. Part of this decline was due to the recruitment of soldiers for the Anti-Japanese War. In addition, many residents left Jiangchuan to earn a living in Kunming, where industry and commerce were rapidly developing with the war effort (JCXZ 1994, 107). Because of growing competition with textile factories there, the loss of income by village producers probably contributed to this migration. The census for 1944 reported a high level of unemployment (21 percent); we estimate that as much as 75 percent of this was female unemployment due to the decline of home spinning and the textile-weaving industry (JCXZ 1994, 113).[40] Villages like Zhibu Village in Tonghai County were well placed to buy up factory yarn and increase their weaving for the market. Jiangchuan villages, however, were farther from the cotton markets and the railway bringing raw cotton from the south and closer to the new competition from factory-made cloth (coming from Kunming). When women could no longer contribute income from weaving, they began to abandon it or turn to other handcrafts to earn a living. The Communist government, established in Jiangchuan in 1950, furthered the transformation after 1953 when the state-owned weaving industry and rationing displaced domestic manual weaving and dyeing (392, 240). Although some households continued to produce cloth for their own use if they could get cotton or yarn, government suppression of markets curtailed commerce, and by the late 1950s, collectivization meant that work in the fields or on massive water management projects took precedence over home-based cloth production.

Girls' and Women's Work in Jiangchuan

The interviews conducted in Jiangchuan County covered several different villages with distinct specialties. The largest number of interviews (140) was in Bulao (Fish catcher) Village located near the lake where making fish nets was one of the local forms of hand labor. Ranbu (Dye cloth) Village, with 42 interviews, was known for its cloth-dyeing shops where home weavers had cloth dyed. In the total sample from Jiangchuan ($N = 211$) 68 percent of the households owned spinning wheels, and 43 percent owned looms. These were used by multiple female members of the family, usually the woman interviewed, her mother and sisters, and occasionally grandmothers. More than a third (37 percent) of women spun cotton, and nearly a third wove it (32 percent; $N = 211$) at their natal homes.[41] The fact that households owned more spinning wheels and looms than they used suggests women gave up these occupations when they became less profitable. With Xingyun Lake and Fuxian Lake nearby, fish nets of many kinds and sizes had a market (JCXZ 1994, 211). The women who married into Bulao

Village from surrounding villages performed cotton textile work, twisted hemp into twine, and made fish nets. In our Bulao interviews, all of the thirty-nine women who made fish nets for sale also spun and wove cotton or hemp for income. Most likely women trained in one kind of handwork took up other handwork as market conditions shifted. Taking all handcrafts together, including making fish nets, dyeing cloth, and twisting various fibers such as straw and pine needles into bundles for fuel, half of the women in the full Jiangchuan sample (119 of 240) produced a handcraft product for income before marriage.

Footbinding in Jiangchuan

Our interview data show that binding was nearly universal for those born 1910–1924 but already dropping for those born 1925–1929, with a gradual but steady decline over the next twenty years (Figure 5.4).[42] This is consistent with a decline in textile work due to increased competition with machine-made thread and cloth. Cotton products reached Kunming via the new railway, radiated into nearby markets, and were distributed to areas previously served by Jiangchuan textile producers. By 1935–1939, when

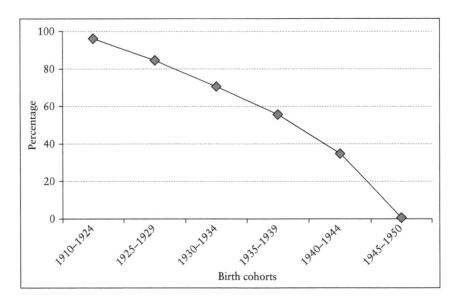

Figure 5.4.   Percentage footbound by birth cohort, Jiangchuan, Yunnan
NOTE: N = 208.

girls born in the late 1920s or early 1930s reached binding age, footbinding had declined to just over 50 percent of this cohort, and most of those were temporary. About one-third of the women born 1940–1944 still experienced attempts at binding, but few stayed bound for more than a very short time once the Communist government came to power and reorganized the labor force. Because Jiangchuan County villages had varied forms of fiber-related skilled handwork, the shift of girls to agriculture and less sedentary work outside the home was not abrupt.

LULIANG COUNTY: A CONSERVATIVE VILLAGE WITH STRAW HANDCRAFTS

Yunnan colleagues describe this largely Han eastern region of Yunnan as very conservative. Han dominance appears in early nineteenth-century accounts of military colonization and economic transformation:

> Luliang, the largest basin [*bazi*] in Yunnan . . . was swarmed with military migrants. . . . With the dramatic increase of villages, ethnic patterns were transformed. The gazetteer compiled in the Daoguang reign (1821–1850) listed over 220 villages in Luliang, among which nearly half were named after the above military terms. (B. Yang 2009, 151, citing LLZZ 1844, juan 1, 15a–18b)

> Many dams, channels, and man-made reservoirs were built and many rivers, lakes, ponds and fields were improved. These water systems created many mini-Han agricultural regions in Yunnan. . . . As soon as military farms were established, an irrigation system was gradually completed, making Luliang into a store-house of rice. (B. Yang 2009, 153)[43]

These profound transformations gave rise to a population that is over 98 percent Han. Sanchahe Township, which includes our research site, is essentially 100 percent Han with just a few hundred Hui and Yi in a population of over one hundred thousand (LLXZ 1991, 128; YSRP 2002, 183–263).

Early eighteenth-century sources report that textile production in Luliang used specialized techniques brought from central China and that handmade cloth brought prosperity.[44] One hundred years later in 1845, local sources report that Luliang had "men who did not plow the fields, but *no* women did not weave. A large number of ordinary families do not have even one *mu* of land. There are many whose specialty is to spin and weave for clothing and food" (LLXZ 1991, 307). Despite the economic significance of women's textile work in the mid-nineteenth century, in the early twentieth century, the spinning and weaving occupations were in decline (307). In 1921 a local report described the decline in handmade textiles:

> The county has about ten thousand working people. Farmworkers are about four in ten (at planting and harvest time this doubles); spinners and weavers are about three in ten; each person's daily salary averages about one *jiao*. The textile producers do not group together to create specialized establishments; they continued to weave local cloth in the old way. Each day is gradually worse; they cannot sell well. (LLXZ 1991, 307)

> In 1928, Ma Jie [a nearby town] established the Hongyuan Dyeing and Weaving Factory[45]—with more than seventy workers and more than seventy looms, of which fourteen were iron looms and the rest were level hand-pulled shuttle, modified, superior looms. These were the greatest technological transformation in Luliang's hand looms. After the modification, the superior looms could automatically push the shuttle, and work efficiency greatly increased output. Products included cloth for clothing, plus broad cloth, small cloth, economical cloth, and various colors of dark blue, light blue, and white handmade cloth. Apart from what was sold in Luliang, this cloth was also sold in Shi Zong, Luo Ping, Qiu Bei, etc., Counties.
>   In the 1940s, Luliang County seat opened three private-enterprise cloth-weaving factories that had forty to fifty looms. The county city, Ma Jie, and nearby villages, had numerous independent weaving and dyeing households. Weavers produced and dyers sold; for the county weaving and dyeing households, this was a prosperous period. (LLXZ 1991, 307)

Girls' and Women's Work in Luliang

Dong Village in Luliang did not specialize in cloth weaving. The location was east of the north-south caravan routes and the new railroad corridor in central Yunnan. According to the women we interviewed, one town in their local market system did specialize in weaving. In Dong Village, only 15 percent of the women ($N = 114$) had looms at their natal homes.[46] Only 13 percent spun cotton, and only 10 percent wove cotton cloth at their natal homes. Significantly, the county gazetteer LLXZ notes that some women produced footbinding cloth for sale. The rates of spinning and weaving dropped for women born in the 1940s. Yet Dong Village women produced a variety of commercial handcrafts, with 60 percent of women ($N = 102$) engaging in some form of handwork for income before marriage. One woman described working from an early age:

When I was age five or six, I started to make hats. One hat was 3.5 *jiao* [0.35 *yuan*]. My mother bought six pounds of cotton; then together we spun yarn. This could make 30 hats. In one day from morning to night, except for eating, I could make 2.5 hats. At that time my older brother and sisters, four of us, made hats together. At night we went to bed after 10 p.m. Every evening we made hats to sell in the market. When market day came, we sold them all.[47]

Most Dong Village women specialized in making products out of straw: weaving straw mats, hats, shoes, and ropes using rice straw and other fibers but little cotton. Because the market for their handmade products did not face competition from factory-made textile products, they persisted longer in performing handwork at home and selling or exchanging their products. The importance of these other handmade products is supported by the county gazetteer, which devotes several sections to hand labor in bamboo and straw products (LLXZ 1991, 280, 309, 313).[48]

Footbinding in Luliang

Footbinding in Dong Village, Luliang, was nearly universal and very persistent (Figures 5.5 and 5.6). Nearly all women born before the 1940–1944 cohort had their feet bound, at least for a short time (Figure 5.7). Attempts to bind girls' feet came to a complete halt only after the Communists reorganized production. An earlier study of female labor and footbinding in a different village in Luliang County found a very similar association between women's straw handcrafts and late persistence of footbinding (Bossen 2002, 2008). These findings are also supported by the succinct statements about footbinding in LLXZ (1991, 859). Income from straw handcrafts meant that families continued to reap value from sedentary daughters with bound feet even when daughters in other areas lost their value as cotton spinners.

LUFENG COUNTY: *EARTHBOUND CHINA*'S LU VILLAGE REVISITED

Lufeng County is located west of Kunming on the old road between Kunming and Dali in western Yunnan. Lu Village has been the subject of considerable ethnographic study and restudy, as described in *Earthbound China* (Fei and Chang 1948) and other sources (Qian, Shi, and Du 1995; H. Zhang 2005; Bossen 2002, 2005, 2008). Located in an irrigated valley a half-hour's walk from the county seat, Lu Village was established as a

Figure 5.5.   Seated woman with bound feet in tiny
shoes with straps in Luliang, Yunnan

Han military base in the Ming period (Qian, Shi, and Du 1995; H. Zhang
2005; Wang family tree (*jiapu*), Bossen's files). (Relatively poor Miao and
Yi communities lie scattered in higher, mountainous areas lacking good
roads to the county seat.) Lu Village residents firmly assert their Han identity, though some Han military colonists likely intermarried with local minority women. The region suffered depopulation after the Muslim Rebellion and was resettled in the late nineteenth century. In the mid-nineteenth
century, travel and trade between Yunnan and Guangzhou intensified as
Chinese demand for cheaper, Yunnan opium rose: "The single most important reason for this increase in trade was the development of a Canton-
ese distribution network in Guangxi and Guangdong for opium grown in

Figure 5.6. Seated woman with bound feet, taped ankles, and a cane in Luliang, Yunnan

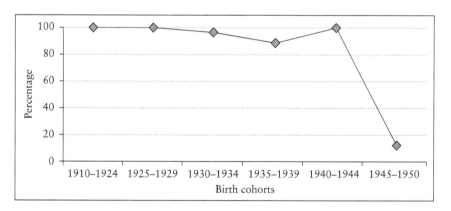

Figure 5.7. Percentage footbound by birth cohort, Luliang, Yunnan
NOTE: *N* = 113.

Yunnan" (Benedict 1996, 51).[49] Lu Village was highly integrated into a wider trading system by virtue of local opium cultivation and its position as a caravan station for the long-distance salt trade. Opium, once an important cash crop in the region, was prohibited by the government in the 1930s, but women born in the 1910s and 1920s remembered that it was widespread. In the early twentieth century, Lu villagers engaged in wet rice farming in the irrigated valley and dry rice farming in its hillier hamlets. Men and sometimes women supplemented farming by seasonal work as porters, miners, and merchants.

Girls' and Women's Work in Lu Village

In the 1930s, Lu Village women performed a great deal of farmwork, putting in as many days as or more than their menfolk in planting, transplanting, weeding, and harvesting rice, beans, squash, and vegetables, as well as raising pigs (Fei and Chang 1948; Bossen 2002). As girls, many women had done farmwork for other families, sometimes for hire or as exchange labor, usually during the busy season of rice transplanting or harvesting. Older girls also sold vegetables, collected firewood, and pastured animals. Some women admitted (despite the sensitivity of the topic) harvesting and processing opium from poppies as girls; they recalled being paid in cash at the rate of two to three *mao* per *jin*, or five *jiao* per day. Poppies required skilled hand labor for scoring the growing pods and scraping the coagulated juice from them. The juice then had to be carefully cooked and dried before marketing.

Regardless of birth cohort, none of the Lu Village women surveyed were taught to spin or weave cloth as girls or after marriage. None of the women from this area saw their families use spinning wheels or looms.[50] However, work in the fields did not mean that Lu Village women were exempt from Chinese traditions of domestic handcrafts. Over two-thirds of the women learned embroidery, and 80 percent stitched cloth shoes for their families.[51] Women and girls were skilled at plaiting straw shoes, stitching cloth shoes, sewing and embroidering cotton clothes, and making straw mats and pads.

Were domestic sewing and embroidery and straw work valuable enough to justify the constraints of footbinding when women were expected to contribute labor to rice farming? The idea that household sewing and embroidery were important economically seems dubious initially. Economic historians have not viewed sewing and embroidery as economic activities with the same attention given to food production or even to spinning and weaving. Today, the very term "embroidery" suggests embellishment rather than economy—a female pastime rather than income-earning work. Yet the assumption that women's embroidery and shoemaking were purely domestic must be scrapped. Cloth, both ordinary and ornamented by embroidery, has always been something that people value, motivating gift exchange and trade. Embroidered garments were important marks of social distinction and class.[52] When crops failed, the sale of textiles and needlework could provide households with an alternative source of income and keep family poverty at bay. In the nineteenth and early twentieth centuries, most Lu Village girls learned embroidery, sewing, and shoe- or sandal making in their natal families and continued this tedious work after marriage, sometimes commercially. In the early twentieth century, a widowed woman could, with difficulty, support herself and even her children independently through her needlework. The woman who could skillfully embroider elegant designs on shoes and garments (e.g., sleeves, bibs, vests, hats, shoes, baby carriers) with exceptional artistry found her handiwork in demand and salable through private contract or in the market.[53]

Wealthy families did not need to sew their own shoes or clothing; they could hire others to do it. Women in families that were less well-off devoted considerable hand labor to keeping family members shod, given the speed with which cloth shoes wore out.[54] A large family made more work for women and girls to keep members decently clothed and shod by stitching, repairing, and patching (Figure 5.8). Cloth shoes lasted longer than straw sandals.[55] With normal use, they might last several months, but with heavy wear—such as porters trudging along cobbled roads or mountain paths—they wore out faster. Men who left home for seasonal work in construction, mining, or transport and merchants supervising their caravans of animals and human porters often depended on replacing straw sandals along their route. Roadside teashops and the many inns of Lu Village were common venues for locals to sell such products.

The complete absence of home spinning and weaving and of spinning wheels and looms in the experience of Lu Village women is striking. In the early part of the twentieth century, Lu Villagers depended on purchased cloth. Cotton was not grown locally, and overland transport of bulky bales of raw cotton was costly, but opium was a cash crop of long standing. With

Figure 5.8.   Woman making soles for shoes in Lufeng, Yunnan. Layers of cotton cloth are glued and stitched together.

earnings from opium and the minerals for which the state prized the region, they bought handwoven cloth from well-located weaving towns in the south.[56] To this common cloth, village women added embroidery as their version of traditional female textile work. The wealthy purchased finer fabrics, and later factory-made cloth, imported from outside the province.

Footbinding in Lu Village

Until the 1930s, slightly more than half of Lu Village women had bound feet, at a rate considerably lower than in other areas and declining by the early 1920s (Figure 5.9). Women said that they were bound only a short time, cucumber or *banpojiao* style, so their feet did not take a fixed shape. Such footbinding did not prevent girls from working natal village fields when they were growing up. Uniformly they told us that women with bound feet could and did work in wet rice fields as well as hoe vegetables in dry fields. Some brought an extra pair of bindings and shoes to the flooded fields, changing to go home. Unlike those with natural feet who went barefoot into the irrigated fields, women with bound feet may have needed the

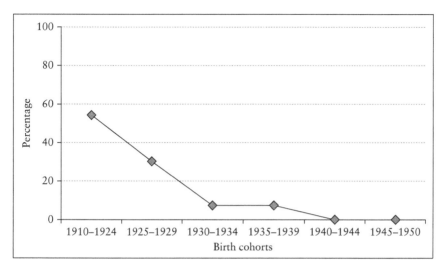

Figure 5.9.   Percentage footbound by birth cohort, Lufeng, Yunnan
NOTE: $N = 105$.

support of their bindings when walking in deep mud. Work in paddy fields was not convenient, but it was manageable if they owned extra binding cloth, especially for those with the less severe form of *banpojiao*.

The significant participation of Lu Village women in farm labor in the 1930s does not conform to the usual assumptions about the incapacity of women with bound feet (P. Huang 1990). Footbinding, at least the kind most common in Lu Village, did not prevent women from working in the fields. Its impact on their productivity is unknown. We suggest that the nineteenth-century increase in opium as a profitable cash crop alongside labor-intensive rice and vegetable farming drew girls away from any domestic handcrafts and hastened the decline of footbinding. Even though binding was more common among the oldest women, the small size of these cohorts means that we cannot be sure that it was ever locally prevalent or especially demanded of brides marrying into Lu Village.

ANSHUN PREFECTURE: PERI-URBAN VILLAGES
ON AN EAST-WEST TRADE ROUTE

Neighboring Guizhou Province is similar to Yunnan, with mountainous terrain and many ethnic minorities. After the Mongol conquest and during the Yuan dynasty, indigenous people lost ground to the Han, who reached an estimated 60 percent of the population by 1851 (Jenks 1994, 29). From 1854 to 1873 the province was devastated by a series of revolts known as the Miao Rebellion, with huge population losses estimated at up to 70 percent (164).[57] Today, the Han constitute roughly two-thirds of the population. Always one of the poorer provinces, nineteenth-century Guizhou had little farmland, few exportable products, and poor transportation to the rest of China. Anshun City, whose peri-urban villagers constitute our Guizhou interview sample, was exceptionally well connected—a thriving town on one of the main river and road routes from the Yangzi to Kunming. It benefited from the trade in opium as well as other goods. Opium, recorded in Guizhou in the eighteenth century, enabled many people to pay for imports of salt, cotton, and cloth.[58] Estimates of Guizhou's annual opium production increased from four hundred *piculs* in 1863 to nine thousand in 1887 (1 *picul* = 133 pounds or 60.5 kilograms), becoming its main crop (23). Hosie (1914) estimated that it reached forty thousand to fifty thousand *piculs* (5.3 to 6.7 million pounds or 2.4 to 3.0 million kilograms) by the early twentieth century, a one hundred–fold increase in four decades.[59]

Girls' and Women's Work in Anshun Villages

In Anshun, women's labor included textiles and fieldwork. The early history of women's handwork in Anshun is illustrated by a poignant (undated) poem titled "Weaving," by Liu Lunxun, honoring an old widow's lifelong support of her family by weaving silk for income:

> The loom sounds: "ga-ga," finger marks are an inch deep,
> Fingertips' blood has already dried; broken is the chaste mother's heart.
> Aged is the white-haired mother-in-law; what can be used to make meals?
> The baby sobs "Waaa, Waaa," waiting to be fed; as the sun sets
> The evening meal depends on exchanging cloth; holding back tears, she swallows her sobs.
> Her cloth pays for the tutor; the orphan finally becomes famous.
>
> Why does heaven have no feelings? The fatherless orphan dies before his mother.
> When young grandson borrows to get married, she again starts reeling silk.
> She returns to gaze at the old loom, finger marks bearing blood.
> Please leave the marks on the loom, her labor recorded in history. (ASFZ 2007, 1229–1230)

Such poems typically reflect the conditions of the Han literate elite (here fallen on hard times), but they also attest to the commercial value of women's handwork for buying food, paying for tutors, and paying a grandson's debt. The Anshun gazetteers for the Ming and Qing dynasties include numerous poems mentioning women's textile work to support themselves or their families. While the elites could afford silk, villagers generally used cotton or hemp clothing. Many women of both peasant and elite families engaged in textile work for income to support their families (ASFZ 2007). Because of high transport costs, the demand for their products was probably limited to local markets.

By the late nineteenth century, the transition to industrial textiles had already affected Guizhou spinners and weavers:

> The penetration of imported cotton yarn and cloth, much of it from India, created a new division of labor in the rural household economy by the late nineteenth century. Because of the higher quality of the imported cotton, most households stopped growing and spinning their own. Instead, a local weaving industry developed rapidly. A survey in Xingyi, which was one of Guizhou's principal cotton markets due to its proximity to both Yunnan and Guangxi, indicated that households with looms jumped from 10 per cent in 1861 to 80 per cent in 1896 (Chen et al. 1993:41). Another survey indicated that by 1890, 80 per cent of all yarn sold in Guizhou was imported, while this was true for only 10–20 per cent of the woven cloth sold (Chen 1989:16). Industrial development along the coast was also creating a demand for many raw materials which Guizhou could provide. (Oakes 1998, 99–100)[60]

Here we find two common effects also observed in Yunnan. The market for hand-spun yarn dried up when factory yarn flowed in, and households with access to factory-made yarn initially expanded their handweaving for local markets, becoming regional weaving centers.[61]

The survey sample for Anshun involves villages located at the edge of the prefectural city. Interviews were conducted in neighborhoods that were farming villages before the revolution but have recently been absorbed by the city.[62] In the Republican period, proximity to city markets gave these villagers access to imported trade goods, including factory-made textiles that more distant communities lacked. In our sample, women earning income from handmade textiles were uncommon. Only 16 percent of the natal households ($N = 199$) owned looms, and even fewer (8 percent) wove cloth for income (see Table A.1). On the city outskirts, villagers would have had access to factory-made yarn. By 1926, Anshun merchants with over one hundred shops imported factory-made cotton yarn on a large scale (ASSZ 1995, 646). Yet spinning required relatively little capital and was a common part of female training in earlier times: 46 percent of women spun yarn (mostly cotton) at their natal home, and 34 percent had spun cotton for sale. Possibly there was market demand for homespun yarn as weft, to add body to cloth that used factory yarn for the warp. Although many women made straw shoes and a few made straw belts and nets or dyed yarn, they produced very few other handcrafts for sale.[63] Commercial demand for textile handcrafts seems to have been declining.

Women's farm labor usually receives little attention in historical accounts. In 1851 opium production was mentioned in the Anshun prefectural gazetteer (Jenks 1994, 23). The work was light (hand) labor, so young girls worked in the fields, moving from plant to plant.[64] Combined with girls' work in other crops such as rice, the handwork of opium collection might not have provided incentive for mothers to bind their daughters' feet.[65] Opium was always a delicate subject in our interviews; despite the general reluctance to acknowledge work in a forbidden crop, thirteen women mentioned that their families had grown opium.[66]

Most Anshun women in our village sample worked in the fields before marriage.[67] The main food crops were rice, followed by corn, wheat, and beans. Eighty-four percent of the households grew rice, with most women participating in the many forms of field labor (transplanting, weeding, harvesting) that rice requires.[68] Proximity to the city gave women access to more types of employment than villagers in more isolated settings. Almost one-quarter of our sample had worked as a servant or hired laborer before marriage. Often, their only income was in the form of meals while they were employed, without any additional grain or monetary payment. In addition, some girls worked in a city weaving workshop.[69]

Did the low proportion of girls working at home to earn handcraft income in the Republican period reduce the incentives to bind girls' feet? The combination of hired labor on farms and as domestic help in this peri-urban setting suggests that the imperative for girls to acquire hand skills for making textiles was weak and getting weaker. From the late nineteenth century onward, imports of yarn and cloth from India to Anshun markets, followed by the establishment of local factories, eroded the market for hand-spun yarn and bit into markets for local handwoven cloth (ASSZ 1995, 638).

Figure 5.10.   Percentage footbound by birth cohort, Anshun, Guizhou
NOTE: N = 196.

Footbinding in Anshun

Figure 5.10 shows that for women born 1910–1924, footbinding was already far from universal at 69 percent and declined early to 43 percent for the 1925–1929 birth cohort. This latter group would have encountered binding around 1932–1937 (assuming binding age of seven), which is well after the large-scale introduction of factory yarn and cloth reported earlier (ASSZ 1995, 638–639; Cheng 1989). Most likely factory-made cloth had also reached peri-urban and local markets by that time. In the Republican period, Anshun girls were already contributing to farm labor. As factory-made replaced homespun thread, the incentive to bind dropped rapidly.

Footbinding in Yun-Gui

The environmental conditions that influenced the distribution of the Han and the ethnic minorities of Yunnan and Guizhou also influenced the gender division of labor and the spread of footbinding. Footbinding was practiced in the valleys and plains, and villages in such areas constitute most of our evidence. Footbinding tapered off earlier in areas where the terrain was steeper and more of women's time had to be spent carrying crops, fodder, wood, and water. Rugged, mountainous terrain and lack of roads meant much greater expenditure of human labor for carrying loads. When women had to perform these carrying tasks on a daily basis, footbinding was impractical. Yunnan's village women often commented that women who lived in mountainous villages did not have bound feet. Thus, footbinding was more common in the relatively level, fertile valleys where farmers could use draft animals to plow and transport goods. This freed more female labor from farming and carrying loads to concentrate on handcrafts. On Yunnan plains, cotton supplies had to be imported for the women to specialize in commercial weaving. Where transport was comparatively cheap—near a good road or the new railroad—women could concentrate and even specialize in commercial spinning and weaving. Where they had no opportunities to earn income through handcrafts or where high-value cash crops (such as opium or tobacco) brought high returns to labor, women increased their agricultural work.[70]

Late nineteenth-century footbinding rates in Yun-Gui reveal different patterns among our sites. Senior kinswomen of our surveyed respondents in Tonghai, Jiangchuan, and Luliang were nearly universally bound from the 1860s to 1920s at a rate of 98 percent (N = 1,085), with only a slight hint of decline at the end of the period in Jiangchuan and Tonghai. Lufeng and Anshun women, in contrast, reported a significantly lower rate among their elder kinswomen, averaging only 61 percent bound (N = 637) over the period. While Anshun declined gradually from 78 to 53 percent, Lufeng rates showed greater fluctuation, averaging 48 percent for the period.[71]

A definite decline occurred in all five sites over the years from 1920 to 1949. Figure 5.11 shows the percentage of footbound women for each village by birth cohort from the 1910s and 1920s up to 1950. Lu Village includes data from a previous study (Bossen 2002) as well as this one.[72] Two sites, Anshun and Lufeng, had comparatively low rates of footbinding for those born in the 1920s and declined below 50 percent by 1930. The two sites from south-central Yunnan, Tonghai and Jiangchuan, experienced a later drop, falling below 50 percent a decade later, by 1940–1944. The remaining site, Luliang, in east-central Yunnan dropped below 50 percent only for women born after 1945.

Once industrial technology allowed efficient conversion of cotton into cloth and its transport to distribution hubs, nearby village producers could no longer compete for sales; their cloth production for cities declined. In Yunnan's southern Tonghai, handweaving had depended in part on access

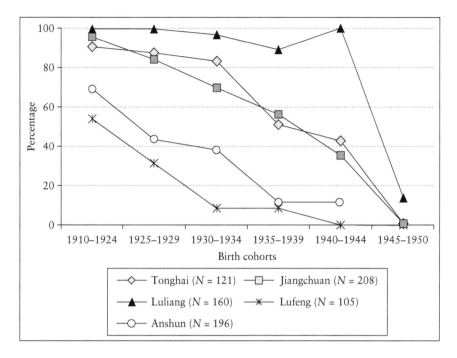

Figure 5.11. Comparison of percentage footbound by birth cohort, Southwest China

NOTE: *N* = 790.

to raw cotton and factory-spun yarn coming from Southeast Asia. Change was stimulated by the completion of the railway from Vietnam to Kunming in 1911 that eliminated the bottleneck created by the slow pace of hand spinning. But Tonghai did not make its handwoven cloth for the city of Kunming, which could import finer goods and was establishing its own modern textile factories. Using the newly available machine-spun yarn, Tonghai's handloom weavers increased their output for yet more rural markets to the south and west of the capital, where modern transport was less well developed. Han villages such as Lu Village in Lufeng County one hundred kilometers west of Kunming purchased handmade *tubu* from other towns specializing in textiles (Bossen 2002; Fei and Chang 1948; Osgood 1963).[73] In Guizhou, villages near Anshun City (subsequently absorbed into the growing city) were receiving imported factory yarn and cloth by 1900 (ASSZ 1995, 638; Feuerwerker 1970, 32, 36).

In Yunnan's Jiangchuan and Luliang sites we find less reliance on women to make cloth than in Zhibu Village in Tonghai. Jiangchuan was better integrated into the Yuxi-Kunming market corridor, so its decline in handmade products closely paralleled that of Tonghai, somewhat mitigated by sustained local demand for fish nets. In Luliang, the handicrafts practiced in our sample village did not emphasize cotton textiles at all; rather, they produced a variety of straw and bamboo products such as hats, mats, and saddle pads for horses. These were less affected by industrial technologies that could not (yet) compete with handmade products. In Lufeng, the tradition of working indoors at spinning and weaving was not established (or had vanished earlier). Lacking homegrown cotton and imported cotton supplies, Lufeng villagers bought handmade cloth in the market. Women engaged in handcrafts such as embroidery and shoemaking, but this was limited in scope. The local economy depended heavily on female labor for farming, while men supplemented household farm income by working in transport, trade, and mining. Opium growing, using much female labor, had also been important around Lufeng and Anshun until, and even after, it was banned by the Nationalists (Hosie 1890, 17; Gao 2011, 27; Derks 2012, 666).

As we piece together the complexities of rural household economies, markets, and women's commercialized hand labor, we note that until the late nineteenth century, a large proportion of Han women across all of these sites had bound feet. Binding was universal for the preceding generations in Luliang, but it was also above 50 percent for women in Lufeng and Anshun, two sites with lower footbinding rates and earlier rejection of the practice. This examination of Yunnan and Guizhou village women's experience allows us to see the unraveling of footbinding in several additional contexts as the intense demand for girls' hand labor declined.

SICHUAN PROVINCE

Collected in the 1990s, the Sichuan data have particular value to the study of girls' work and footbinding for three main reasons. First, Sichuan sits at the center of a northeast to southwest arc, a completing link in our extensive research sweep across China. Second, with their rich and varied ecology and economic heritage of diverse Han immigrants, the Sichuanese practiced an unusually wide variety of cropping and crafts that used the labor of little girls lavishly. Third, the Sichuan data take us deeper into the past than data presented in other chapters of this study because Gates collected them fifteen years earlier, in 1991 and 1992. What Sichuan women told her helps us sketch the longest evidence-based trajectory into the past for rural footbinding that exists now or likely ever will.

Well buttressed by geography against all but the most aggressive Central Asian conquerors, Sichuan maintained a degree of autarky from political and commercial centers far to the east. The "four rivers"—the literal meaning of *si chuan*—merged to become the Yangzi River, which carried high-value goods to eastern China. Two main imperial roads crossed the core basin: one leading northeast from Chengdu to Beijing, requiring many months for the full journey on foot or by slow pack animal; the other almost directly east from Chengdu to the Yangzi port of Chongqing, a trip of about two weeks. Porters and caravans took cloth and tea south and east over difficult mountain tracks, although land carriage was prohibitively costly for food staples and common goods.

The 1911 revolution that ended imperial rule further diluted central control. Warlords and Sichuan's local elites maintained loose connections with the emerging Republican government. As Japan's influence expanded on the coast, the GMD saw the value of Sichuan's agricultural wealth and protected location. In 1937, the GMD's armies and government; the universities, banks, and factories; and a multitude of refugees took Chongqing as China's wartime capital. This immigration of "outsiders," who spoke and ate differently and who quickly monopolized local power, imposed an enormous burden on ordinary Sichuanese. Immense numbers of rural folk were impressed into construction works or drafted into military service. To feed and clothe them all, villagers were taxed heavily, often in advance. Civil war with the Communists followed rapidly after the Japanese surrender, ending only in 1950.

Early Western imperialism had left Sichuan's economy at the headwaters of the Yangzi nearly untouched for over a century after it began to transform China's coast. Even after treaty-port status was forced on middle Yangzi River ports in the 1860s, the slow and uncertain transport of goods farther up the Yangzi by human boat pullers was not replaced for a generation. Difficulties of passing through the Yangzi gorges delayed the ability of steamships to reach Sichuan. Treaty-port status was imposed on Chong-qing in 1891 (Matthews 1999), and after the 1895 Treaty of Shimonoseki, China also had to allow Japan free navigation to the Yangzi River trade all the way up to Chongqing. Only in 1905 was steamship transport for goods moving upstream into Sichuan reliable. Even then, adventurers and commercial missions complained about the Sichuanese lack of interest in Western products.

Booms and busts in England's cotton textile industry drove anxious searches for new markets, a pressure increased by the development of cotton factories in India.[74] Indian cotton yarn shipped from Bombay to British Burma slowly infiltrated China's southwestern provinces by mule train and backpack from as early as the 1880s, well before a flood of factory-spun yarn began to steam upriver from Shanghai. Sichuan had a backdoor for cotton imports as well as the better-known route from Shanghai up the Yangzi. Transport networks that brought factory-made yarn and woven cloth via French colonies in Southeast Asia and British Burma into Yunnan and Guizhou also passed northward into Sichuan. During the long Anti-Japanese and civil wars, the province's rudimentary factories could scarcely meet the needs of China's military and civil elite, much less those of the indigenous population.

While the arrival of machine-made cotton textiles diminished the value of girls' labor, the persistence of many other indigenous products almost certainly slowed this decline. Girls' labor was essential to many of Sichuan's most valuable products, some of which are not well documented. They helped in tending silk cocoons and reeling silk floss. They also collected the fruits of several important tree products, notably the sources for tung oil and an insect-derived wax (Gates 2015, 125–126). Modern alternatives began to replace such things in the early twentieth century, but many remained in use among ordinary people. Kerosene, for example, was far too costly to replace rape oil or vegetable tallow for home lighting; many Sichuan women recalled spinning at night by the light of an incense stick stuck in their footbindings. Also persistent were handcrafted everyday goods such as reed sleeping mats, hemp and jute sacks for goods transport, straw sandals for porters, and fruit and vegetable preserves. Tea, opium, and Sichuan's famous herbal medicines were commercial products that employed girls' labor. The factory-spun yarn that began to arrive in the 1880s and 1890s was, of all the novelties industrialism provided, the one most likely to affect the use of girls' labor.

The Sichuan Survey: Ten Counties

The Sichuan survey is both earlier and much larger than our other provincial samples. It captures the experience of girls and women in late imperial and very early Republican China. The 4,977 women interviewed in ten counties by Hill Gates's teams in 1991 and 1992 were all born prior to the Anti-Japanese War. The oldest women, born between 1878 and 1900, were old enough to work by the time of the 1911 revolution that ended the empire and were middle-aged by 1937, while the youngest were only eight years old when the GMD moved its capital to Chongqing in 1937 and mostly married by the time the Communist Party took control.

Because Gates (2015) has explored those lives in detail elsewhere, here we aim only to summarize the main findings about the girls' and women's handwork in textiles and the changing distribution of footbinding over time. This important body of data, by its sheer magnitude, gives us an additional opportunity to explore the relationship between girls' labor and footbinding in China's most populous province. The Sichuan sample, as we use it here, is drawn and aggregated from ten counties. While Gates has examined the distinctive characteristics of the local economies, here we are interested in their contribution to the larger view of change across the north, northwest, and southwest arc of inland China.

Girls' and Women's Work in Sichuan

Viewing the Sichuan survey as a whole, we find that hand labor in textiles (cotton, hemp, ramie, silk) was an important part of girls' premarital work for more than half (53 percent) of those born between 1887 and 1904 (Figure 5.12). This declined to 48 percent for those born 1905–1919 and dropped to 41 percent for those born in the 1920s (N = 118, 2,128, and 2,731, respectively). This decline of 12 percent by girls working in textiles over the course of about forty years suggests that a long-term shift in customary forms of hand labor by girls and women was under way. In the aggregate, this shift was not abrupt, as women attempted to alter their handcraft skills for new uses, but the decline in textile work suggests that the incentive to train girls for sedentary work with bound feet also declined.

Figure 5.12.   Early twentieth-century village woman with tightly bound feet spinning cotton in Sichuan, 1917–1919. Her plain homespun clothing shows that footbinding was not confined to the wealthy.

SOURCE: Sidney D. Gamble Photographs, David M. Rubenstein Rare Book and Manuscript Library, Duke University

Footbinding in Sichuan

Sichuan's decline in footbinding by birth cohort is consistent with the decline in girls' hand labor in textiles. Footbinding rates were above 80 percent for those born up to about 1915. After that, particularly for those born in the 1920s, footbinding declined rapidly to less than 50 percent. Although the Sichuan sample does not include later birth cohorts that would overlap with those in our other sites, there is little doubt that footbinding continued its decline as in the other provinces we have examined (Figure 5.13).

SOUTHWEST CHINA'S LOCAL DIFFERENCES

Our findings from Yunnan, Guizhou, and Sichuan complete our exploration of local differences in patterns of female labor and changes in foot-

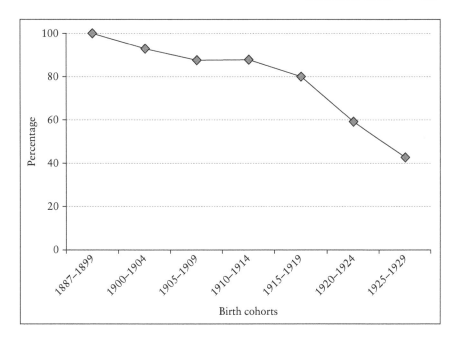

Figure 5.13.   Percentage footbound by birth cohort, Sichuan (ten counties)
SOURCE: Gates 2015
NOTE: $N = 4,977$.

binding in China's macroregions and provinces. As we examined the various ways girls and women labored at textiles and handcrafts at individual village sites in the very different environments of China's vast hinterland, we also documented the changes in rates of footbinding over time. The evidence of local economic changes, often stimulated by larger economic transformations and political upheavals, shows how profoundly the forces of modern industry and transportation disrupted the value and tradition of training girls to submit to footbinding and perform hand labor. Analyzing hand labor and footbinding by birth cohort and place has allowed us to identify the prevalence, timing, and pace of footbinding's decline and relate it to the timing and pace of changes in trade and technology that affected villages and households across China's hinterland. We now combine these village-based findings and turn to a more general analysis of the relationship between female labor, footbinding, and industrialization in early twentieth-century China.

CHAPTER SIX

Bound Feet Across China

The intensified employment of female labor within the peasant household—because that is essentially what the spinning component in particular of handicraft cotton textiles meant—was thus the major industrial contribution to maintain per capita output levels in the two cycles of premodern economic growth in late Ming and early Ch'ing (Qing) China.
> —Albert Feuerwerker, "Handicraft Industry in Ming and Ch'ing China" (1995b)

The actual distribution of footbinding throughout China, and its relationship to female confinement and women's work, is still poorly understood.
> —Gail Hershatter, *The Workers of Tianjin, 1900–1949* (1986)

In the preceding chapters we examine the links between female hand labor and footbinding in the context of local economies that were quite diverse and changing in many ways during the early part of the twentieth century. Our research and travels from region to region and province to province demonstrate just how widespread girls' labor and footbinding were in China's interior provinces. Can we discern a general pattern among these local cases? How best can we describe this pervasive linkage, and how did footbinding finally come to an end?

Here we construct a large-scale test of our hypothesis that footbinding declined more rapidly when girls' handwork at home lost economic value. Then we review the history of China's hand-textile sector and the

138

nineteenth- and early twentieth-century industrialization that disrupted its connection with footbinding.

Interviews and data collected from our diverse rural sites generally support our hypothesis that strong demand for girls' handwork reinforced footbinding as their mothers trained them to use their hands. Painful feet reminded girls that they should sit still and, while they sat, help with the endless work of spinning and weaving. We now ask whether this relationship holds up in the aggregate, across our samples of China's rural communities. To address this larger question, we combine the data from our village sites in North, Northwest, and Southwest China and call this data set the Eight Provinces survey. We also draw on Gates's earlier large Sichuan survey for comparison. The results of our quantitative analysis are best understood in the context of China's industrialization and its implications for homebound female work.

Did footbinding persist longer when girls were involved in regular, intense handwork than when handwork was an occasional, intermittent activity? Additionally, did footbinding persist longer when girls performed handwork for income than when they did not earn income from hand labor?

THE HAND-LABOR VARIABLE

Because hand labor is intrinsically more varied and complex than footbinding, assessing its intensity presents many difficulties. Young and teenaged girls performed a wide range of tasks at their natal homes for roughly ten years between the ages of six and sixteen (Gates 2015).[1] Because duties shifted and increased during their girlhood, women's memories are not fine-tuned for measuring time spent at multiple tasks at different ages, seasons, or years.[2] Although some described in detail the amount of spinning they were required to perform daily, we could not establish a precise quantitative measure for comparing the intensity or amount of time that girls devoted to each type of hand labor. These included a great deal of hand spinning and weaving of cotton but also a variety of other handcrafts such as making fish nets, straw hats, straw shoes, and reed mats. Since nearly all girls, even those who performed heavier tasks, learned some types of handwork,[3] we had to determine who had worked regularly and who worked rarely at handcrafts. This was particularly challenging for a period when the growing volume of industrial substitutes and imports began displacing homemade goods. The phrase "handwork for income," as we use it, indicates commercialization, but these were commercial activities in which payment often took the form of goods: raw cotton, grain, salt, oil, or simply meals. The income girls earned was informal and scarcely legible to those outside the family.[4]

To combine disparate data from different regions, we simplify the handlabor and footbinding data to binary, categorical variables corresponding to survey responses. A common denominator for handwork as a predictor of footbinding must distinguish between limited, intermittent, or rare production of handcrafts and more intensive regimes that regularly enlisted young girls in hand labor. In the Eight Provinces survey, we use "handwork for income" as a measure of intensity—that is, handwork performed for exchange, sale, or wages and not solely for family use. This condenses complicated divisions of labor into a simple binary for each girl: she either performed handwork for income at her natal home before marriage or did not.[5]

"Handwork for income" provides a rough gauge of labor intensity. We assume that when a girl's handwork was associated with an income, parents had an incentive to have her produce beyond family needs. When she earned no income, the incentive was weaker. A lack of income also suggests that handwork had low market value. Nevertheless, a large family that required cloth for its own consumption could also require a great deal of sedentary work from a girl's young hands in the preindustrial era when there were few affordable alternatives.[6] Even after local homemade cloth began to lose market share to yarn and cloth imported from other parts of China or abroad, in families that grew cotton or other fibers, women often spun and wove for home use. Producing goods at home saved money and trips to the market but could also take the form of disguised unemployment.[7] When a girl or woman could earn income from her handwork, however, she was likely to work more intensively and continuously.[8] Poor families often depended on income from women's weaving and girls' spinning to pay taxes and rent; to supplement small plots and poor harvests; or to exchange for grain, salt, oil, or cotton.

There are two conditions in which dichotomous coding might misrepresent girls' handwork intensity and underestimate the strength of the handwork-footbinding relationship:

1. When a girl was burdened with continuous handwork for use by a large family (one with many males and only one daughter), a lack of outside income for handwork would wrongly predict never-bound feet.

2. When a girl rarely performed handwork but occasionally sold or exchanged handmade items, she would be classified with those doing intensive handwork and erroneously expected to have bound feet.

Both types of misclassification would dilute the expected relationship between intense handwork and footbinding.[9]

Because the gamut of different kinds and degrees of handwork during girlhood could not be converted to one continuous or numerical-scale variable, we use a simple dichotomous variable. For the Eight Provinces survey the dichotomy is between handwork for income and no handwork for income. (Even as handcrafts declined, limited handwork for family use persisted for years.) We thus distinguish between hand labor that formed a smaller part of a girl's duties and hand labor that was part of a more intensive regime. This is a reasonable proxy for estimating the amount of hand labor a girl was expected to do.

THE FOOTBINDING VARIABLE

As in the preceding chapters, we use a binary variable for footbinding. Did the respondent ever have her feet bound when she was a girl? If she was ever bound, we classified her as "bound," even if the binding did not last very long. This simplified the complexities of trying to get accurate information on how long and how severely she was bound and how much her feet were deformed with arch bones buckled and toes twisted. If she was ever bound, the point was that someone in her family, or the girl herself, felt it important enough to attempt binding—it was still an expected part of girlhood and bodily training.[10] On the other side of the binary, a woman classified as "not bound" was therefore "never bound." This created a clear distinction among those who were bound in some form and those who were never bound.

LINKING HANDS AND FEET IN CHINA

In view of the diversity of our village sites, the challenge has been to find a way to compare the economic importance of handwork in different villages and for different individuals as it declined and to do so in the context of the changing household economies in which girls were trained to work. Skills learned and practiced for generations do not evaporate or cease entirely when new technology makes them unprofitable or obsolete. The tradition of teaching girls to do certain forms of handwork and needlework often continues even when it is no longer economically useful.[11] At first, families wonder whether the new technologies are going to be permanent or vanish with the next economic downturn or disruption of trade. Thus, families that grow cotton continue to spin and weave some of it at home, even though nearby markets sell stacks of lower-priced cloth imports. After all, families that already have spinning wheels and looms at home can keep family members at work and possibly save money on purchases, even if they can no longer sell their products locally.[12] Even when factory cloth is cheap, women's lack of cash and lost income from sales encouraged them to produce as much as possible at home or find alternative employment. Factory employment was rarely open to married women with children or unmarried village girls, who had to leave home to work in shops or factories, where they incurred new costs for food and lodging. Factory girls also risked their reputation and marriage prospects, as they were assumed to be "broken shoes"—"loose" women outside the purview of family supervision and protection (K. Johnson [1983] 2009, 78; Rofel 1999, 74). Even more important, the number of factory jobs for girls was vastly smaller in the period studied than the number of girls losing work to mechanization.

RELATIONSHIP BETWEEN HANDWORK FOR INCOME AND FOOTBINDING

Treating footbinding as a binary dependent variable (ever bound or never bound), we tested the impact of two independent variables: women's year of birth and handwork for income. The birth-year variable is quantitative, while the handwork-for-income variable is binary and categorical, as is the dependent variable, footbinding. That is, we tested the impact of (1) the birth year and (2) participation in handwork for income (before marriage) on footbinding. The analytic tool of choice for such a test is a logistic regression (Pampel 2000).[13] This produces a multiplicative result most easily presented as the odds of the dependent event (footbinding), given the values of the independent variables.

Using the data from our Eight Provinces survey, we present the logistic regression results in Table 6.1. Our results show that for girls who did handwork for income, the odds that they would be footbound were 2.144 times greater than if they did not do handwork for income. Our results also show that with the passage of every year, the odds were 0.857 times the prior year's odds that they would be footbound. Odds less than 1.0 indicate a decreasing proportion of girls bound in each succeeding year; that is, the odds of any girl being newly bound decreased by 14.3 percent (1.0 minus 0.857) per birth year. The effects of birth year and doing commercial handwork are both statistically significant at the 0.01 percent level. The value for handwork for income (0.762) divided by the value for birth year (−0.154) is used to calculate how many more years (4.95) that footbindings were initiated if daughters performed handwork for income than if they did not (see Appendix B for equation).[14] If girls earned income from textile handwork, initiations of footbinding continued around five years longer than if girls did not do handwork for income. The logistic regression thus allows us to estimate separately the effect of each independent variable, birth year and handwork for income. As it is in any regression result, this should be understood as indicating the direction and magnitude of the effect, not precise measurement.

These results are very convincing. Even though some individual sites do not have enough cases to reach statistical significance, the aggregate sample suggests that the relationship is significant and quite strong for much of early twentieth-century China. It is not surprising that year of birth has an important influence, since footbinding drops from nearly universal in the oldest age groups to completely absent in the younger cohorts of women.

TABLE 6.1

Eight Provinces survey: Logistic regression analysis of footbinding

	Value	Pr > chi-square	Odds ratio
Intercept	298.002	<0.0001*	
Birth year	−0.154	<0.0001*	0.857
Handwork for income	0.762	<0.0001*	2.144

NOTE: Pr = probability. Surveys cover fourteen sites; N = 1,735 women born 1912–1950. Excluded are Hebei Pang (few cases) and Anhui Linquan (missing data). The Pang survey included only 58 women, with 6 footbound born in the 1920s.

For girls who did handwork for income, the odds that they would be footbound were 2.144 times greater than if they did not do handwork for income. (See Appendix B for equations.)

*Generally considered significant at or below the .05 level

In essence, "birth year" stands for all the other variables that were producing change in early twentieth-century China. However, the effect of girls' commercial handwork on footbinding offers solid evidence that our hypothesis is correct. Footbinding was more than an aesthetic practice. When young daughters were trained in hand labor to produce textiles and other goods for sale or exchange, they were more likely to have their feet bound.

Table 6.2, a powerful illustration of the effect of handwork for income on footbinding, presents the results for the odds and probability of being footbound for five-year intervals from 1920 to 1940. Every five years decreases the odds of footbinding by 2.16 times. Doing handwork for income increases the odds of footbinding by 2.14 times. This is another way of noting that doing handwork for income prolonged the practice of footbinding by almost five years, other things being equal. (Our regression estimates 4.95 years exactly, hence the slight difference between 2.16 and 2.14 in this illustration.) Thus, the odds of being footbound for the 1925 birth year and no handwork for income are almost identical to the odds of being footbound for the 1930 birth year and doing handwork for income (see the italicized numbers).

Tables 6.1 and 6.2 show that footbinding did not instantly stop when commercial opportunities for hand-spun or woven cloth declined. Obviously, the decline in commercial opportunities for handcrafts itself was not instantaneous or linear—as we show in the next section. (Local spikes and troughs followed the openings of railroads and wartime blockades.) As commercial opportunities declined, mothers would still start binding their

TABLE 6.2

Eight Provinces survey: Footbinding odds and probabilities by five-year periods

Birth year	HANDWORK FOR INCOME		NO HANDWORK FOR INCOME	
	Odds	*Probability*	*Odds*	*Probability*
1920	21.846	0.956	10.196	0.911
1925	10.115	0.910	*4.721*	*0.825*
1930	*4.683*	*0.824*	2.186	0.686
1935	2.168	0.684	1.012	0.503
1940	1.004	0.501	0.469	0.319

NOTE: Survey covers fourteen sites; N = 1,735 women. These data are a powerful illustration that doing handwork for income extended initiations of footbinding by almost five years, other things being equal. The odds of a woman being footbound if she was born in 1925 and did no handwork for income are almost identical to the odds of her being footbound if she was born in 1930 and did handwork for income (see italicized numbers).

daughter's feet, believing, perhaps, that these traditional activities would always have value. But a variety of adjustments could be made in the face of uncertainty about future markets and gains from disciplined handwork. Binding at a later age and binding more loosely were intermediate measures that mothers could use as they hesitated. When few gains were to be had, mothers no longer strictly enforced the painful binding ordeal and began to give way to their daughters' protests.

We now compare the Eight Provinces analysis to data from the Sichuan survey. The procedure is similar, with three differences relating to content, cohorts, and coding. The Sichuan survey systematically collected information on hand labor with textile fibers—cotton, hemp, ramie, and silk. In contrast, the Eight Provinces survey included a wider range of handwork specialties, including hats, mats, nets, bags, and shoes. Second, the Sichuan data were collected earlier and report on birth cohorts that range from the late nineteenth century only up to 1929. The median birth year of the Sichuan survey was 1908; for the Eight Provinces survey, 1931.[15] This means that when most of the Sichuan women were girls, industrial substitutes for hand labor were still relatively rare in Sichuan's rural areas. Because there was less displacement of handmade textiles by factory goods, nearly all women who produced textiles did so regularly and had heavy workloads. Thus, the third difference is that we include all women who reported any labor in textile handcrafts, without distinguishing whether they worked for use or for income. As we show later, the labor committed to handmade textiles, whether for use or income, was enormous before new forms of transportation and industrial goods arrived. Thus, for Sichuan the binary variable divides between women who worked with textile fibers and those who did not. The footbinding variable that we use is the same for the Sichuan survey as for the Eight Provinces survey.

The result for Sichuan's handwork in textiles also confirms that there was a very strong relationship between hand labor in textiles and footbinding. If the Sichuan women born between 1887 and 1929, inclusive, performed hand labor in textiles before marriage, the odds were 2.5 times greater that they would have bound feet than if they did not do hand labor (Table 6.3). Both birth year and handwork in textiles are again statistically significant at the 0.01 percent level. If girls did textile handwork, initiations of footbinding continued 5.7 years longer than if they did not do textile handwork. While quite similar, the earlier and larger sample from Sichuan

TABLE 6.3
Sichuan Province: Logistic regression analysis of footbinding

	Value	Pr > chi-square	Odds ratio
Intercept	309.446	<0.0001*	
Birth year	–0.161	<0.0001*	0.851
Textile handwork	0.924	<0.0001*	2.519

NOTE: Pr = probability. Survey covers ten counties; N = 4,977 women born 1887–1929. For Sichuan girls, the odds of being footbound were 2.5 times greater if they did textile handwork, and initiations of footbinding continued 5.7 years longer than if they did not do textile handwork. (See Appendix B for equations.)

*Generally considered significant at or below the .05 level

suggests that the relationship between textile handwork and footbinding was at least as strong at the turn of the century.

The evidence and statistical tests show we can have great confidence in our hypothesis. The results are highly significant, and the effect of hand labor before marriage is evident for a large sample across widely separated provinces of China. Year of birth (implicitly including dramatic events and changes that affected local economies) is also a significant variable, even before the 1949 revolution began to clamp down on domestic commercial production by women. Of course, year of birth is not an agent of change in itself but a proxy for a range of variables that affected rural China during the early twentieth century. As trade and technology changed, so did long-standing labor practices and gender expectations at the core of rural family traditions.

FROM HANDCRAFT TO INDUSTRIALIZATION
OF COTTON TEXTILES

Although the end of girls' labor in home handwork was liberating and meant that their feet were no longer hobbled at an age when children yearn to run and jump, there were other consequences. The industrialization of cotton textiles and the subsequent decline of handcrafts entailed the loss of income-producing activities for a large proportion of Chinese rural women who had been trained for such work. This contributed to a devaluation and widespread loss of respect for girls and women themselves. The larger social and economic processes accounting for this devaluation were scarcely perceptible to those it affected or to most of those who wrote about women at the time. Historians and anthropologists wrote about the hardships inflicted on the peasant family, but the gender dimensions usually escaped them. They wrote about the need for women to work without appreciating the degree to which urban textile industrialization created disguised unemployment in the countryside.

Today, experts are quick to inform the public when unemployment has a greater effect on particular groups, such as male blue-collar workers or female civil servants. In the early twentieth century, the reformers of the May Fourth Movement and the modernizers of Nationalist and Communist movements agreed that women needed to leave the home and join the modern labor force, whether in factory work or agriculture. Yet to do this, women had to struggle through many layers of cultural admonitions that they belonged at home.

The connections that we have emphasized between forms of girls' hand labor and footbinding seem reasonable and obvious once we examine the evidence. Thus, we pose the questions: Why was this relationship missed by so many for so long? Why has there been such a resistance to seeing women and girls as economic agents? Why has the interpretation of footbinding been so heavily focused on the idea that it attracted a husband when in fact it was usually the parents who selected marriage partners?

One reason for missing the connection may be that people tend to focus on the evidence they can see. Girls working indoors at spinning wheels or looms were not often seen or described by travelers. Social customs restricting interactions between unrelated men and women limited the ability of male foreigners to observe the labor of young girls. Yet even nineteenth- and twentieth-century women travel writers have given few accounts of the interior workings of peasant households that take into account child rearing and child labor. The customs of elite women and observations of women working outdoors predominate. All this suggests that educated urban writers had little access to the inner quarters of the peasant household. The labor of children was mainly recorded when they worked in public places. Thus, observations of children, especially young girls, working in early twentieth-century textile mills are more common.[16]

A second reason for failure to consider the link between hands and feet is the reluctance to believe that women might forcefully impose footbinding on their daughters to make them work. After all, mothers are supposed to be nurturers—how could they knowingly inflict pain on their own daughters? We believe that when mothers had few ways to earn income and keep the family clothed and fed, the control of girls in their own women's domain allowed for an intrafamily division of labor that let mothers be more productive. In the context of patriarchal households, it is difficult to perceive mothers as agents.[17] Their sacrifices for their families have been celebrated in a genre of writing that emphasizes their devotion to their sons; the sacrifices they demanded from others have been ignored. Yet their daughters were their subordinate labor in the women's domain until they reached the age of marriage. The daughters' labor was supervised by their mothers. In our interviews with women, almost all said their footbinding was done by their mothers, and accounts of beatings by their mothers (not their fathers) abound. Binding may also have kept fathers from demanding their help in the fields. Yet most historical writing has looked at the footbound woman in relation to patriarchal authority and assumed it was done primarily to please men.

Third, as Gates (2015) has emphasized elsewhere, we must also recall that into the early twentieth century, life expectancy in China was short. There was not much time to learn technical skills before teenage marriage, with its ensuing pregnancies and interruptions for child care. Women often died young (as did men). Consequently, many wives had no mother-in-law to help with domestic work and child care. Mothers needed help and consequently found footbinding a convenient way to rein in young daughters and assign them simple but essential handwork that allowed mothers to do more skilled and complex tasks.

TEXTILE INDUSTRIALIZATION REVISITED

Economic historians have carefully studied the decline of domestic textile production and the shift to industrial production. Information about the impact on female hand labor, usually out of sight inside the courtyard, has been limited, and the role of mothers as commercial textile and handcraft producers training, supervising, and disciplining their daughters and daughters-in-law has been overlooked. How did hardworking mothers restrain, train, and keep their energetic young girls seated at work spinning, weaving, plaiting mats, or knotting nets? Footbinding appears to be part of the answer. How did older women evaluate the discipline and hand skills of an incoming daughter-in-law? Bound feet wrapped in homemade cloth bands and embroidered tiny shoes spoke directly of sedentary habits and well-developed hand skills.

The magnitude of girls' and women's contributions of hand labor to China's preindustrial economy remains poorly understood, even though it enters larger debates about China's economic development. Put in demographic terms, the labor of girls assumes its proper proportions. In a society where death came early, the decade between a small girl's capability for light work and marriage into another family constituted about one-third of the female working years in a lifetime. And those years could be very productive, because they were unencumbered by pregnancy, lactation, and (often) child care.[18] Although we do not pretend to estimate total hours or days of labor by girls of different ages and abilities, our survey has shown that girls started work early and were an important part of the rural labor force well before marriage. The ability of young girls to spin was also noted by Kang Chao: "The single-spindle wheel was so simple that a girl of seven or eight could learn to operate it" (1977, 182). Industrialization transformed China's deeply entrenched division of labor, dramatically reducing the need for girls' hand labor in the home and changing the value, expectations, and training of girls as a result. After enduring for centuries, footbinding declined rapidly across China following the spread of new technologies of textile production and transportation. We pay particular attention to the transformation of widespread production of cotton thread and cloth in a rural, female-centered, home-based system using simple equipment to large, impersonal, capital-intensive, mechanical production in urban centers. This was not the only handcraft to be affected by industrialization, but it is the one for which there are abundant data and that played the greatest role (outside farming) in the lives of rural people.

In the eighteenth and early nineteenth centuries China possessed an extensive handcraft industry in textiles and exported handwoven cotton cloth, called "nankeens," to Japan, European countries, and the Americas (Chao 1977, 49–51, 82; Zurndorfer 2009, 61). Cotton nankeens made entirely with hand-spun yarns were exported to Japan by the seventeenth century, to Europe and North and South America by 1730. By 1805, exports of cotton cloth increased to an annual peak of around 1.6 million bolts (nearly six million pounds) (Chao 1977, 51).[19] Although quantitative estimates of the proportion of spinning labor done by children are impossible to derive, there is no doubt that the burden fell mainly on young girls and contributed to the long reign of footbinding in textile-producing villages across China.

The nineteenth century witnessed a reversal from Chinese handwoven cotton exports to factory-made textile imports, which began when cotton yarn and cloth from the industrializing countries began encroaching on Chinese markets. By 1833, exports of nankeens had dropped to only thirty-one thousand bolts. Exports thus fell to less than 2 percent of the peak in under three decades as the industrial cotton mills of Lancashire and America expanded and began to seek foreign markets (Chao 1977, 51, 82).

When the treaty ports opened after 1870, China's yarn and cloth producers began to encounter direct competition from industrial imports on home ground. From 1870 to 1910, imported factory-spun cotton yarn increased thirty-three-fold, from about nine thousand to more than three hundred thousand pounds per year, as shown in Figure 6.1 (Feuerwerker 1995a, 34).[20] As a result, economic historians estimate that the proportion of domestic yarn used in making Chinese textiles declined from nearly 100 percent in 1870 to around 76 percent for 1900–1910.[21] These three to

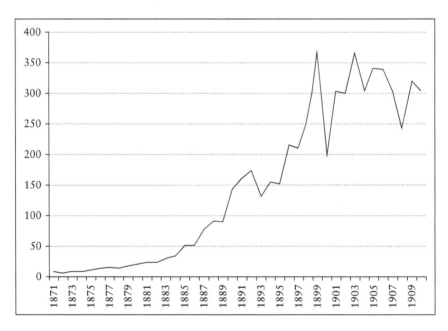

Figure 6.1. China's yarn imports (million pounds), 1871–1910
SOURCE: Data from Feuerwerker 1995a, 34

four decades undoubtedly affected those households for whom hand spinning was a source of income, although the change was earlier and more complete along the coast than in our interior sites.

Transport by rail and steam accelerated the distribution of new products and the machinery that made them. In 1895, China had only 288 kilometers of railway. By 1912 two north-south railways linked the eastern coast cities of Shanghai, Nanjing, Ningbo, and Qingdao to the northern cities of Beijing, Tianjin, and Taiyuan (Feuerwerker 1995a, 70–72, map 3).[22] These railways linked the North China Plain and the Yangzi Valley. Other lines linked Kowloon to Canton and Haiphong to Kunming (Yunnan).[23] In the 1930s, the main north-south railway connected Beijing all the way to the South China ports at Guangzhou and Hong Kong. The east-west (Longhai) line linked coastal Shanghai to Baoji at the western edge of Shaanxi. By1936, China had 10,730 kilometers of railway, excluding Manchuria and Jehol. With relatively dense branch lines in the east and northeast, China lacked railways in most of the west and southwest (Map 6.1).[24] The growing railroad network in conjunction with steamships on the Yangzi and other navigable rivers greatly enhanced commercial transport and allowed industrial yarn from China's coast to percolate into China's interior, depriving a large portion of China's rural population, particularly women and girls, of a time-honored, customary way to earn income.

Spinning

Spinning and weaving were differentially affected by industrialization. Why pay attention to the spinners, whose work was not an end in itself? We have argued that the intensified employment of female labor prior to the modern period conscripted very young footbound girls for spinning. This child labor was never very obvious since it took place indoors at home. Yet village girls who spun and wove by hand were linked along with their mothers to local agents and markets and thence to vast commercial networks beyond their own small circumscribed ambit. Local traders carried homemade textiles to village markets, to town merchants with cloth shops, and then to well-capitalized long-distance cotton merchants who amassed and transported cotton, yarn, and cloth for distant domestic and foreign markets.[25]

During the early lives of our interviewees, home spinning was done almost entirely on very simple, wooden, locally made spinning wheels.

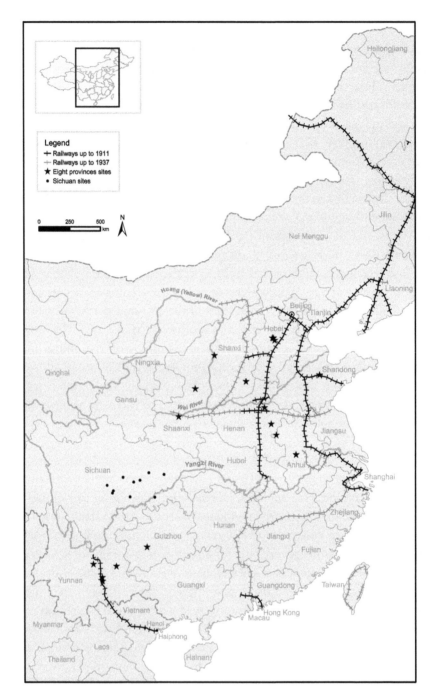

Map 6.1. China's completed railroads, 1911 and 1937

SOURCE: Adapted from Feuerwerker 1995a, 72, 139; Chen and Farley 1937, 167

Noting that multi-spindle wheels had been invented in China long ago, historians have wondered why they were not generally used in the nineteenth and twentieth centuries.[26] Chao claims that "when factory yarn came into wide use, native spinning wheels with 3 or 4 spindles were the first ones to disappear, leaving the most primitive one-spindle wheels in operation" (1977, 182). The spinning wheels with three or four spindles required older girls with more skill to operate, but older girls could earn more by weaving (182–183).[27]

Chao reasons that

> older girls could easily earn more from other handicrafts than from spinning.
> In short, . . . the least efficient spinning tool was preferable because it just
> fitted the marginal labor which had no opportunity cost, whereas spinning
> wheels with 3 or 4 spindles were unprofitable despite their relatively high
> productivity because the opportunity cost of labor inputs exceeded their ben-
> efit. (1977, 182–183)

Young girls were the source of "marginal labor which had no opportunity cost"—meaning they had no alternative way to earn income. Because older girls and women could earn more by weaving, it is not surprising that demands for intensive hand spinning were passed down to the younger girls, who had to make themselves useful by spinning with the single-spindle wheel.[28] Many young girls were inducted into such sedentary handwork by force of footbinding. Machine spinning alleviated that demand. China's supply of factory-spun yarn increased continuously from 1871 to 1936.[29] As a result, the production of hand-spun yarn fell rapidly after the 1870s (Figure 6.2).

The rapid growth during the late nineteenth century in imported machine-made yarns foreshadowed even greater displacement by machine spinning in China in the early twentieth century. From 1905 to 1909 China's annual average of machine-spun yarn rose from 415,000 to roughly 2.3 million bales in 1928–1931. According to Chao, in 1905–1909 the share of hand-spun yarn was 76 percent of China's supply, but by 1928–1931 it had dropped to 26 percent (1977, 232, table 26). Thomas Rawski's estimates (Figure 6.2) show a similar decline over six decades (1989, 93).

In the 1890s mechanized textile mills began to be established in China. Despite some failures along the way, the number of cotton mills climbed rapidly after 1915, reaching 140 in 1936 (Lai 1967).[30] In four decades, the quantity of power spindles increased rapidly from less than 200,000 in 1895 to 1 million by 1915 and 5.5 million in 1935 (Chao 1977, 301, table 40). (See Figure 6.3.)

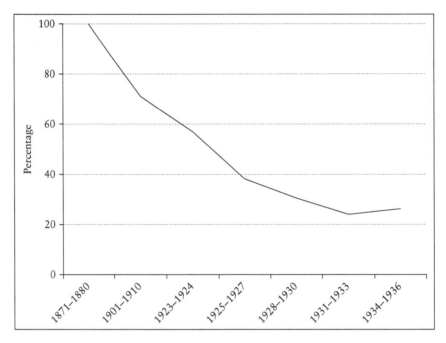

Figure 6.2. Percentage of China's hand-spun yarn output by weight, 1871–1936
SOURCE: Data from Rawski 1989, 93, table 2.10
NOTE: Data exclude net imports.

Where were these multi-spindle factories located? More than half of the textile mills and spindles were concentrated in Shanghai (Figure 6.4). Including Shanghai, two-thirds of the textile mills and spindles were in Jiangsu Province, where yarn merchants had access to the Yangzi River network (Lai 1967, 125; Chao 1977, 127, 302; Tang Chi Yu 1924, 442).[31] About 20 percent were in other eastern cities, Qingdao, Wuhan, and Tianjin. The North China Plain (Hebei, Henan, and Anhui) had about 9 percent of the machine spindles, while the northwest (Shanxi, Shaanxi, and Xinjiang) had only 2 percent. Southwest China, Yunnan and Guizhou, had none (Lai 1967, 125). Even populous Sichuan Province lacked modern factories into the 1930s.[32] Chongqing, capital of Sichuan and China's wartime capital, had only one mechanized textile mill before the Japanese overran eastern China in 1937 (Howard 2013, 1896).[33] The concentration of mills points to an uneven impact on handcraft spinners in the interior provinces, depending on their access to or insulation from expanded, cheaper yarn supplies.

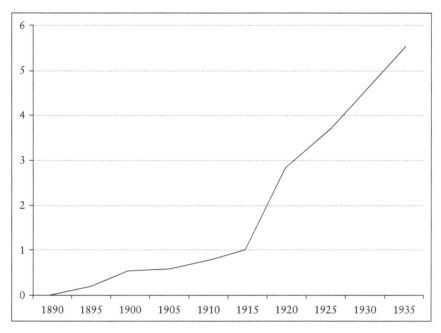

Figure 6.3.   Total industrial cotton-mill spindles (millions), 1890–1935
SOURCE: Data from Chao 1977, 301, table 40

Like the earlier imported factory product, yarn from the newly established mills in China quickly cut into markets for Chinese hand-spun yarn.
The long-term decline of China's hand spinning seems to have paused in
the 1920s because of increased handloom weaving that used both machine-
spun and hand-spun yarn.[34] The limited data on spinning, however, do
not show where or how hand spinning increased in volume of output. The
higher labor productivity of spinning mills pushed the market price of
homespun yarn down until it approached the purchase price of raw cotton. When machine yarn was readily available and cheap, it drew urban
and town buyers away from homespun well before dispersed rural households stopped spinning and weaving for their own use. Paradoxically, the
increased supply and lower cost of machine yarn encouraged hand weavers
to produce more cloth even as the spinning of yarn by hand lost much of
its market value. Handloom weavers who switched to machine-spun yarn
preferred it as warps for strength, cross-cutting them by homespun wefts
for added thickness. This loosened, for a time, the bottleneck that spinning

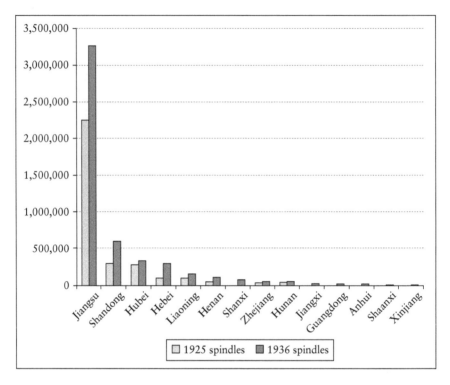

Figure 6.4. Number of cotton-mill spindles by province, 1925 and 1936
SOURCE: Data from Lai 1967, 87, 125, tables 18, 34

had always made in textile production. Another response to imports was to shift from hand spinning to handweaving with factory yarn. Yet this was not always possible: looms were more expensive than spinning wheels, and girls had to be older and physically larger to operate them.

Beyond supplying the integrated mills and handloom weavers of eastern China with factory yarn at low cost, the new railways and steamships allowed merchants to bring cheap factory yarn into the interior provinces (Map 6.2). The growth of inexpensive, uniform-quality yarn from the new mills was initially overwhelming for hand spinners but a boon for weavers. The labor productivity ratio of machine spinning to hand spinning in the 1930s was at least 40:1 (P. Huang 1990, 98; 2002, 519).[35] Hand spinning for income was severely squeezed and ultimately doomed, but it enjoyed a brief revival when handweaving combined stronger machine-spun warp yarns with thicker, weaker hand-spun wefts.[36] As a result of increasing

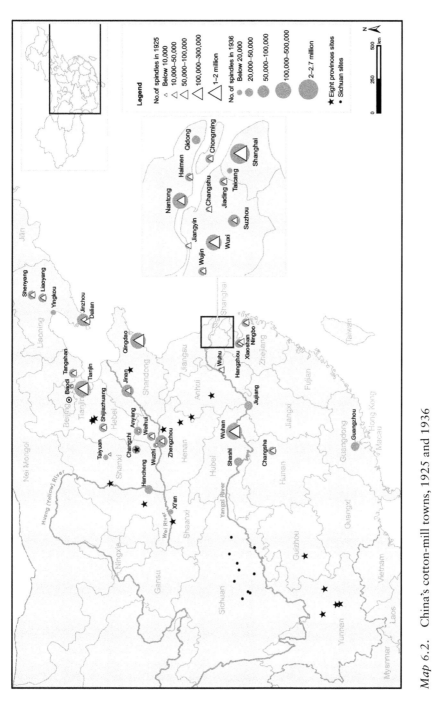

Map 6.2. China's cotton-mill towns, 1925 and 1936

SOURCE: Adapted from Lai 1967, 89, 123

competition from cheaper machine-spun yarn, opportunities for village girls to earn income from hand spinning dried up and presaged the abandonment of footbinding first in the coastal cities and later in the interior provinces, as we describe in Chapters 3–5.

Figure 6.5 shows that China's cotton yarn production more than doubled by 1924, with a rising proportion provided by factory yarn.[37] Between the 1920s and 1936, the divergence between rising machine-spun and

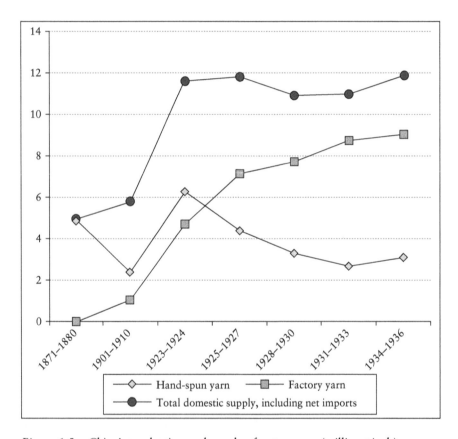

Figure 6.5. China's production and supply of cotton yarn (million *piculs*), 1871–1936

SOURCE: Data from Rawski 1989, 93, table 2.10

NOTE: 1 *picul* = 133.33 pounds. Hand-spun yarn production dropped from 1870 to 1900, rebounded from 1910 to 1923 (when domestic handloom weavers combined factory and hand-spun yarns), and dropped again as China's cloth factories spread in the 1920s. Factory yarn production, starting from zero in 1871, rose rapidly from 1901 to 1927 and less rapidly in the 1930s during the world economic depression. For data, see Table A.7.

declining hand-spun yarn is striking. Spinning did not stop abruptly (or entirely) nationwide, but the possibilities for families to sell or exchange the yarn produced by girls and women grew increasingly limited, particularly in the areas well served by yarn and cloth merchants and modern transportation. The areas with best access to industrial yarn were eastern cities and seaports such as Shanghai, Hong Kong, Guangzhou, and Tianjin, as well as lower and middle Yangzi River ports. Handcraft spinning and footbinding declined earliest in these areas.

Weaving

Handloom technology also changed. Where families had access to good distribution networks and could purchase the more productive improved looms, handloom weavers temporarily increased cloth output for internal markets. With larger investment in new iron-gear looms, families and workshops could get better returns with regular, full-time weavers. As a result, men, who could work without disruptions from babies, child care, and cooking, started to supplement and replace women at the more capital-intensive looms (Grove 2006, 81–83). Weavers who could not afford the investment in improved looms and lacked location or transportation advantages faced declining incomes. But by the 1930s, even the iron-gear handloom weavers were going bankrupt as cheap cloth made in industrial textile mills progressively won over urban and rural customers. As industrial textiles expanded, spinning wheels and handlooms were often discarded.

Some historians have stressed that the vigorous response of the handloom-weaving sector is a sign of the dynamic market forces operating in China in the Republican period. We review the handloom data with a different aim—to clarify the unexplored and undocumented effects on girls' labor. The early twentieth-century resilience of handloom weaving is linked to three significant changes—in technology, location, and the division of labor—which we examine in turn.

China's handloom cotton weaving had long been held back by the comparatively slow pace of hand spinning and thus limited yarn supplies. It typically took three to four days of hand spinning to provide enough yarn for one day of weaving (Chao 1977, 179; Gates 2015). The rapid growth in yarn supplies coming from power spinning mills unleashed handloom weavers and allowed them to increase output by weaving more continuously. Mechanized weaving did not, at first, have a huge advantage over

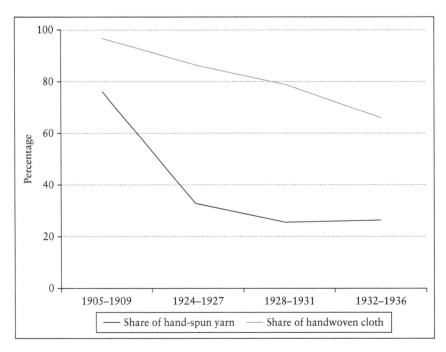

Figure 6.6. Handcraft production of cotton yarn and cloth, percentage of total yarn and cloth output, 1905–1936

SOURCE: Adapted from Chao 1977, 232, table 26

handweaving (Chao 1977). Historians stress that a smaller productivity gap for weaving than for spinning explains the more successful resistance of handwoven cloth to the competition of factory cloth in the early twentieth century (Figure 6.6). Handloom weavers were able to compete against the machine for decades after the introduction of large integrated textile mills, in part because they produced cloth that was generally preferred by rural Chinese—it was thicker, warmer, and more durable than factory cloth— but also because they could employ family labor at low cost (Figure 6.7). Using simple technology and flexible family labor, they could also hold down fixed costs. However, handloom technology was not static. Profiting from access to cheaper, more abundant factory yarn and favored locations, Chinese weavers copied and designed innovative handlooms and reorganized handloom weaving.

Using the old methods of spinning and weaving, households had relatively small investments in equipment. Spinning wheels and the traditional,

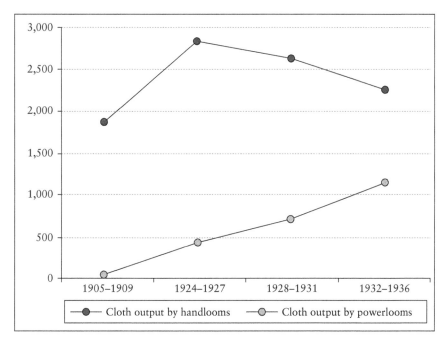

Figure 6.7.   China's cloth output by hand and power looms (million square yards), 1905–1936

SOURCE: Adapted from Chao 1977, 32

"clumsy" (*ben*) looms cost little and could be made by local carpenters but could weave only narrow cloth at a slow rate (Chao 1977, 70–71). These looms produced

> the traditional narrow goods, usually 11 to 15 inches wide. The width was restricted by the effective reach of the weaver. On the traditional Chinese loom the shuttle had to be thrown back and forth from one hand to the other. The weaver sitting with both arms raised, throwing and catching the shuttle all day long simply could not maintain any sort of speed and straddle a width wider than that given above. (Kraus 1980, 122)[38]

The narrowness of cloth from traditional looms had an advantage, however. Cloth woven about a foot wide made efficient use of material when sewn into the square-cut styles of peasant shirts and pants, for it resulted in almost no wasted offcuts. Narrow looms produced cloth in widths adapted to making simple, comfortable clothing that required minimum cutting and tailoring.

The adoption of improved wooden looms with hand-operated fly-ing shuttles around the turn of the twentieth century, even as early as the 1880s in some locations, increased productivity for those who could af-ford them.[39] Flying-shuttle looms could produce twice as much cloth per day as the traditional wooden loom (Kraus 1980, 132–133; Gamble 1954; Chao 1977). The iron-gear loom, produced in China after 1907,[40] was more expensive but four times as fast as the clumsy loom as described for Ding County in Chapter 3 (P. Huang 1990; Chao 1977, 184). Adoption of the iron-gear or treadle loom allowed weavers to continue producing *tubu* for China's extensive markets, holding at bay the finer machine-made cloth from the many factories springing up along the eastern seaboard and major cities. The ratio of labor productivity between a power loom and the iron-gear hand loom was about 4:1 (Chao 1977, 185), which, in turn, suggests that a power loom was sixteen times more productive than the traditional wooden handloom.[41]

Accounts comparing handwoven and factory-woven cotton cloth offer little information regarding the changing distribution of the three types of handlooms—traditional wooden looms, improved flying-shuttle looms, and iron-gear looms—in China's interior cities and towns. The iron-gear looms were more expensive and wider and made use of foot pedals, or treadles, a feature that seems to have been less compatible with footbind-ing. "The foot pedals controlled all movements, including the pulling of warps and the rolling of cloth" (Chao 1977, 184). Production of iron-gear looms in China began in Tianjin in 1907 (Hershatter 1983, 1986). "By 1921 they had been reported in such widely scattered and relatively out of the way places as Beihai, Guangdong; Jinhai, Zhejiang; and Tengyue, Yun-nan" (Kraus 1980, 134–135).[42] As improved flying-shuttle and iron-gear looms spread inland, rural weavers using the simple clumsy looms were increasingly at a disadvantage. In Ding County in just twenty years, clumsy looms dropped from 260 to 48, a decline of 82 percent. Table 6.4 shows the rapid shift to improved types of looms in a weaving village of Ding County.

The influx of cheap factory-produced yarn affected handweaving in two phases. Initially, by breaking the bottleneck requiring three or more days of spinning labor to supply one day of weaving, machine-yarn from India and Japan promoted the growth of handweaving in rural households (Gates 2015; Chao 1977, 179). Those nearer the sources of imported fac-tory yarns were able to increase output more readily, and handweaving even

TABLE 6.4
Percentages and types of handlooms in a Ding County village

Year	Clumsy (%)	Pulling (%)	Iron-gear (%)	Total (N)	Index of productive capacity
1912	93	7	0	280	100
1917	83	17	0	270	105
1922	66	28	6	255	124
1927	51	34	15	246	146
1932	20	51	29	239	190

SOURCE: Data from Kraus 1980, 133, table 5.7; Gamble 1954, 315, table 96

NOTE: Productive capacity ratios are 1:2:4 for clumsy (simple wooden), pulling (flying-shuttle), and iron-gear (treadle) looms (Gamble 1954, 302).

expanded into areas not particularly known for it.[43] After the introduction of more expensive, improved looms just after the turn of the twentieth century, the dispersed pattern of household weaving shifted into a second phase. Beginning in eastern coast metal shops in Tianjin and Shandong, handweaving became more concentrated in areas that had access not only to ample yarn supplies (factory or hand spun) but also to locales capable of manufacturing the superior looms. Gradually, manufacture of more-sophisticated flying-shuttle and iron-gear looms began to diffuse to the interior, and the looms themselves were shipped by merchant-entrepreneurs to urban handloom factories in major cities and river ports.[44] In the 1930s, in areas like Yan'an, Shaanxi, cut off from eastern cloth supplies, efforts were made to build and disseminate more efficient spinning wheels and looms modeled on innovations in other parts of China (Schran 1976).

Figure 6.6 juxtaposes China's hand-spun yarn and handwoven cloth output over time. From 1905–1909 to 1924–1927 handloom weavers increased output by using mixed machine- and homespun yarn (Chao 1977, 232). After 1924–1927, handwoven cloth output fell again as integrated industrial textile mills continued to increase output.

Shift in Weaving

Up to the late nineteenth century, spinning and weaving "were not concentrated in cities, but rather in the countryside. . . . Women and children who did most of the spinning and weaving within the households were themselves scattered throughout the cotton-growing regions and beyond" (Hamilton and Chang 2003, 181–182). Emphasis on the vitality of handcraft cloth production obscures the massive shift from small wooden handlooms to iron-gear hand and foot looms. It also overlooks the massive shift from dispersed home-based weaving to the concentration of new-style handloom weaving in specialized weaving centers with access to modern transportation and handloom technology. In these areas, looms were often supplied on credit to weavers who produced in a putting-out system (Chao 1977; Walker 1999).

Handloom weaving became more concentrated in specialized weaving centers known for particular kinds of cloth. Chao (1977, 188) describes the growth of handweaving and the rise of a succession of centers such as Ding County, Baodi, and Gaoyang in Hebei and Wei Xian in Shandong as they acquired new iron-gear looms.[45] These new weaving centers were often close to local manufacturers of iron-gear looms in Tianjin (Hebei) and Qingdao (Shandong) (Hershatter 1983, 1986; Chao 1977, 195). More-over, they were located near major railways and roads. Dispersed villagers produced cloth at a slower rate, had higher transportation costs to reach the cloth markets, and had few means to invest in or acquire the expensive new looms. Weaving households and workshops concentrated in towns and villages near modern transportation networks could buy factory yarn and improved looms to increase their weaving output.

> The newly emerged centers of handicraft textiles differed from the old centers in that they were not cotton-growing areas, hence commanding no intrinsic advantage. Their hand loom cloth industries depended decisively on the skill of weavers and the quality of products, namely their adaptability to new technology and new products. (Chao 1977, 197)

Summing up the shift in the locus of handweaving, Chao writes,

> Hand-weaving factories tended to appear in places other than the [old] cen-ters of native cloth. Furthermore, those units preferred the locations just out-side the city limits but not in the countryside. To keep away from the coun-tryside meant to avoid direct competition with the subsidiary production of rural households; besides, it was easier to get full-time workers in urban areas than in rural areas. (1977, 214)

Increasingly, specialized weaving centers and their distribution networks supplied China's city and town markets with hand-loomed cotton cloth. Famous cotton weaving centers like Gaoyang, Baodi, Ding County, and Wei Xian not only became more efficient;[46] they also created known brand names that attracted urban and town consumers (see Chao 1977;

Feuerwerker 1995a,113; Hamilton and Chang 2003). From 1912 to 1929, Gaoyang increased the number of iron-gear looms from eleven hundred to twenty-seven thousand sets and produced 3.2 million bolts of cotton cloth annually, which was sold in "more than 20 provinces plus Outer Mongolia and Southeast Asia" (Chao 1977, 193–195; Grove 2006). Gaoyang was served by the Beijing-Hankou railway.

Dispersed rural home-based weavers lost the urban working-class markets to cloth distributed from well-known handweaving centers (Kraus 1980). Apart from the smaller rural markets and remote interior markets, where warm, durable cloth was still in demand, weavers saddled with the older looms had fewer buyers—mainly other peasants like themselves.

The growth of the new handweaving industry sustained and even increased employment for weavers in some areas but left many village women with reduced opportunities to earn income. Rural home-based weavers outside the new handweaving textile centers were besieged by both industrial and new handloom competition. Together, textile mills and improved handloom weaving centers contributed to the collapse of female incomes from home-based textile work in many parts of rural China. Those who could not obtain the new flying-shuttle and iron-gear looms first lost out to hand-loomed cloth produced in the new weaving centers, but even with new looms, "the regional competition among the new centers of hand weaving was acute. . . . One place rose at the expense of another" (Chao 1977, 197).

In many areas, especially in the interior, small handloom enterprises continued to operate. In 1933 in Chongqing, "over 90 percent of the 1,300 factories remained family-run workshops, with 24,000 looms producing over one million bolts of cloth" (Howard 2013, 1896; see also Gates 2015). By the 1930s, however, the heyday of handloom weaving drew to a close. "Virtually all empirical surveys on local hand loom weaving mention that it declined seriously in the early 1930s" (Chao 1977, 197). Figure 6.7 shows, after a peak in the mid-1920s, a decline in handwoven cloth in the late-1920s, while the output of machine-woven cloth rises steadily for three decades.

After Japan invaded and occupied eastern China in 1937, the disruptions of warfare, bombings, and relocation of Chinese industry to the west make it difficult to trace changes in yarn and cloth production at the national level. When blockades disrupted supplies, some areas reverted to older hand methods while others sped up efforts to modernize their technologies in response to severe wartime shortages of cloth.[47] When war cut supply lines for machine textiles, officials needing to clothe their armies put girls and women, and sometimes boys and men, to work spinning and weaving—an important but temporary hiatus in the slow decline of handcraft textile making. Where cotton grew well, hand spinning and especially handweaving sometimes have persisted to the present day. Although handweaving is rare today, we have been shown *tubu* produced in the early years of the twenty-first century in our research sites. During the lifetimes of our research subjects, however, the great majority of rural women who would once have specialized in spinning and weaving, proud of both their handwork skills and their bound feet, came to find such work and footbinding, its bodily symbol, permanently devalued.

Rise of Industrial Weaving Mills

In emerging weaving centers in Hebei, the larger capital investment in iron-gear looms and greater returns to labor led men to take up weaving to keep looms in full-time operation.[48] In Gaoyang, "in 1933, there were 30,000 iron gear looms in the weaving district spread across a five-county area in more than one hundred villages" (Grove 2006, 89).[49] With a productivity ratio of at least 4:1, iron-gear looms may have displaced more than ninety thousand weavers working on cheaper clumsy looms. Although total handcraft cloth production increased, rural women and girls across China who continued to depend on the simple clumsy loom to earn income had to work much harder to earn anything or find a way to shift to other work.[50] While we cannot determine how commonly the shift in looms led to a shift to weaving by men,[51] the increased output of the improved handlooms alone would have changed the economic outlook for vast numbers of rural women outside these favored centers.

Women who began their lives as footbound spinners in mother-daughter teams were ill-prepared physically to operate the new iron-gear treadle looms.[52] Chao suggests that initially the iron-gear loom was "not widely adopted because it was not constructed to suit the bound feet of the Chinese women in those days. With some modifications subsequently made by the Chinese manufacturers in the foot pedals the new loom finally became popular in the 1920s" (1977, 84). By that time, increasing numbers of girls in eastern coast cities like Shanghai and Tianjin, long rendered superfluous as hand spinners because of the importation of factory yarn and rise of cloth mills, were able to avoid foot binding. Their mothers, perhaps sensing the futility of such training, had become less insistent about it. Abundant anecdotal evidence exists for earlier decline of footbinding in cities where modern textile mills were first established. Lu Lihua, born in 1900 in a town near Shanghai to a shopkeeper family, is one example:

> My mother was illiterate and had bound feet. When I was six, she began to bind my feet, too. But I cut the wrapping cloth off at night. I usually obeyed my parents, but not with this footbinding. I was afraid of the pain and did not like bound feet. With bound feet, a girl could be distinguished as a girl. I wanted to be the same as boys—without distinction. They said, "You will harm yourself by having big feet in the future. You will not be able to marry into a good family." I said, "Let me harm myself. I cannot take this pain." Blood oozed from my feet, and I showed this to my mother. "Mom, look, how can I bear this?" She said, "There's no other way. You have to bear the pain." With those words, she continued binding my feet. I quietly resisted. She bound my feet during the day; at night I went to my grandma, who lived just across a bridge, and cut the wrapping cloth off. Mother said, "If I fail to bind your feet, how can I be a mother? Won't you blame me in the future?" I said, "No . . . Let me have my big feet so long as I can walk." Three times I cut the wrapping cloth off. . . . Finally my mother gave up. (Wang Zheng 1999, 146)

Lu Lihua's older sister, born in 1898, had bound feet. Lu Lihua, the second daughter, disappointed her father because he did not have a son. He decided to "raise her as a boy" and allowed her to attend school in 1906. In Shanghai, she was able to attend a girls' school and went on to found her own school. The fact that Lu Lihua's account makes no mention of handcrafts is consistent with their displacement by industrial textiles in the cities.

Little quantitative evidence is available to make a direct connection between the decline of footbinding and the rise of factory cloth production in the eastern coast cities. One study done in 1929 in Tianjin found that in the total female population of 543,366, the footbinding rate was only 27 percent, so the rate for Tianjin girls and young women must have been very low even by 1900 (Hershatter 1986, 258n42).[53] This can be compared to the Ding County study of Dongting, where in the same year the proportion of footbinding in the female population as a whole was still as high as 52 percent (N = 1,736) (Gamble 1954, 48, 60). In Ding County's Dongting district, footbinding had stopped among those born after 1916, when iron-gear looms displaced simple handlooms.

The rise of the cotton textile industry in China provided jobs to women and girls who lived in proximity to the factories and to some who migrated and lived in dormitories. Foreign visitors to Shanghai's cotton textile mills commented not only on the high proportion of women but also on the omnipresence of young girls "running" around the mills. Child labor was still common, and girls as young as eight were learning textile factory work. Footbound women and mothers with babies strapped to their backs, in the mills that would still hire them, were considered too slow and inefficient although diligent (Moser 1930). However, despite the preponderance of girls and young women in the textile mills, these jobs numbered just over one hundred thousand in Shanghai's cotton industries in 1929, in contrast to the millions of rural woman with vanishing incomes from spinning and weaving (Honig 1986, 23–25).[54] No doubt the nature of factory work favored young girls with natural feet who could move quickly about the factory as needed (191).

As cotton textile mills spread across the land (see Map 6.2), the number of power looms increased from twelve thousand in 1922 (Tang Chi Yu 1924) to roughly fifty-two thousand in 1936 (Lai 1967). Industrial cloth output increased from around 6 million square yards in 1890 to over 400 million by 1925 and reached 1.4 billion in 1936 (Chao 1977, 313). (See Figure 6.8.) The share of handwoven cloth dropped in just thirty years from nearly 100 percent in 1905 to 66 percent of the total cotton cloth produced in China in 1936, a severe drop yet still less dramatic than the drop in the share of hand-spun yarn (see Figure 6.6). We cannot determine what percentage of this handwoven cloth was still produced by women and girls in dispersed villages on old-style looms and how much production had shifted to iron-gear looms and centralized handweaving workshops located near towns with access to railways or river ports. As transportation improved, the new textile mills and specialized handloom weaving centers shipped their products across China and beyond. The century-long process of shrinking home employment for female cotton spinners and weavers forced rural women in many parts of China to seek other forms of income, at considerable disadvantage, in overcrowded labor markets, particularly in the 1930s (Walker 1999). In the 1950s during the collective period, female participation in the labor force was no longer a matter of choice. State policy explicitly sought to bring women out of the home to make them more productive.

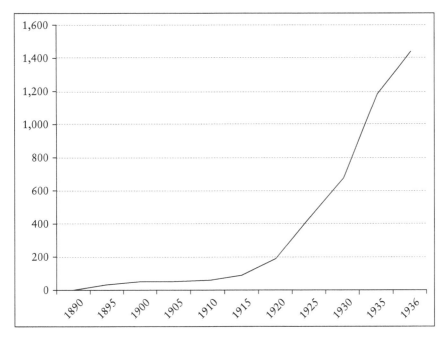

Figure 6.8.   Cotton cloth output from modern mills (million square yards), 1890–1936

SOURCE: Data from Chao 1977, 313, table 43

Kraus summarizes the effects of the decline of handweaving as follows:

> Weaving in the rural areas of China was a very commercialized affair, and very specialized. . . . The effect of the resulting but even more rapid decline in hand-woven cloth production would have been focused on those households which had previously decided to specialize in spinning and/or weaving. Their position must have become particularly acute by the early Thirties. This distress must have been evidenced by a desperate search for new cash income. (1980, 142)

These speculations are supported by many accounts, but after the Japanese invasion in 1937, the distress from lost livelihoods was compounded by the increasing loss of lives due to violence. The fact that Shanghai and Nanjing, in the heartland of Chinese factory textile production, were occupied by the Japanese created a massive relocation of China's modern textile production to the west and even stimulated some areas to revive hand spinning and weaving during the war years.

DEVALUATION OF WOMEN'S WORTH

Francesca Bray has written about changing perceptions of Chinese women's work over time: "Where women were still seen as primarily or solely responsible for the production of a valuable commodity, the value of the work they performed does seem to have translated into respect" (2013, 112). In view of the massive changes in the textile sector that reduced the time-honored respect for and reliance on rural women's handwork, it is no wonder that urban and rural segments of Chinese culture came to denigrate rural women as backward and "unproductive." To the extent that their skilled hand labor no longer produced a product that people valued and were willing to pay for, society began to look down on these women. In the early twentieth century, the changed economic circumstances put pressure on women to work outside the household and participate in "productive" labor. The values of female propriety, confining women to work at home and praising them for their modesty, diligent handwork, and small feet, were at odds with women's new economic situation. Social barriers to female employment in public places had to be overcome, while family expectations prioritizing domestic service were at odds with modern economic conditions. Reproductive technologies of the first half of the twentieth century did not enable women to prevent pregnancy, so their reputations were at risk if they were unmarried; if they were married, work outside the home came at the expense of their (many) children.

National figures tell a story of handcraft resilience and survival (1850–1950). Missing is an account of the decimation and displacement of rural home-based, woman-centered worksites in which women wove and girls spun. This enormous loss of employment by women and girls, stuck at home with bound feet, was also a disempowerment that lay, invisibly, behind the overt folk sayings that girls were not worth anything or that they were merely "goods on which you lose money."

Even a well-known reformer, Liang Qichao, who favored women's education, espoused the view that women at home were worthless. As historian Wang Zheng puts it,

> He argued that because Chinese women were not allowed to have an education and were confined to the women's quarters and restricted by custom, they had become "as lazy as vagabonds and as stupid as barbarians."

He asked rhetorically, with two hundred million vagabonds and barbarians, how can our country not be harmed? (1999, 172)

The ideological devaluation of women that accompanied the devaluation of the work they traditionally performed is not unique. It finds its parallel in an ideological shift in England during industrialization (Valenze 1995).[55] Beyond the many literary examples of women's devalued status in the late nineteenth century, Mao's revolutionary generation, following Marxist thinking, viewed the household as an unproductive (and politically unreliable) place. The inability to see or measure the devastating impact of new technologies and capital investments on a domestic labor force has led to a misrecognition of the intensity of commercial hand labor prior to the industrialization as well as the hardship caused as it wrenched footbound girls and women from their homes to participate in what was considered productive labor in fields and factories. Historians have puzzled over the cultural factors that may have inhibited women's shift to other types of work but rarely considered footbinding in the context of changing economic conditions. In many respects, Chinese have been swift to respond to market forces, but when these forces entail deployment of female labor outside the home, a range of questions arise concerning female safety, morality, and the obligations to bear and care for children and the aged. When women labored at home with bound feet, these contentious issues of domestic responsibility and multitasking were solved by limiting their options.

When handwork for income became less and less viable, women whose feet were permanently deformed by binding had to go out to work on heavier tasks despite the difficulties and pain it caused. This conflict between expectations of work at home and rising need to supplement incomes by work outside, would account for reports of women with bound feet working in the fields. Women might justifiably object that this is not the work they were fit for, but that was little help when the family was short of food.

Ideological change is complex, and we do not claim that the loss of handcraft income is the only explanation for the decline of footbinding and the pressure on women to work outside the home. A case can be made that the flood of new commodities and fashions contributed to desires for change (Dikotter 2006; Finnane 2008). This is undeniably true for the coastal cities and their surrounding villages. But rural populations had much less exposure and incentive to adopt new fashions when they could barely afford sturdy everyday clothing. In the memories of our respondents, their articles of clothing were almost always minimal, with new garments appearing only one year in three. Village girls were not unbinding their feet so they could buy fashionable shoes.

When a large category of people lacks access to work, the group loses social value. Some of the repercussions of rural women's invisible mass dis-employment from 1850 to 1950 could be connected to abundant evidence of skewed sex ratios that reflect the devaluation of girls. Historian Kathy Le Mons Walker, commenting on the "interlocking of economic growth and rural decline," wrote about rural economic changes:

> By the 1920's the features of the rural family system bearing directly on women—female infanticide, child marriage, contract prostitution-concubi-nage, and the buying and selling of females—were clearly on the rise. . . . Rural decline . . . unquestionably became one of the key factors influenc-ing rural families to sell their daughters or to place them, in return for a cash payment, into some form of servitude for a specified period of time. (1999, 192)

RETOOLING

In the mid-twentieth century, women had to "retool" themselves, to learn jobs where they needed to stand on their feet, as in the new textile factories where women walked rapidly while tending their machines as well as using their hands. Factory owners preferred to hire young, unmarried women and girls, but not if they had bound feet.[56] That women should come out into society, out of household-based work, was mandated by the revolutionary government in 1949 and fully enforced during the late 1950s. Revolution-ary technological changes of the Republican period combined with the po-litical revolutions of the mid-twentieth century to push rural women out of the home into the fields and factories as China continued its quest to build a modern economy.

Viewed from a distance, the new late nineteenth- and early twentieth-century technologies of transportation and textile production appear to have been significant factors in the eradication of footbinding. Our data linking the persistence of handcrafts to the persistence of footbinding clearly point in this direction. Footbinding, a permanent mutilation, was inflicted by mothers who needed to ensure girls' early compliance with demands for disciplined handwork. It was expected that such handwork would continue throughout their lives. The twentieth-century movement for universal education of girls as well as boys also contributed to a new outlook and opportunities for girls, generally reinforcing natural feet by the very act of sending girls outside to a classroom. Certainly, educators promoted the idea that girls could seek work outside the home by using their education. Yet our data indicate that formal education was not the decisive factor that led to the demise of rural footbinding in the 1930s. Very few women in our village sites were literate or had had any education at all until after the Communist government was established in 1949. A strong motivation for the elimination of the practice was the growing disrespect for the low productivity of women confined to domestic labor. The widespread critique of female idleness entered into the discourse of reformers. But we believe that underlying the critique was the recognition that domestic handwork had become unprofitable. Economic change made reformers recognize that families had to seek livelihoods for their daughters, and these were not compatible with footbinding.

Binding was initially reinforced and intensified by the commercialization of handmade cotton yarn, cloth, and other handcrafts. The further economic and technological changes that put an end to the widespread practice of disabling daughters' feet also brought a distressing loss of income and social esteem for girls and women. An incredibly difficult transition to gainful employment outside the home awaited many rural women who were illiterate, unprotected, and ill-prepared for physical labor (Hershatter 1986; Honig 1986; Dikotter 2010). For rural girls, the modernizing economy meant that a once-respected cloistered, sheltered, and thus morally unassailable life within the walls of the house and courtyard was no longer possible. Social criticisms of the morality of rural girls who stepped outside the gate or migrated to work outside the village or in factories would linger for decades.

Mainstream accounts of China's industrial transformation have been skewed by failing to notice how an enduring system of handcraft production favored and tolerated the infliction of painful deformities on hundreds of millions of girls and women. Just as labor conditions in subcontracted offshore plants tend to stay outside the scope of economic analysis until a large factory burns down with workers locked inside, so were the harsh labor conditions of young girls ignored as long as they were dispersed, out of sight, in the family home. The deformities of bound feet, a sight that troubled nineteenth-century foreign observers who saw women hobbling outdoors, were curiously never connected to the work that young girls did indoors. The historical record has perpetuated the notion that footbinding was imposed on girls primarily to make them beautiful, without considering that young girls first had to learn to be useful. By noting the oversights and omissions of economic history in regard to young and powerless girl laborers, we can achieve greater transparency and understanding of the complex social and economic pecking order and the transformations in process.

DEMISE OF DEBILITATING GENDER PRACTICES

In recent years there have been attempts to draw lessons from the demise of footbinding to change other customs that are damaging to women and girls (Appiah 2010a, 2010b; Mackie 1996). Some advocates, with the best of intentions, interpret footbinding in the conventional manner, as a practice designed to attract men in marriage. They believe that footbinding was eventually defeated by proselytizing, teaching men and women about the harm it did, and by promoting group reinforcement. They suggest that current human rights advocates should adopt similar methods against other customs, such as female genital cutting, widely practiced in parts of Africa and the Middle East.

Appiah's account emphasizes the campaigns of Christian missionaries and Chinese literati as moral reformers. No doubt these groups had some influence in urban centers where they created a core of converts, but ignorance of the widespread economic pressures and motivations that impelled vast rural populations to abandon footbinding leads to a superficial account. Gates (2015), in her Sichuan study, and our more extensive research among thousands of elderly rural women in many provinces of China, paint a very different picture, one in which moral reforms and public campaigns often had little impact. What in many cases did have an impact was a drastic change in rural livelihoods. The explanation given by Appiah and Mackie completely ignores the economic incentives that propelled the demise of footbinding in China. In Appiah's view, eliminating the practice of female genital cutting is to be achieved through moral suasion, a core of converts, and respect for traditions of the community. These methods may be helpful, but in misunderstanding the demise of footbinding in China, would-be reformers may be led to ignore the specific socioeconomic drivers of the practices they wish to end.

Examining the link between the young hands of cotton spinners and their bound feet has significance well beyond the demise of a debilitating custom. Our research confronts the accumulation of gender and class bias that has inhibited a thorough understanding of the economic conditions confronting China in the late nineteenth and early twentieth centuries. Lack of attention to the economic activities of women and girls was buttressed by assumptions of footbound women's idleness. Lack of interaction with rural women or observation of their domestic working conditions led scholars to focus on the gendered lives of the elite, and even then they rarely considered women's skills in economic terms. By demystifying footbinding and examining it as a part of economic life in large parts of the rural population, we can transcend reliance on literary sources emphasizing elite ideals, sexuality, and aesthetics. Moreover, we have shown that the intensive hand labor demanded of young girls lends credence to the claim that much of rural China was experiencing involutionary growth, increasing output through more intensive use of family labor.

Our evidence firmly demonstrates how the family economy of rural China incorporated girls' labor and sustained the practice of footbinding. Young hands were taught to work, and their labor underpinned China's preindustrial textile prowess. Footbinding declined when girls' hand labor at home was displaced by industrial developments. Thus, we must revise the conventional explanations of footbinding based on speculation and reinforced by repetition. These explanations have obliterated the economic roles of women and stressed the role of Christian missionaries, the ideologies of social reformers, and men's attraction to small feet. In their recollections, women who managed to unbind as girls often credit their own resistance in the face of beatings and dire warnings. Yet it was parental resolve to enforce the combination of footbinding and hand labor that weakened as mothers came to terms with industrial expansion and capitalist development in China. Thus, it is time to lay to rest the mythical pursuit of idle beauty as the force that drove hundreds of millions of women to bind their young daughters' feet.

Appendix A: Tables

TABLE A.1
Research sites: Cotton and hand labor at natal home by girls born 1910s–1940s

Province	County/city: site	Natal family grew cotton (%)	Spun cotton (%)	Spun cotton for income (%)	Had a loom (%)	Wove cotton (%)	Wove cotton for income (%)
NORTH CHINA							
Hebei	Ding County: Qingfengdian	68	86	68	28	51	28
	Ding County: Pang	69	81	75	43	46	30
Shandong	Qingzhou	36	39	2	6	8	0
Henan	Kaifeng	38	95	75	35	53	9
	Huaiyang	36	48	10	20	9	3
Anhui	Linquan*	85	70	53	48	30	23
	Liu'an	75	92	25	22	11	7
NORTHWEST CHINA							
Shanxi	Changzhi	4	58	12	18	19	4
	Lin County: Qikou	61	93	49	57	55	25
Shaanxi	Zhouzhi	82	90	18	57	73	15
	Luochuan	8	72	3	66	38	5
SOUTHWEST CHINA							
Yunnan	Tonghai	0	66	26	87	64	39
	Jiangchuan	0	55	13	57	32	26
	Luliang B	0	13	8	15	19	8
	Lufeng	0	0	0	0	0	0
Guizhou	Anshun	0	46	34	16	15	8

NOTE: Families at most sites in North and Northwest China grew cotton. Sites that grew little in Northwest and none in Southwest China depended on the cotton trade. In all but two sites (both in Yunnan) spinning cotton was common (39 to 95 percent of those surveyed), while the percentage of weaving was more variable. Blank answers were excluded in constructing percentages. The number of responses for each site varied, as not all women answered questions for every category but, except for Linquan, were generally close to the full sample.

*The Linquan figures for percentage with income are estimates based on four interviews reconducted in 2011 because original survey wording overlooked income-in-kind commonly found in putting-out systems. Since three of four had earned income-in-kind from spinning and weaving, the estimates for income are three-fourths the percentage who spun or wove cotton. The full Linquan survey data concerning natal homes with a loom and percentage of women who wove cotton before marriage suggested a recent abandonment of weaving.

TABLE A.2

Percentage footbound by birth cohort, Dongting and Qingfengdian-Pang, Ding County, Hebei

	DONGTING		QINGFENGDIAN-PANG*	
Birth cohorts	Footbound (%)	Number	Footbound (%)	Number
≤1880s	99	492	81	70
1890s	94	212	100	24
1900s	71	259	84	169
1910s	12	310	74	102
1920s	0	463	38	114
1930s			1	211
Total		1,736		690

SOURCE: Data for Donting from Gamble 1954, 60; Qingfengdian-Pang data from authors' surveys

NOTE: In Dongting, the experimental area, footbinding began to drop quickly for those born in 1900–1910. Combining Qingfengdian and Pang shows that footbinding declined later and more gradually outside the experimental area.

*The Qingfengdian and Pang surveys include the woman interviewed and information on her elders (mothers, mothers-in-law, grandmothers from natal and marital families) and sisters. Elder generations' birth years were estimated as born twenty-five years earlier per generation and sisters as five years older or younger. The Pang interview sample is small (N = 63), with no one born in 1915–1919 in the interviewee's generation and no one born in 1890–1894 in the elder generations.

TABLE A.3

Percentage of improved looms and percentage footbound by binding cohort, Ding County

Birth year	Year to bind feet*	Total number of women and girls	Footbound by binding year (%)	Pulling and iron-gear looms (%)
1900–1904	1907–1911	130	83	0
1905–1909	1912–1916	129	57	7
1910–1914	1917–1921	149	20	17
1915–1919	1922–1926	161	6	34
1920–1924	1927–1931	169	0	49
1925–1929	1932–1936	294	—	67
Total		1,032		

SOURCE: Data from Gamble 1954, 60; Bossen 2002, 47

NOTE: Footbinding percentages are from a sample of 515 families in the experimental district (district 3). Loom percentages are from a single village in Ding County, location not identified. As the proportion of more efficient looms increased, the proportion of Dongting girls being bound decreased (see Figure 3.4).

*Assuming an average binding age of seven, we add seven years to reported birth years.

TABLE A.4

Percentage footbound by birth cohort, North and Northwest China

Birth cohort	Shandong Qingzhou % (N)	Henan Kaifeng % (N)	Henan Huaiyang % (N)	Anhui Liu'an % (N)	Anhui Linquan % (N)	Shanxi Lin (Qikou) % (N)	Shanxi Changzhi % (N)	Shaanxi Luochuan % (N)	Shaanxi Zhouzhi % (N)
1910–1914			100 (1)				100 (1)	100 (1)	100 (4)
1915–1919	100 (2)	86 (7)	100 (7)	100 (5)	86 (7)	75 (4)	100 (3)	100 (3)	100 (3)
1920–1924	67 (6)	100 (6)	93 (14)	69 (13)	100 (5)	25 (4)	71 (7)	100 (16)	86 (14)
1925–1929	74 (26)	73 (23)	95 (20)	76 (21)	84 (25)	11 (18)	88 (17)	84 (19)	83 (24)
1930–1934	51 (43)	50 (20)	92 (13)	40 (25)	52 (31)	6 (34)	63 (32)	27 (22)	33 (15)
1935–1939	26 (58)	44 (18)	65 (17)	22 (9)	15 (13)	6 (33)	30 (23)	0 (15)	36 (11)
1940–1944		0 (8)	33 (6)	15 (13)	11 (9)	0 (3)	0 (7)	6 (16)	8 (12)
1945–1949		0 (9)	13 (16)	0 (9)	0 (8)		0 (4)	0 (9)	0 (15)
1950		0 (4)	0 (4)	0 (2)	0 (1)			0 (2)	0 (4)
Total N	135	95	98	97	99	96	94	103	102

NOTE: Table excludes Hebei; for Hebei data, see Table A.2. In the village sites in Shandong, northern Henan, northwest and central-west Anhui, and central Shanxi, footbinding declined rapidly in the 1930s. In the Shanxi Lin (Qikou) site, footbinding was already dwindling in the 1920s cohorts, but in a mat-making village in Huaiyang, Henan, it declined later in the 1930s and early 1940s.

TABLE A.5
Percentage footbound by birth cohort, Southwest China (Yunnan and Guizhou)

Birth cohort	Yunnan Tonghai % (N)	Yunnan Jiangchuan % (N)	Yunnan Luliang % (N)	Yunnan Lufeng % (N)	Guizhou Anshun % (N)
1910–1924	91 (11)	96 (25)	100 (17)	54 (24)	69 (16)
1925–1929	88 (24)	84 (32)	100 (26)	31 (13)	43 (35)
1930–1934	83 (29)	70 (54)	97 (35)	8 (25)	38 (52)
1935–1939	51 (35)	56 (70)	89 (57)	0 (25)	11 (84)
1940–1944	43 (14)	35 (20)	100 (17)	0 (12)	11 (9)
1945–1950	0 (8)	0 (7)	13 (8)	0 (6)	
Total N	121	208	160	105	196

TABLE A.6
Percentage footbound by birth cohort, Sichuan (ten counties)

Birth cohort	Footbound	Cohort (N)	Footbound (%)
1887–1899	18	18	100
1900–1904	93	100	93
1905–1909	271	309	88
1910–1914	633	719	88
1915–1919	882	1,100	80
1920–1924	897	1,525	59
1925–1929	514	1,206	43
Total	3,308	4,977	

NOTE: The Sichuan percentage of women footbound declined gradually up to the 1915–1919 birth cohort. In the next decade, those born in the 1920s, footbinding declined significantly from 80 to 43 percent.

TABLE A.7
China's cotton yarn imports, 1871–1910

Year	Imports (million lb)	Year	Imports (million lb)
1871	9	1891	161
1872	7	1892	174
1873	9	1893	131
1874	9	1894	155
1875	12	1895	151
1876	15	1896	216
1877	15	1897	209
1878	14	1898	261
1879	18	1899	366
1880	20	1900	198
1881	23	1901	303
1882	25	1902	300
1883	30	1903	365
1884	35	1904	304
1885	52	1905	341
1886	51	1906	339
1887	79	1907	303
1888	91	1908	243
1889	91	1909	321
1890	144	1910	304

SOURCE: Feuerwerker 1995a, 34

NOTE: *Piculs* converted to millions of pounds (see Figure 6.1).

TABLE A.8
China's production and supply of cotton yarn (million piculs), 1871–1936

Period	Hand-spun yarn	Factory yarn	Net imports	Total domestic supply including net imports	Hand-spun yarn as percentage of total domestic supply
1871–1880	4.9	0.0	0.1	5.0	98
1901–1910	2.4	1.0	2.4	5.8	41
1923–1924	6.3	4.7	0.6	11.6	54
1925–1927	4.4	7.1	0.3	11.8	37
1928–1930	3.3	7.7	−0.1	10.9	30
1931–1933	2.7	8.7	−0.4	11.0	25
1934–1936	3.1	9.0	0.2*	11.9	26

SOURCE: Rawski 1989, 93, table 2.10

*For 1934–1936, for domestic supply to total 11.9, net imports in source table should be −0.2 (see Figure 6.5).

Appendix B: Equations: Logistic Regression Results

The odds ratio of being footbound can be expressed more completely as

$$P_{FB} / (1 - P_{FB}) = \text{Odds ratio of being footbound}$$

Given the odds, the probability of footbinding is

$$P_{FB} = \text{Odds}_i / (1 + \text{Odds}_i)$$

For the Eight Provinces survey,

$$P_{FB} / (1 - P_{FB}) = (e^{298.002})(e^{(-0.154)(\text{birth year})})(e^{(0.762)(\text{handwork for income})})$$

$e^{(-0.154)(\text{birth year})} = 0.857 =$ a 14.3% decrease in the odds of footbinding per year

$e^{(0.762)(\text{handwork for income})} = 2.144 = 114.4\%$ increase in the odds of footbinding if girls did handwork for income

For the Eight Provinces survey, the value for handwork for income (0.762) divided by the value for birth year (0.154) yields 4.948, the number of years longer that initiations of footbinding continued if girls did handwork for income.

For the Sichuan survey,

$$P_{FB} / (1 - P_{FB}) = (e^{309.446})(e^{(-0.161)(\text{birth year})})(e^{(0.924)(\text{textile handwork})})$$

$e^{(-0.161)(\text{birth year})} = 0.851 =$ a 14.9% decrease in the odds of footbinding per year

$e^{(0.924)(\text{textile handwork})} = 2.519 = 151.9\%$ increase in the odds of footbinding if girls did textile handwork

For the Sichuan survey, the value for textile handwork (0.924) divided by the value for birth year (0.161) yields 5.739, the number of years longer that initiations of footbinding continued if girls did textile handwork.

Chapter One

1. We conservatively estimate that hundreds of millions of Chinese women grew up with bound feet. The practice has been so poorly documented that any estimate has a large element of guesswork. A rough method of estimation is as follows: The late Qing dynasty population was about 450 million in 1900. Judith Banister (1987, 3) states that there were 430 million in 1851 and 583 million in 1953. Roughly 90 percent of 450 million (405 million) would be considered Han Chinese. If almost half of these 405 million people were female (using an estimated sex ratio of 110 males to 100 females that conservatively takes into account excess female mortality due to female infanticide, abandonment, and neglect [Jiang et al. 2012; Mungello 2008]), then there were around 192 million females. If only half of those women lived in regions where footbinding was practiced, then roughly 96 million would have been bound during the last half of the nineteenth century. If life expectancy was generously estimated at about forty to fifty years, and assuming a smaller population of 430 million in the early nineteenth century, another 92 million women could have been bound in the early nineteenth century, or nearly 200 million for the nineteenth century alone. These assumptions about the distribution of footbinding are not arbitrary, as shown by our survey data on mothers and grandmothers.

2. The late imperial period usually refers to the Ming-Qing period (1368–1911), while our interest is primarily in the later late imperial period, the nineteenth century, the latter part of the Qing dynasty.

3. The dates of these conflicts indicate the frequency of political clashes in the late imperial and early Republican periods. They include the Opium Wars (1839–1842, 1856–1860); the Taiping Rebellion (1850–1864); the Nian Rebellion (1851–1868); the Muslim Rebellions in the southwest (the Panthay Rebellion, 1855–1873), in Gansu (1872–1878), in Shaanxi (1862–1873), and in Xinjiang (1864–1876); the Miao Rebellion (1854–1873); the Boxer Rebellion (1899–1900); the First Sino-Japanese War (1904); the Xinhai Revolution (1911–1912); the Anti-Japanese War (1937–1945); and the Chinese Civil War (1927–1937, 1945–1949).

4. The North China famine of 1876–1879 killed nine to thirteen million people. The drought and famine of 1920–1921 affected some thirty million victims, with estimated mortality at half a million. The North China famine of 1928–1930 killed an estimated ten million. See Lillian Li 2007, 284, for a list of major disasters and famines during 1850–1950, although the list curiously omits the 1887 flood when the Yellow River changed course and killed nearly one million people (Yellow River casualties include another nine hundred thousand during the 1937–1945 period).

5. Up to the mid-twentieth century, Chinese wives were often referred to as "inside people," reflecting their responsibilities for indoor work in the home (Jacka 1997, 122).

6. Kaifeng (then called Bianjing) was the capital of the Northern Song dynasty (960–1127); Hangzhou was the capital of the following Southern Song dynasty (1127–1279). Both capitals were centers of textile production, and the Song dynasty as a whole is associated with commercial expansion.

7. Ko explains that in the four southernmost provinces of Guangdong, Guangxi, Guizhou, and Yunnan "only those in the provincial capitals imitate it, not those in the countryside" (2005, 131). The countryside includes Han colonists and a variety of conquered minorities.

8. Footbinding disappears in the northeast; northern provinces of Heilongjiang, Jilin, and Inner Mongolia; and western provinces of Xinjiang and Tibet. Its incidence decreases in western Sichuan, Gansu, and northern Liaoning.

9. The Hakka, a distinctive group of early Han migrants to Guangdong, were usually unbound. Women in parts of Yangzi delta region were not bound, and some in Beijing were also not (Fei 1983; McLaren 2008; Walker 1999; Elliott 2001, 247). Howard Levy notes, "Within a single province, natural and bound-foot areas existed side by side. The natural foot predominated in such southern provinces as Fukien, Kwangtung and Kwangsi" (1966, 273).

10. Although footbinding was viewed as an ethnic marker in frontier settings such as Manchuria or Taiwan where Han colonists interacted with native or aboriginal populations, footbinding was not strictly limited to or diagnostic of Han populations. In some areas, minority women also bound feet, while in others, Han women, including most notably the Hakka, did not bind. Non-Han groups seem more likely to have adopted footbinding when the local household economy involved settled farming and handcrafts. Neighboring populations practicing shifting agriculture or more nomadic ways of life generally did not adopt footbinding. In settled farming populations with a mixture of non-Han and Han characteristics, footbinding was sometimes used to identify women as sinicized, or Han. For more on binding among the Manchu and Yi (called Lolo in eighteenth-century texts), see Ko 1998; 1997, 14, 24. For information on the Tujia, see Brown 1996. For a discussion of the Bai, see Hsu 1967.

11. The Manchu populations were state dependents, originally pastoralists and military horsemen. Manchu women commonly knew how to ride horses.

Alain Peyrefitte cites Aeneas Anderson (1795) regarding Manchu women observed in Beijing: "'Their feet free from the bandages [referring to footbinding] . . . were suffered to attain their natural growth.' Staunton commented on the beautiful horsewomen: 'A few Tartar ladies were on horseback, and rode astride like men'" ([1992] 2013, 125).

12. Brown (2004), Ko (1997, 1998), and Shepherd (2012) observe that footbinding in Taiwan at times acted as an ethnic boundary, distinguishing the practices of unbound aboriginal women from the "civilized" practices of Han women. Thus, in border areas, footbinding could be a way for women to reinforce a claim to Han identity. This implies that Han bound girls' feet mainly to distinguish themselves from aboriginals who were otherwise culturally similar. Similarities and differences in aboriginal and Han women's economic activities have yet to be considered. Anthropologist Francis Hsu, describing the ethnic Bai in Dali (a large market town in Yunnan) as Chinese in 1941, noted that older women had bound feet and more than half worked at commercial hand spinning and weaving—without making any connection between footbinding and hand labor or questioning the bilingual Bai identity as Chinese (1967, 18, 69; see also Cohen 2005, 46, 48).

13. This includes areas such as densely populated Henan Province in the North China Plain, where the Han are an overwhelming majority.

14. Further research on origins and timing of its regional diffusion awaits the discovery of new records about commoner women and analysis and dating of women's foot bones in Chinese burials. When China's archeologists turn their attention to common burials, their findings will reveal more about the prevalence and distribution of footbinding in different regions and earlier centuries.

15. The maxim obscures the fact that rural woman in many part of China also performed a variety of agricultural tasks in continuously evolving divisions of labor (Jacka 1997; Bossen 2002).

16. Explanations that mothers gave to their daughters, implying that footbinding led to better marriage opportunities, are discussed in Brown et al. 2012.

17. This was equally true in urban areas where artisan women recruited their daughters to produce a wide range of handcrafts; where girl servants in wealthy households specialized in spinning, weaving, and embroidering; and where gentry women themselves had been taught fine embroidery skills as girls (Mann 1992).

18. Data from our samples suggest that women born up to 1939 had an average of seven pregnancies and six live births.

19. Chinese couples' ability to control fertility (and hence population growth) claimed by Lee and Wang (1998, 1999, 2002), Li Bozhong (1998), and Pomeranz (2002) has been disputed by Engelen and Hsieh (2007), Sommer (2010), A. Wolf (1985, 2001), and Wolf and Engelen (2008). An average of six or more pregnancies per woman and six surviving children is already a heavy burden in terms of domestic labor, as well as in relation to pregnancy, birth and postpartum recovery, breast feeding, and carrying infants and toddlers. The reproductive burden

alone would have decreased the time most women could devote to textile labor. Economic historians who estimate women's labor inputs rarely take this into account.

20. Fei Xiaotong characterized the child-care burden of village women in Kaixiangong as follows: "The children of the village cling to their mothers all day long. . . . The period of suckling lasts three or more years. . . . Whenever the child cries, the mother will at once put her nipple into the child's mouth to keep the child quiet. Moreover, women in the village do not go to the farm, but work almost all the day in the house" (1983, 31–32).

21. Bray cites the Ninghe gazetteer, quoted in Tong 1981, 306.

22. One source reports that "foreign families have adopted more than 50,000 Chinese abandoned babies since the 1990s" ("Foreign Parents" 2003). In 2011, the US State Department reported that sixty-four thousand Chinese children were adopted in the United States between 1999 and 2010 (Leland 2011).

23. Levitt, author of *Freakonomics*, was speaking in support of Half the Sky Foundation, an organization founded to help Chinese orphanages raise their standards of care. Bossen has also seen such scars on children adopted from China and, while in China in the 1990s when volunteering at an understaffed orphanage in Yunnan, saw forty to fifty babies lying in cribs with bottles propped to feed them because caregivers lacked time to hold the babies.

24. Examples of exclusive focus on fashion and beauty are abundant in novels as well as history and anthropology textbooks.

25. This was not just a Western view. The May Fourth Movement of 1919 and the Communist Revolution both incorporated feminist reforms aiming to rescue women from patriarchal oppression.

26. A problem of regional representation has also been identified for Chinese women writers. Using data from a 1957 survey, Susan Mann found that over 70 percent of women writers in Qing times were from the Lower Yangzi region, which in 1843 held only 17 percent of the total population outside Manchuria (1997, 229–232).

27. See Fong 2004, 14, 17–21, 32, 52, 64; 2008, 15, 31; and Mann 2007, 26, 174–175, 198–199. Eyferth (2012) discusses handmade textiles in the rural gift economy; Gates (2015, 143–148) describes the use of embroidery to extend and maintain female networks.

28. Reports that some female servants also had bound feet contradict the view that binding marked elite status.

29. Ko's title, "Cinderella's Sisters," for her study of footbinding is a case in point. Nineteenth-century Chinese reformers often echoed Western missionaries' vocal criticisms of footbinding.

30. Bray notes that *nügong* can also be translated as "womanly work." She describes Confucian moralists' and officials' writings praising regions where women wove cloth as "culturally and even morally superior" to regions where

women did not weave. Weaving diligently at home gave women a dignified gender identity (Bray 1997, 245, 256–257).

31. Bray writes, "The productive role of wives was largely masked in the course of the late imperial period" (1997, 366).

32. Fred Blake suggests that "the impairment of women's feet served more to mask than to completely restrict their participation in economic production" (1994, 700). Of the prior studies that do explore connections between women's labor and bound feet, see Gates 1997a, 1997b, 2001, 2005, 2015; Bossen 2002, 2008, 2011; Bossen et al. 2011; and Brown et al. 2012.

33. G. William Skinner (1964, 1965) emphasized physiographic features (mountains and river drainage basins) that shaped regional retail markets and steered and enabled commerce and the differential accumulation of wealth in China's regions. His analysis, though powerful and widely used, has found critics (e.g., Gates 1996, 63–72).

34. For all the detailed efforts to document change, the debate implicitly enlists attitudes (and passions) regarding Western development models (Eurocentrism), Chinese models (Sinocentrism), and pro- and anti-Communist/Marxist or market interpretations of China's twentieth-century economic potential, alternative development paths (capitalist or Communist), and the necessity (or lack thereof) for Communist revolution. See, for example, Allen et al. 2011; Brenner and Isett 2002; De Vries 2011; P. Huang 2002, 2003; Kung, Bai, and Lee 2011; Lee, Campbell, and Wang 2002; Li Bozhong 1998, 2000, 2009; Lillian Li 2007; Little 2010; Ma and Wright 2010; Pomeranz 2002, 2003a, 2003b; Sommer 2010; and A. Wolf 2001.

35. Writing about Jiangnan, Huang maintains, "Growth in annual household income came not so much from increased returns per workday as from the fuller employment of household labor: of the women, children, and elderly who had been at best partially employed in production, and of the adult male during his spare time. It was growth without development, or involutionary growth" (1990, 77). Huang's (1985) examination of economic involution in the North China Plain runs closely parallel, arguing that expanding population and commercialization did not lead to capitalist production but rather strengthened the institutional and economic significance of small farms employing family labor.

36. We have not found reports of boys learning to spin, although men did learn to weave in some areas, particularly when a household or workshops invested in large, complex looms.

37. Huang calculated that an average *mu* (666.7 square meters) of cotton yielded 30 *jin* (33 pounds, or 15 kilograms), enough for 22.7 bolts of cloth (weighing 1.32 *jin* each with 4–5 percent wastage). On average a spinner could spin about 5 ounces (*liang*) of yarn a day (presumably 16 *liang* to the *jin*) from about 5 ounces of ginned cotton or 15 of unginned. In the eighteenth and early nineteenth centuries, returns from spinning ran "around 30 to 50 percent of

the worth of the raw [unginned] cotton." Each *jin* of raw cotton "was worth two times its weight in rice." Spinning one-third *jin* of ginned cotton was worth 30–50 percent of 2 *jin*, or 0.6–1.0 *jin* of rice. Huang (1990, 84) gives earnings as 10–15 ounces of rice per day of spinning. We assume he means husked rice since he says 44 catties (*jin*) (unhusked, 63) per month was the present-day ration for an adult female peasant laborer, and 47 catties for males in Huayangqiao (1990, 85). The adult woman's ration would be 1.5 pounds of rice per day. Li Bozhong (2009, 393–394) estimates much higher returns in the Songjiang textile region in the eighteenth and early nineteenth centuries.

38. Huang emphasizes that family members whose earnings did not cover the cost of their maintenance would still be supported as kin: "A family farm could not simply fire its excess family members" (1985, 8). Huang's belief that ties of kinship kept family members from being fired is largely true, yet he may be over-confident that unneeded family members were always kept. Adopting out and/ or selling boys and girls and illegal wife selling were not uncommon responses to family distress (Sommer 2015).

39. Mark Elvin (1972) and Harriet Zurndorfer (2009, 58) have described and analyzed China's slowness to adopt known labor-saving spinning and weaving technologies in cotton textile production.

40. Pomeranz draws from historian Li Bozhong, who maintains that women were drawn to textile work by the higher incomes rather than driven away from farmwork by cultural constraints.

41. Huang (2003, 157) responds that he did indeed misplace a decimal, pointing out that Pomeranz "mentions this particular error no less than one dozen times in his response [see Pomeranz 2002]. He almost makes it his central theme." Indeed, Pomeranz (2003a, 168, 169, 171; 2005) continues to dwell on the misplaced decimal in further rejoinders.

42. Huang notes that it takes seven days to produce a bolt of cloth, includ-ing one day of weaving and four for spinning yarn, whereas Pomeranz assumed weaving took three days (Huang 2002, 513). Women in different parts of China (from Fujian to Sichuan) have told Gates that they weave "*yi tian, yi zhang bu*" (one day, one *zhang* of cloth, about 3.6 meters), assuming that the work of sizing warps, putting them on the loom, and preparing bobbins of weft thread had al-ready been done.

43. Such claims are attributed to Li Bozhong (2000, 63–65).

44. Pomeranz continues, "But . . . there appears to have been relatively little yarn for sale," suggesting that yarn markets were weak (2005, 247). After previ-ously defending the use of price data (Pomeranz 2003a), Pomeranz seems to ac-cept Huang's criticism that the retail price of cloth sold by town merchants does not necessarily reflect returns to rural woman weavers (Pomeranz 2005; Huang 2002, 217). Speculating about higher returns for more specialized types of cloth (around 1750), he confesses doubt about how much of the cloth price was cap-tured not by weavers but by cloth finishers such as dyers and calenderers, usually

men, in towns (Pomeranz 2005, 247). Neither author clarifies the nature of the original data. Most everyday handwoven cotton cloth, however, went from loom to use without dyeing or calendering.

45. The data he bases this reduction on, though, are drawn from Huang's work and related to heavy farmwork—in other words, boys' work, which probably was not equal to adult male productivity. In a note he explains, "I have decided not to discount women's labor, because it makes my calculations more conservative and because the usual method of discounting—by comparing wage rates for men and women—will not work here. First of all, we lack good wage data for eighteenth-century China. Secondly, assuming that differences in wage rates accurately reflect productivity differences would be to assume an efficient labor market, and whether anything even remotely like that existed is one of the points at issue here. In the twentieth century, children were paid anywhere from 12.5 percent to 37.5 percent of the wages of adult males (Huang 1990:66); not much to go on, but enough to suggest that by counting their labor as one-third of an adult labor unit I am unlikely to be discounting it too much" (Pomeranz 2002, 548n10). The data for child wages that he takes from Huang refer to long-term laborers in farming, most likely boys, at (Western-style) ages ten and above. Unlike in spinning, the lesser strength of young boys would likely make a difference in farm labor productivity.

46. Pomeranz repeats the discount procedure when he calculates that "180 days of labor (much of it by children) was probably the equivalent of no more than 100 days of adult male labor, this would be [worth] 13 pounds of grain per day" (2002, 550). But if adult males were no better (and probably worse at spinning with hands roughened by farmwork), then their labor would be worth only 7.2 pounds of grain per day.

47. Eyesight can deteriorate with age, but so did Beethoven's hearing. After a lifetime of work spinning and weaving, some women could probably still do it blindfolded. We have witnessed many elderly women in their seventies and eighties still exercising their skills in handcrafts.

48. Here, "yarn" and "thread" are used interchangeably, much as people used them in rural areas. In English, yarn is generally assumed to be thicker than thread, the former used for knitting and the latter for sewing. Yet in February 2012, when Laurel Bossen spoke to a weaver with thirty years' experience tending machine-powered looms at the Lowell, Massachusetts, textile mill, she was assured that the terms were used interchangeably. While in some sense "thread" may refer to the finer counts and "yarn" to thicker counts of material used in weaving, there does not seem to be a clear distinction between the two. Depending on the abilities of the spinner and intended use for the yarn, the hand-spun product could be finer or thicker.

49. Pomeranz concedes that "the economics of textile production are not completely understood, and scholars have not sufficiently traced the differences between more skilled tasks, often done by women in the prime of their lives, and

other tasks taken on by girls or the elderly." However, he does not disavow his earlier discounting by two-thirds the work by girls and older women, or even mention his earlier arguments for discounting child labor (2005, 240).

50. Many historians instead emphasize cultural preoccupations with femininity and fashion or the ideologies of missionaries and Communist movements. China scholars largely ignored connections between footbinding and women's handcraft labor. Exceptionally, Blake suggests that footbinding helped "mystify" appropriation of women's labor power by the "male-dominated family system" by "masking" a woman's labor (1994, 700). But where Blake points to the abstract father-dominated family system as the agent, we propose that mothers themselves, striving to increase their output (under a male-dominated gender- and class-stratified system), employed this method to squeeze more labor from their subordinate daughters' hands.

51. H. D. Fong (1933, 46) surveys a wide range of rural handcraft industries in 1928 with special emphasis on Hebei Province.

Chapter Two

1. Gates has more limited evidence for approximately four thousand Fujian women gathered in a project in the early 1990s by colleagues from Xiamen University, but little has been published from these data (Gates 1997b, 2001).

2. The bulk of the survey data collected here was funded by the National Science Foundation Grant BCS#0613297, Melissa J. Brown, principal investigator, and Bossen and Gates, co-investigators. Gates and Bossen collected data in the northern and southwestern provinces. Brown conducted surveys in provinces along the Yangzi Valley. A study of footbinding and marriage mobility draws on data from all the sites (Brown et al. 2012). Bossen's research in China was also supported by a grant from the Social Sciences and Humanities Research Council of Canada, and Gates's research in Sichuan was funded by the Harry Frank Guggenheim Foundation. A Carl and Lily Pforzheimer Foundation Fellowship (2011–2012) at the Radcliffe Institute for Advanced Study at Harvard University also provided support for Bossen and a two-month visit by Gates to work on this project.

3. Southeast China includes the provinces of Zhejiang, Fujian, Guangdong, and Guangxi.

4. The eight provinces include four in the north (Anhui, Hebei, Henan, Shandong), two in the northwest (Shaanxi and Shanxi), and two in the southwest (Yunnan and Guizhou). We surveyed seven northern village sites and four northwestern sites. In the southwest, we surveyed five villages, four in Yunnan, including an earlier Yunnan site studied by Bossen (2002, 2008), and one in Guizhou. The concept of nineteenth-century macroregional systems developed by Skinner (1977) informs much regional research on China (e.g., Benedict 1996, 13, maps 1 and 2). Defined by geography and river drainage basins, China's macroregions form territorially based systems of transportation, trade, communication, and

culture within the larger nation-state. Our sites are drawn from three of Skinner's nine macroregions: the North, Northwest, and Yun-Gui (Yunnan and Guizhou).

5. Sichuan Province here refers to Sichuan before it was divided to create the new province of Chongqing.

6. Melissa J. Brown also played a significant part in these revisions.

7. To protect the privacy of individuals interviewed, we do not use their names, or we use pseudonyms.

8. For example, a woman would know her approximate age and if she was born in the year of the horse. The Chinese zodiac is a cycle of twelve years, so matching the animal year with a calendar year close to her approximate age allowed us to determine the year of birth.

9. When villagers gave age in traditional or nominal years, *xusui* (the number of calendar years they had lived in), we converted them to *zhousui* (full years), as used in Western age counts.

10. Those who helped us are too numerous to list here; we thank many of them in our acknowledgments.

11. This is not unique to this project. Rather, it is an intrinsic but unacknowledged characteristic of all surveys. Interviewers are human beings with a range of skills and shortcomings and personality differences. Despite the best efforts to standardize questions, both the interviewee and interviewer inevitably reflect their individual abilities. Sociologists may contend that these difference average out; anthropologists are more likely to encourage informants to speak at length, trying to reduce misunderstanding through dialogue.

12. A persistent language problem for all of us was the difference between prerevolution vocabularies of work and social status and those learned in "the new society." The modern use of *gong*, labor or work, differs from rural terms formerly used for agricultural work, handwork, or housework. The core meaning of *gong* during the Maoist period was "work assigned by the state." Its meaning now slides between that and its prerevolution and post-"reform" senses, each of which is embedded in a particular political-economic context.

13. We aimed for two counties per province, but in Shandong and Guizhou we include only one county. For Yunnan, where Bossen began ethnographic research in the late 1980s, we include four counties.

14. See Dikotter 2010, 255–261, for a discussion of Great Leap Forward hardships and abuses specific to women when women were forced to work in the fields; the author does not mention footbinding. Helen Snow reported that in the 1930s, she saw footbound peasant women refugees who were "actually dying because they could hardly *walk*. Their feet were stumps" (1984, 43; emphasis in original).

15. Quantitative data on mortality of women with bound feet are not likely ever to be available.

16. Villages normally have concentrations of fathers, sons, and brothers linked with other patrilineal kinsmen. China's patrilineal property rights and

incest taboos generally require sisters and daughters to marry out, dispersing to other villages.

17. The majority of wives came from nearby villages, often within the same market area, so that parents and go-betweens could negotiate marriages based on face-to-face networks (Bossen 2002, 2007; Lavely1989; Skinner 1964). Occasionally wives came from distant regions, fleeing famine conditions in other provinces. Very few women grew up in the same village as their husband or shared the same natal village with other wives.

18. We strove to collect information on the prices or exchange values of girls and women's labor. Fully systematic and comparable collection, however, proved to be too complex for survey work. During the different decades in which these women grew up, prices and currencies fluctuated greatly, and units of measure were far from uniform despite Republican efforts to standardize them; we encountered much variation by locality and time period. The Republican period witnessed the spread of industry and railroads, economic growth and depression, wartime blockades, Japanese occupation, and inflation. Given uncertain, fluctuating monetary values, we asked women about incomes in terms of quantities of the staple of grain, but not many could give firm answers. They better remembered the rate at which spun yarn could be exchanged for cotton. This differed from Gates's (2015) surveys of an earlier generation in Sichuan when many women did know the value of their income in grain.

Chapter Three

1. The number of sites initially planned was eight. A second Shandong site, near Linyi City, was surveyed in part by a field assistant local to the area, but because we were unable to visit it and the sample was small, it was excluded.

2. Chao 1977; Feuerwerker 1995a, 1995b; and Zurndorfer 2009 describe the expansion of cotton growing and cotton cloth production in northern China.

3. Zurndorfer (2009, 52) points out that initially the dry climate in Hebei, Shandong, and Henan hindered cotton spinning until spinning in damp cellars solved the problem (Chao 1977, 21; Bray 1997, 217; Elvin 1972, 1973, 214; Zurndorfer 2009).

4. Table A.1, column 3, shows the percentage of our survey families that grew cotton.

5. Banister (1987, 6) and Chris Bramall (2009, 295, table 9.2) cite George Barclay et al. (1976), who estimated that in 1929–1931, the life expectancy at birth of rural agricultural families was only twenty-four for females and twenty-five for males, and 30 percent of babies died in their first year. William Lavely and R. Bin Wong (1998, 724) give an estimated life expectancy in 1930 of thirty-two years.

6. See Blunden and Elvin 1983, 164–165, for a map based on Japanese sources. Snow 1938; Hanson 1939, 280–281; Tschiang 1986, map 9; Esposito

1959; and Chesneaux, Le Barbier, and Bergère 1977, 90, 102, 291, describe areas of Communist resistance under Japanese Occupation.

7. Ding City was the seat, or capital, of a county (*xian*) that administered the towns and villages of the county. Ding Xian includes both Ding County and Ding City.

8. The Mass Education Movement founded by James Yen (Yan Yangchu) and others set up a village campaign in Ding County in 1926 with People's Schools, technical innovations, and cooperatives that operated until the Japanese invasion in 1937 (Hayford 1990).

9. Li Jinghan's lengthier study of Ding, although less used by later scholars than Gamble's, is especially valuable for its ethnographic detail.

10. We chose 1930 as a cut-off date to avoid cases where women were brought into spinning as a duty of wartime. A discussion of women's wartime textile teams follows in the section on Shanxi in Chapter 4.

11. Kang Chao gives a labor productivity ratio between 1930s power spinning and the simple spinning wheel as at least 44:1. The hand spinner could produce about half a pound of yarn per day (eleven working hours), whereas power spindles with same amount of labor could produce twenty-two pounds per day (Chao 1977, 180).

12. This quotation from Huang draws on Chao 1977, 185, citing Zhang Shiwen (1936) 1991, 427. For a discussion of machine spinning in Ding County, see Gamble 1954, 288–289, 298–300.

13. Users and sellers overlap. That is, sellers also produced for their own use and are included within the 46 percent who wove for home use.

14. Somewhat inconsistently, Gamble elsewhere says Ding footbinding disappeared in "30 years," by 1919 (1954, 46).

15. The Pang Village sample size is small ($N = 63$). To reduce distortions from small numbers, we combine it with Qingfengdian because both sites are in Ding County.

16. In Ding County reformers were able to build on the previous work of local, education-minded authorities (Gamble 1954, 185, 188).

17. Gamble describes five samples. The footbinding data are from a 1929 survey of 515 families (3,571 persons) in the experimental district. This sample and two others "cannot be considered typical community figures as the groups were not random samples. They all included more than an average number of middle class and well-to-do families . . . [and] no one-person 'families'" (Gamble 1954, 24).

18. Gamble gives occupations of those over age twelve for the study of 515 families (1954, 62, table 14); only three females (0.3 percent of 1,176 females) and forty-eight males were students. In the experimental district (district 3), girls were 16 percent of the pupils in the sixty-three lower primary schools, but fourteen villages had no school. In Ding County fewer than one in seven children age six

to fourteen were in school (Gamble 1954, 195, 198). Gamble does not indicate whether schools required unbound feet.

19. In Qingfengdian, 63 percent of our sample had never attended school; another 7 percent attended after the 1949 revolution.

20. See Bossen 2002, 45–48. Gamble shows changing loom technology in one village. Original wooden looms declined from 93 percent in 1912 to 20 percent by 1932, while flying-shuttle looms introduced in 1908 increased to 51 percent in 1932. Iron-gear looms first appeared in 1922 and reached 16 percent ten years later. The total number of looms, however, decreased from 280 to 239 in the same period (Gamble 1954, 314). See Chapter 6 for further discussion of the shift to improved looms.

21. Esherick divides Shandong into six regions: Peninsula, Northwest, North Slope, South Hills, Jining, and Southwest (1987, 7–10). Our site, Qingzhou, is on the North Slope.

22. The port at Tianjin imported roughly 8.9 million pounds of factory yarn in 1889 and more than 35.8 million pounds in 1899. In Zhenjiang in 1899, "cotton yarn represented 40 percent of the goods sent inland under transit passes, and piece goods another 22 percent" (Esherick 1987, 69).

23. Esherick considers the possibility of exaggeration by missionary Smith "to direct attention from the religious to the economic causes of Chinese anti-foreignism" but believes, as we do, that Smith wrote from firsthand experience in Northwest Shandong. Prior to the Boxer Rebellion Smith had also written about the competition of machine-spun cotton yarn that was "severely felt in the cotton regions of China and many who had just managed to exist in former days are now perpetually on the edge of starvation" (Esherick 1987, 361, quoting Smith 1899, 276).

24. In 1980 Esherick interviewed Shandong villagers in Pingyuan, bordering En to the east, and found that none recalled buying factory yarn (*yangsha*) before about 1920.

25. Martin Yang's home village is in Taitou, about fifty kilometers north of Qingzhou, our Shandong site.

26. During the Yuan dynasty Qingzhou was linked by road to the capital, Jinan, and then southeast to the sea, and Muslim troops were stationed there. By the eighteenth century, Qingzhou women's handcraft textiles were recognized as economically important (Jing and Luo 1978). Early English-language ethnographic writings on Shandong describe village life on its coast and plains, not Qingzhou's hilly region (Johnston [1910] 1986; Pruitt 1945; M. Yang 1945).

27. Wild silk from Shandong's wooded mountains was a major provincial crop, but our Shandong survey did not ask specifically whether women had raised wild silk larvae or mulberry silkworms.

28. Spun yarn was probably requisitioned after warfare cut off Qingzhou's supplies of trade goods. The fifty-four women who spun learned late, at an aver-

age age of fifteen instead of the more typical ages of seven or eight, and none learned before 1933. This suggests the villagers had little need to make their own cotton yarn and cloth before warfare disrupted supplies.

29. While 43 percent of natal families had a spinning wheel and 39 percent spun cotton, only 6 percent had a loom and only 8 percent wove cotton (see Table A.3).

30. Ding County and Gaoyang are two well-studied sites (Gamble 1954; Grove 2006). Chao (1977, 195–203) mentions the rise and fall of other handloom weaving centers, such as Deping and Weixian in Shandong and Baodi in Hebei. Weixian was on the Jiaozhou-Jinan railway, about 114 miles from Qingdao.

31. See Beresford 1899, map facing p. 1.

32. The Qingzhou area has long had substantial local cultural variation. There are numerous mixed Hui (Muslim) and Han villages as well as a Roman Catholic missionary presence (QZSZ 1988, 43–55). We did not systematically survey ethnic-religious identity. About one-third of families in the villages closer to Qingzhou City were Hui, with religious symbolism displayed at the doorway and main room. Farther from the city, the Hui were not prominent. Villagers declared there was no difference in footbinding practices between the local Han and Hui in either the city or villages. We observed that Hui women of Qingzhou also had bound feet. Indeed, in Qingzhou's old Muslim area, some elderly footbound women wore Muslim headscarves.

33. Li gives two Hebei village examples. In Nangong in Jizhou, where farmers grew cotton, women spun and wove cotton. In swampy Yongqing County Xin'an Township, where farmers could not grow cotton, women used reeds to make mats and curtains for sale (L. Li 2007, 106–108).

34. Our two Henan sites echo differences between cloth-making Qingfengdian and mat-making Pang Village in Ding County.

35. Kaifeng village women did not report other major forms of handcraft production besides textiles.

36. Only twenty of the women in our sample were married in 1945 or before.

37. See Eyferth 2012 for a discussion of post-Communist persistence of weaving in parts of Sichuan and Shaanxi, and see Jack Chen 1973 for information on rural Henan during the Cultural Revolution.

38. No looms survived; we did not find out if they were used for mats or for cloth.

39. Some 48 percent ($N = 100$) spun cotton, and 9 percent of them also made hemp twine; an additional 2 percent made only hemp twine.

40. In the Weixi site, Huaiyang County, some interviews may not have recorded items as produced "for sale" if the woman interviewed was not the selling agent when she was a girl.

41. Village woman of Kaifeng County (born 1923), interview by the authors and/or team, May 2007.

42. The rate of decline in Kaifeng is almost identical with that in our two other Anhui village sites. All three are on the North China Plain but south of the Yellow River.

43. It is difficult to know if Feng's policy had an impact at that time or if later media instilled this view. Feng was defeated by Chiang Kai-shek (Jiang Jieshi) in the 1930s. Ruth Hayhoe (2007, 78) notes Feng became governor in 1922 and established university education in Kaifeng at Henan University in 1927.

44. Although all but the oldest women in our Kaifeng sample later had their feet unbound, only one woman unbound as early as 1929. Eleven unbound in the 1930s, and thirty-seven women unbound in the 1940s. Most unbinding (twenty-nine women) took place in or after 1945.

45. Both counties were included in Buck's ([1937] 1964) massive agricultural survey. Linquan belongs to Fuyang prefecture; Buck shows Fuyang as a wheat-sorghum area and Liu'an, to the south, in a "Yangzi rice-wheat" area. Buck's survey shows both Linquan and Liu'an produced cotton (table 11), as do our research sites.

46. In the Republican period Huaibei commerce was poorly developed because of low population density and expensive, inefficient transportation—dirt roads. "Villages near rivers could use boats to import and export commodities," but periodic flooding disrupted commerce (Perry 1980, 33).

47. The north-south Beijing-Hankou line (completed in 1906) passed through Henan to the west of Anhui. The north-south railway from Tianjin to Nanjing (the Jinpu line, completed in 1912) crossed eastern Anhui. By 1916 the east-west Longhai railway crossed the northern tip of Anhui (Han 2001, 18). Between 1932 and 1936 another north-south railway linked Huainan City in central Anhui to Nanjing on the Yangzi. Perry (1980, 33–34) describes how the construction of railroads changed Huaibei trade patterns in the 1920s, shifting from small boats on the Huai River and Grand Canal to trains going to Shanghai, Xuzhou, and Kaifeng.

48. With little manufacturing, the "commercial potential [of Huaibei] went unrealized." Although silk and cotton were suited to the Huaibei climate, in the twentieth century, Anhui counties that had been centers for silkworm cultivation since ancient times were "bare of mulberry trees, and few looms were to be found" (Perry 1980, 36–37). See also LAXZ 1993.

49. Horse carts were rare because dirt roads were often impassable.

50. Our research site in Linquan County belongs to Fuyang Prefecture, which was "from ancient times famous for its textiles" (FYXZ 1994, 148).

51. Han states, "Because they were unable to convert their labor into cash, their status was low" (2001, 72). Elsewhere, however, Han reasons that "since more money could be earned by doing farmwork than by cooking or weaving, girls contributed less to the household than their brothers" (71), implying there were at least *some* opportunities to earn from handcrafts. The apparent contradiction between earning no cash and earning (less) may be explained by restrictions on women and girls attending markets themselves to collect their own incomes.

52. More than half reported weaving after marriage. In a few households, both father and mother took turns weaving, but most weavers were women.

53. In 2007, our survey questions in Linquan were too limited. Asked about incomes (wages and sales) for hand labor, women responded "none" for spinning and weaving. Later, through open-ended questioning, we found we needed to ask about "exchange" (*huan*) for payment "in kind," often as a means to obtain additional raw material. Exchange in kind would have (somewhat) protected villagers from monetary inflation. A return visit in 2011 located four women previously interviewed. Three of the four (who previously said they did not "sell" or earn wages for thread or cloth) explained that part of their spun thread and home-woven cloth was exchanged (that is, sold) in the market for other goods. The income took the form of cotton or cloth. By 2011, with most of the village razed and villagers dispersed into new apartment buildings, we could not locate others to interview again regarding production for exchange.

54. Four village men, born 1916–1929, described trade in Linquan and in surrounding markets on the plains in Anhui and Henan. Only one told of home-spun yarn sold in the town.

55. By 1908, Anhui had fourteen textile mills, none in Liu'an but one in Fuyang, the Yongxin zhibuchang, founded in 1908 (Wang and Shi 1991, 33).

56. Linquan woman (born 1925), interview by the authors and/or team, 2007. By comparison, a village woman in our Liu'an sample wove one *kuai bu*, which is four *zhang* (each *zhang* is about 10 feet, or 10 *chi*, long), roughly 13 meters. Other Liu'an women reported weaving from one-half *kuai* (20 feet, or 6.6 meters) to five *zhang* (50 feet, or 17 meters) daily (weaving all day). Here, a *chi* is 0.3 meter.

57. "The rural mountain districts sent bamboo, wood, tea, hemp, medicine, and brooms down the Pi River to Liu'an and north to Huainan and received salt, coal, and everyday consumer goods [*riyongpin*] in exchange" (LAXZ 1993, 235). Although female hand labor made brooms and hemp products in mountainous southern Liu'an, our north Liu'an respondents did not grow or process hemp.

58. In Liu'an 62 percent weeded and picked cotton, and 61 percent spun cotton before marriage. Twenty-six percent sold or exchanged cotton (N = 97).

59. One Liu'an woman explained that her household's wooden loom was used to "burn pots" during the "exaggeration movement" (*fuqua feng*)—referring to the Great Leap Forward campaign to make steel in backyard furnaces when firewood became scarce.

60. In Yang Village, Liu'an County, every household had a wooden loom and wove hemp (used for gunnysacks to transport goods during the war); the number of hemp-making looms rose to eight thousand, and tens of thousands of people made hemp (LAXZ 1993, 187).

61. Several reasons may account for this difference in weaving rates: (1) Liu'an grew less cotton and more rice than Linquan; (2) Liu'an weavers may have already adopted improved looms, possibly operated by men in workshops; and (3) Liu'an's proximity to the Yangzi River made it easier for factory goods to displace Liu'an homespun yarn.

62. Linquan woman (born 1933), interview by the authors and/or team, 2011.

63. In Linquan 51 percent and in Liu'an 45 percent of women interviewed were ever bound—that is, at least temporarily.

64. The duration of binding, ranging from a few months to twenty-eight years, averaged less than five years.

Chapter Four

1. The double "a" in Shaanxi (陕西) is not an incorrect spelling of Shanxi (山西); it is a modern convention for distinguishing between two similar spoken words with different tones and entirely different characters. To add to the confusion, the character for Shaanxi was formerly romanized as "Shensi."

2. Yan Xishan ruled from 1911 to 1949 through the warlord, national, Japanese, and Civil War periods.

3. Roughly three-quarters of the villagers in our sample grew wheat and corn as their staple grains.

4. Woman of Changzhi suburbs, North Village, interview by the authors and/or team, April 11, 2007.

5. A *jin* of raw cotton can produce yarn that weighs more than one *jin* when starch, moisture, and dirt are included in the weight. For more on hand spinning, see Hershatter 2011, 47.

6. Monetary prices were subject to much local variation and rapid inflation during the war. Women often gave the rate at which yarn could be exchanged for cotton.

7. This part of the Shanxi-Suiyuan border region was an area of "intense CCP activity after the second half of 1937" (Goodman 1994, 1009).

8. Women in Changzhi suburbs, North Village, interviews by the authors, April 10 and April 11, 2007.

9. For the political and ritual importance of Black Dragon King temples in this region, see Chau 2006.

10. Laurel Bossen photographed the Qiushui Cloth Shop plaque with this wording in 2011.

11. Qikou now has many public murals (for Chinese tourists) recounting early Communist activities. Strong local Communist influence suggests that nearby Yan'an Communist bases in Shaanxi and Shanxi organized and relied on women as textile producers in Lin County (LXZ 1994, 239).

12. Footbinding is rarely mentioned in this collection of three thousand interviews. This suggests that the party, desperate for cooperation from villagers, was reluctant to push an anti-footbinding policy.

13. Footbinding was avidly discussed by Long Bow's elderly women in Carma Hinton and Robert Gordon's documentary film *Small Happiness* (1984).

14. Ko cites census reports that "in 1928 the proportion of footbound women among the female population" was 18 percent for the province, and in 1934, just six years later, it had dropped to 9 percent, or 534,497 females. Curiously, a different census for 1932–1933 counted "almost one million women aged

thirty and under who had bound feet" (Ko 2005, 62). Given the contradictory findings and the possibilities of different definitions or deceit regarding the practice, like Ko, we doubt their reliability and note that unbinding may have been temporary to avoid fines.

15. Extensive CCP media repetition of revolutionary war films and the CCP's liberating mission over the years most likely influenced women's memories of what they had heard about as girls. The difference between the two sites is slight but is consistent with more direct intervention in Qikou than in Changzhi.

16. With the desperate need for female hand labor, activists did not emphasize unbinding. Of the Shaan-Gan-Ning Border Region Esherick wrote, "Western scholars have been disappointed by the CCP's more conservative record on women's issues in the Yan'an period" (1994, 1061n41). See also Andors 1983; Cong 2013, 188; Davin 1976, 32–52; K. Johnson (1983) 2009, 63–83; Selden 1971; Stacey 1983, 168–169; Stranahan 1981, 1983.

17. CCP influence was more ostensible in Qikou than in the dispersed villages of our Changzhi sample.

18. The Yan'an base itself was famous for establishing women's textile teams to supply the Communist troops with clothing (K. Johnson [1983] 2009, 65; Keating 1994a; Mao Zedong 2004; Schran 1976; Selden 1971).

19. Guanzhong, or "middle passage," is not an administrative district. It is a topographical reference to the central passage across Shaanxi between mountainous zones to the north and south.

20. Trade goods included cotton, hemp, grain, vegetable oils, hides, wool, meat, and draft animals in return for processed products from Shaanxi's plain. Cotton and cotton cloth from Shandong and Hebei weaving centers like Ding County were exported to Shanxi and beyond (Chao 1977; Gamble 1954).

21. For more on Luochuan transport, see Bossen et al. 2011, 369.

22. Hosie (1890, 16) also describes girls and women harvesting opium.

23. For a more detailed description of Zhouzhi and Luochuan, see Bossen et al. 2011.

24. Luochuan village women did not know the source of their cotton or how it was traded. Village men believed it came from Guanzhong rather than Shaanbei. This is consistent with our site remaining within the Nationalist orbit rather than the Communist base area (Keating 1994b, 125, 138). Cotton was also grown in the northeastern part of Shaanbei—Suide, north of Yan'an, and three counties east of Yan'an (Huang Zhenglin 2006, 432)—but Guanzhong cotton may have been better quality.

25. Women reported their marriage age in *xusui*, which is generally a year older than the Western method of counting completed years (*zhousui*). The average in *xusui* was 15.2 years, or 14.2 completed years.

26. Vera Neill Gates, mother of Hill Gates, remembers rough Chinese silk as a favored material for blue-collar work shirts, cheap and tough, in Canada during the Great Depression.

27. Hemp was also used to make paper in Shaanbei, but none of the women in our sample mentioned this work, and we did not specifically ask about paper.

28. Wool weaving was so rare in China that we did not prepare questions about wool processing. Indeed, wool was not commonly spun or woven in North China but was felted.

29. Embroidery made mostly for personal gifts created an important hand-made trove of value used for marking and strengthening personal ties with other women and their families (Gates 2015, 143–148), but such items could also be sold in the face of economic need (Edgerton-Tarpley 2008, 21, 49). The fine work of pictorial paper cutting may have served the same purpose.

30. Cotton production and women's important skills in spinning and weaving declined in northern Shaanbei (Suide) because cotton was replaced by opium under the warlords and because "competition with foreign textiles" and the collapse of trade during the Civil War "all but destroyed the folk textile industry" (Keating 1994b, 139). Kay Ann Johnson also comments that women's spinning and weaving work "had dwindled in the last few generations because of the loss of markets to more efficient modern and foreign industry" ([1983] 2009, 65).

31. Luochuan girls had less cotton to spin, or anti-footbinding pressures of the nearby Communist base area had an effect. The Nationalists in Zhouzhi also promoted unbinding, yet women persisted somewhat longer in efforts to bind their daughters' feet (Bossen et al. 2011). Correspondingly, Eyferth (2012) finds that Zhouzhi women continued hand weaving for many years during the Maoist period because of the scarcity of cloth and their access to homegrown cotton.

Chapter Five

1. Shallow native craft were used in some sections, but gorges, rapids, and seasonality of river flow limited their use for long-distance transport. Thus, travelers rarely comment on their use for trade goods in Yunnan and Guizhou.

2. Bin Yang calls the Yunnan trade route the "Southwest Silk Road" even though silk was not among the major goods traded. He uses the term analogously to the "Silk Road," the northern overland route, and the "Maritime Silk Road" from land to sea to highlight the trade between China and the rest of Asia. Yang contests Sinocentric ideas of Yunnan as a remote, uncivilized place of exile, countering that it was a dynamic central crossroads linking East, South, Southeast, and Central Asia.

3. Guizhou was established as a separate province in 1413 (Oakes 1998, 90–91).

4. David Bello (2003, 1121) cites James Z. Lee (1982, 284) regarding the growth of copper mining and associated population expansion from five to twenty million in Southwest China as a whole (Yunnan, Guizhou, and Sichuan) between 1700 and 1850.

5. This rebellion was not simply a religious conflict between Muslims and Han; there were Han on both the imperial and rebel sides. Muslims specialized in

commerce and tended, like the Han, to be concentrated in towns and along trade routes.

6. Yunnan's "registered" population of 1855 was roughly 7.5 million, but by 1884 after the rebellion it had dropped to roughly 3 million. Military violence, famine, emigration, and plague decimated the population (Benedict 1996, 39; see also Lee 1982, 149). Benedict's population figure for Yunnan in 1855 is lower than Lee's 10 million estimated for 1850, which probably includes Yunnan's unregistered as well as officially registered population.

7. Bin Yang (2008, 163) analyzes the interaction and seesaw processes of indigenization (*tuzhuhua*) and sinicization (*hanhua*). He explains, "Ming military colonization of Yunnan brought male soldiers who came with families. All these campaigns left about 280,000 soldiers in Yunnan. This figure, nonetheless, only constituted about one-third of military immigrants, in that each soldier brought his wife and children to the garrison (it is fair to estimate that each soldier was the head of a three-person family). A rough estimate of the first generation of Ming military households in Yunnan would be over 800,000" (146).

8. Yunnan province has the greatest number of identified ethnic minorities in China, followed by its neighbor, Guizhou. James Lee (1982) examines Han immigration to Yunnan over the centuries.

9. Core regions, identified by Skinner (1977, 214–215), are employed by Benedict (1996, 12–13).

10. Susan Mann notes imperial concerns with female propriety, production strategies, and "expanding the government's tax base," as expressed by a public works minister in the Qing reign of Yongzheng (1723–1736) in a memorial on Yunnan's agricultural development: "The memorial uses the Jiangnan region as a model of economic development," recommending that "women workers must be industrious" (*nü gong zhi yi qin ye*). The minister describes "ways to manufacture and distribute looms to peasant households and explains the advantages of promoting cotton rather than silk weaving in this frontier society" (1997, 148). See also LLXZ 1991, 307.

11. The collection of cotton and cloth as tax from Yunnan was already noted in official sixteenth-century government records (Chao 1977, 20; Zurndorfer 2011). Silk was too expensive for commoners, and Han settlers preferred cotton to hemp. Minorities used hemp, ramie, and other local fibers to make cloth and other goods (Litton 1903, 4). Anthropologist Eric Mueggler (1998) notes that hemp clothing was associated with poverty in northern Yunnan's Yi minority region.

12. "Cloth from Hupei [Hubei] reached northern Yunnan via Szechwan [Sichuan], first by water up the Yangtze [Yangzi] and its tributaries, then on the backs of porters who carried loads as large as 117 pieces of clothing weighing 220 pounds, and then by pack animal on the Yunnan mountain roads. Kweichow [Guizhou] was reached mainly via Hunan employing the Tung't'ing [Dongting] lake and the Yuan river which flows into it" (Feuerwerker 1970, 340). See also Bourne 1898, 259.

13. Among Yunnan's major cotton markets were Dali in the west, Simao in the south, and Kunming in the center.

14. Both Tonghai and Jiangchuan are in Yuxi Prefecture.

15. See also Yunnan roads in the map by George Philip and Son (1948).

16. Luo and Zhong (2000) examine the diverse techniques and tools for spinning and weaving surviving among Yunnan's minority groups, demonstrating the significance of handmade textiles, women's complex textile skills, and concern that this cultural heritage is rapidly disappearing.

17. Lack of schooling and illiteracy rates do not necessarily correspond. Those who attended school for only a year or so may remain illiterate, while a few who never attended school acquired basic literacy as adults from informal literacy classes or from family members.

18. A reminder of the Great Leap Forward (when Communist leaders required families to make steel in backyard furnaces) surfaced when one woman said that the family's wooden loom was burned in 1958. Although only mentioned by one woman, this may explain the fate of many old wooden looms.

19. During the Ming dynasty, Han immigrants to Tonghai brought their methods and tools for spinning, weaving, and dyeing thread from eastern China's Jiangnan. According to the local gazetteer, "Han villages of Tonghai and nearby Hexi counties were known for their 'men plow, women weave' division of labor. Although at first women spun and wove for subsistence, they began to produce textiles to earn a living, and gradually textiles became a large-scale commodity distributed in many counties across the whole province" (THXZ 1992, 139).

20. Unlike the North China Plain, where most villages have access to very similar resources and hence less opportunity to specialize, the varied environment of central Yunnan, with its mountains, plains, and lakes, caused many villages to specialize in particular products and congregate at periodic markets to exchange local specialties and long-distance trade goods.

21. The Chinese width was given as 8 *cun*: 1 *cun* equals 1.3 inches, so this measurement would be 10.4 inches or about 26 centimeters.

22. Many nineteenth- and early twentieth-century explorers comment on caravans carrying raw cotton into Yunnan from Burma and Tonkin (Colquhoun 1883; Davies [1909] 1970; Litton 1903; Rocher 1879). Towns in southern Yunnan purchased the cotton for spinning and weaving. By the late nineteenth century, factory yarn from distant producers had entered the trade and local weavers were starting to use it for handweaving. Litton reported that most cottons "have in the last twelve years rapidly yielded in public favour before 'yangshapu' [*yangshabu*] or cloth locally woven from imported yarns. The great centre of this industry is the Hsinhsing [Xinxing] Valley, three days south of Yunnanfu [Kunming]" (1903, 3). Similarly, Davies ([1909] 1970, 161) reported that in 1895 the principal industry in Qujing City in east Yunnan was weaving cotton cloth from Indian yarn imported from Hong Kong. The Tonghai gazetteer reports that in the nineteenth century special kinds of Shanghai raw cotton were even brought to Yun-

nan through Sichuan (THXZ 1992; XSZZ 1994). In the late nineteenth century, some cotton may have been grown as far north as Yuxi itself, but in 1940 Fei and Chang (1948) reported that Yu Village weavers did not grow cotton because they had become dependent on factory-made cotton yarn bought in the markets. John L. Buck's maps of this region also suggest cotton was grown to the south of Yuxi and Tonghai ([1937] 1964).

23. Tonghai County ethnic groups (besides Han) include Yi, Hui (Muslim Chinese), and Mongol communities. The Hui of Najia Ying were known for hardware skills (*wujin*) and the caravan trade. People in other villages, besides making cloth, specialized in copper pots, stonework, construction work, horse equipment, vegetable knives, wooden furniture, bamboo baskets, or tofu (THXZ 1992, 139).

24. Chao (1977, 186) argues that replacing hand-spun with machine-spun yarn helped hand-loomed cloth remain competitive. He cited the 1896–1987 Blackburn mission report: "Most hand weaving activities in Yunnan began after 1888" (Blackburn Chamber of Commerce 1898, 262). See also China Maritime Customs 1892, 109. Chao suggests that the influx of Indian yarn to Yunnan encouraged the growth of new handweaving centers, which lasted to the 1930s. Tonghai, in this chapter, was such a center. Its growth as a weaving center after 1888 may have included the use of improved flying-shuttle looms.

25. Locally *yangshabu* continued to be called *tubu*.

26. Tim Wright's research on the Great Depression in Yunnan notes that falling prices had a selective effect: "Some handicraft products, such as Yuxi cotton cloth, lost their markets in 1934–35" (2000, 726).

27. During the 1990s, when Bossen visited villages and towns in Yuxi Prefecture, a high proportion of the older women still had tightly bound feet and could be seen in the streets, markets, and villages. The area had also maintained its cottage weaving industry up to the 1949 revolution (Bossen 2008).

28. Names of villages are pseudonyms.

29. Zhibu Village woman (age ninety-one), interview by the authors and/or team, December 10, 2008.

30. One woman who married young learned spinning only after marriage because she was physically too small to weave before marriage.

31. Zhibu Village woman (born 1939), interview by the authors and/or team, August 18, 2009.

32. Zhibu Village woman (born 1935), interview by the authors and/or team, August 18, 2009.

33. Zhibu Village woman (born 1932), interview by the authors and/or team, August 19, 2009; Zhibu Village woman (born 1924), interview by the authors and/or team, August 22, 2009; Zhibu Village woman (born 1928), interview by the authors and/or team, August 20, 2009.

34. Zhibu Village woman (born 1932), interview by the authors and/or team, August 21, 2009.

35. The resulting explanations of income were highly variable. We do not have a method to reliably calculate incomes for different products and years. Wright notes that "Yunnan's currency situation was even more chaotic, particularly up to the mid-1930s when it fluctuated wildly against the national currency" (2000, 718).

36. The Internet features photos of Yunnan's footbound women, baring their feet, often accompanied by recycled theories about footbinding's origin and abolition.

37. We asked women if their feet were bound long enough to have a fixed shape, usually a process of several years. Sixty-nine women were able to answer this question, and thirty-nine said their bound feet had a fixed shape. Of those who unbound, roughly half (49 percent, $N = 68$) did so before marriage.

38. When asked about unbinding, 93 percent who were "ever bound" also said they "unbound" their feet. Most unbinding was done in the 1940s and early 1950s, with an average unbinding year of 1947, before the Communist victory in 1949. Twenty-two women who unbound did so after 1949. What is curious about the seemingly high rate of unbinding is that some of it must have been temporary, because a large proportion of the women interviewed in this village visibly retained bound feet well into their old age, as our photographs also show. Evidently some women unbound temporarily under the threat of fines and surreptitiously rebound later because severely bound feet lacked enough support to walk without the bindings. Ko (2005, 38–49) gives a detailed description of the irreversibility of bound feet once they are formed and the ordeals of those made to unbind. Ko quotes Xue Shaohui (1855–1911): "Now they suggest that those who have already bound should all let their feet out at once. But no magical pill can grow a new set of bones; a severed head cannot be reattached" (40). Like binding, the pain of unbinding could be "severe" (Jackson 1997,154; see also Yang Yang 2001).

39. "According to incomplete statistics, before Liberation, Jiangchuan altogether had 4,911 cloth-weaving households and roughly 6,430 weavers; their annual production was about thirty-six thousand bolts. The main products, 'Feather Blue,' 'Mixed Blue,' and 'Triple Blue' local cloth [*tubu*] were sold to more than thirty neighboring prefectures and counties" (JCXZ 1994, 240). Although the gazetteer does not give the date for these figures, it refers to the peak in the Republican period as over four thousand households (219). Dates are not clear or complete enough to compare numbers of weavers and outputs at different points in the Republican period.

40. The working-age population was roughly 40,000: nearly 15,000 farmers (including a few miners), 1,300 in commerce and transport, 2,000 in public service, and another 500 in liberal and other professions, a total of 18,800, assuming these were all male. Three remaining categories would account for most of the women: handicraft industry, 1,600; service industry (including housework), 11,200; and jobless, 8,350. If we assume that handicrafts are mainly textiles and service industry (housework) is also a catchall for all women's work, the total

is 12,800—far fewer than the number of males. A few women might have been counted in commerce or the professions and possibly public service (although women were very rare in public service then), and a few men counted in handicrafts. The only way this adds up to a reasonable population sex ratio (with the typical male surplus of, say, 110 males per 100 females—despite the war, which would have removed some men) is to assume that women are three-quarters of the jobless, or 6,262. (This would give a total of 19,062 women, compared to 20,888 men, a sex ratio of roughly 110 males per 100 females). Given the stress on textile producers, particularly the loss of work for spinners, this seems plausible. See JCXZ 1994, 219.

41. Spinning was more concentrated in Bulao Village, where 56 percent of the women spun.

42. Although gazetteers typically do not pay attention to footbinding, the Jiangchuan gazetteer confirms our finding of widespread footbinding among the villages, briefly referring to the practice: "From childhood, women deem bound feet as a symbol of beauty. The tips of shoes are embroidered" (JCXZ 1994, 655). The authors interpret the abandonment of footbinding in terms of fashion aesthetics and Republican reforms.

43. Bin Yang cites Yunnan Zhi, juan 1 (Fang 1998), which has thirteen volumes with "almost all official records . . . and scholarly works about Yunnan from the western Han (206 BCE to 209 CE) to the end of the Qing dynasty (1644–1911)" (B. Yang 2009, 16, 21n31).

44. "The history of local cloth [*tubu*] production is age-old. . . . In the Qing dynasty Emperor Kang Xi's fifty-third year (1714) . . . , spinning and weaving techniques came from the Central Plain" (LLXZ 1991, 307).

45. Women we interviewed named this factory and store, Hongyuan ranzhi gong chang, as the source of their cloth.

46. A question concerning spinning-wheel ownership was asked in just twelve supplementary interviews in 2010; none of the families owned one.

47. Dong Village (Luliang) woman (born 1941), interview by the authors and/or team, April 28, 2010.

48. Hosie (1890, 44) observed caravans loaded with hats between Guiyang and Yunnan, attesting to the commercial value of handmade hats. See also Hosie 1914, 2:105.

49. Benedict (1996, 51–54) discusses in detail nineteenth-century trade routes for Yunnan opium.

50. The businessman father of one woman bought a bamboo loom in Kunming. Her mother did not know how to use it, so no one used it. Lu Village woman (born 1927), interview by the authors and/or team, 2010.

51. These data are from Bossen's 1996 survey of fifty-seven elderly Lu Village women about work in their natal village (see Bossen 2002).

52. For a discussion of the relation between embroidery and rank in imperial China, see Steele and Major 1999, 29–30.

53. Some of the older Lu Village women (ten of fifty-seven) had done commercial embroidery before marriage. Others reported that they sold shoes and embroidery after marriage. Unfortunately, our survey did not ask for details about the items that they embroidered.

54. Shoemaking belonged to the female realm of handcrafts like doing needlework, stitching cotton, or plaiting straw sandals. Cotton cloth was used for the upper part of the shoe and glued and stitched into layers for the sole.

55. Delia Davin observed that in China "clothes were usually made at home, and so sometimes were the cloth and the thread that went into them. Cloth shoes stitched by women took two or three days to make but lasted only five or six months" (1975, 251).

56. Southern sources of homespun may have displaced earlier use of hemp or cotton cloth from other Yunnan markets. In the nineteenth century hemp cloth was common among the nearby minorities of Yunnan (Mueggler 1998). In the early twentieth century, Lufeng County had very limited cotton cloth weaving and enormous cotton cloth imports (LFXZ 1997, 322).

57. Drawing on James Lee, Robert Jenks notes that "a vast immigrant tide had brought about a 60 percent preponderance of Han by 1851. Lee may err in stating that this 60 to 40 percent ratio persisted to the present, for the widespread slaughter of minority group members during the rebellions in Guizhou and Yunnan, combined with subsequent minority migrations to Southeast Asia, probably increased the preponderance of the Han" (1994, 29).

58. Jenks reports that "Guizhou did not grow enough cotton to clothe its population, and large quantities of cotton cloth were imported, especially from Hunan and Hubei. Crude cotton cloth was cheap, wore well, and was appropriate to the climate" (1994, 24). See also Hosie 1890, 34.

59. Hosie (1914, 2:278–279) estimates that Guizhou produced opium up to 1906, after which it was suppressed by imperial decree.

60. Xingyi is located in Qianxinan, Guizhou, about midway between Anshun and Luliang, on Guizhou's western border (K. Chen 1989).

61. Cheng Biding (1989) views spinning as female work and weaving as male work but offers no specific evidence for this generalization. Male weaving may have been a recent adaptation to technological change, such as flying-shuttle or iron looms (141). Female concentration on spinning is consistent with our evidence showing women had higher rates of spinning before marriage.

62. The Anshun residents remain in the site of their original village, now mixed with migrants. The population of the prefecture is roughly 61 percent Han; the women surveyed were Han or assimilated to Han.

63. For information on handmade straw hats from Anshun, see Gates 2015, 130, and Hosie 1914, 2:105–106, photos 112, 125. In 1910, Hosie describes his caravan in Guizhou "haggling with old women and girls over the price of straw sandals, many of which changed hands" (1914, 2:104).

64. As Hosie describes opium processing, "Peasants, principally women and children, were busy harvesting the juice . . . moving in the poppy fields, each armed with a short wooden handle . . . [with protruding] 'brass or copper blades' to incise the capsule to make the juice exude" (1890, 16–17).

65. Bossen and Gates disagree on the importance of footbinding for girls who worked in opium processing. Bossen believes that opium processing alone, when it required pod scraping in the fields, would not be a strong incentive to bind daughter's feet for two reasons: (1) it would require walking among the poppy plants, and (2) it was seasonal and not likely to be a girl's main work. The incentive for binding would be greater *if* combined with considerable sedentary handwork rather than farmwork such as rice transplanting, weeding, and harvesting. The answer may lie in the number of weeks of poppy harvests combined with weeks of sedentary handcraft work required from girls. Gates believes that all forms of *light* labor, whether sedentary or not, were an incentive to bind feet. Gates sees binding primarily as a means to teach obedience, whereas Bossen sees it as a means to keep young daughters in place for sedentary handwork. Both obedience and staying put were required of young girls.

66. None of the women born after 1938 reported growing opium, but earlier opium was described as "*pubian*," or commonplace.

67. Some Anshun women combined hand- and fieldwork: for example, an older footbound mother could not work in the fields, so the daughter both worked in fields by day and helped her mother spin at night. The daughter also went to market to buy and carry back coal and to sell spun thread and buy cloth.

68. Of 184 households where agricultural labor was recorded for natal homes, 154 grew rice. Data on rice labor were recorded for only 104 women. Of those, 99 (95 percent) worked in the rice fields. The most conservative ratio for female labor in rice is 64 percent (99 of 154). Women's rice labor included the following: planting, transplanting, weeding, fertilizing, watering, harvesting, carrying heavy loads, threshing, drying, and winnowing.

69. Anshun woman (born 1921), interview by the authors and/or team, July 8, 2009.

70. There is no clear way to estimate whether handcrafts or field labor gave a greater return. Women's wages varied throughout the year, often much higher for peak periods of rice work and very low at other times. The rates of return would depend on supply and demand for each product, and these constantly varied, for example, with good or bad crop years, high or low market prices for cloth, the regularity of shipments of imported goods (not regular then), inflation, labor shortages, migration, and conscription and war.

71. Lufeng rates of binding among elder relatives of the women surveyed ($N = 241$) ranged from 100 percent for the 1860s birth cohorts to as low as 22 percent ($N = 51$) for the cohort born in 1910, only to rise again in the 1920s. Some of this fluctuation may be due to small numbers per cohort, as well as to

varied occupations: some women worked in poppy and rice fields and as porters, while others made straw shoes or embroideries for sale.

72. The individuals in the 1996 and 2010 samples do not overlap. The 1996 sample was concentrated in Lu Village center, whereas the 2010 sample focused on women from the outlying hamlets.

73. By the mid-nineteenth century, western towns may have been getting their cotton cloth from Burma (Giersch 2006, 177).

74. According to Sven Beckert, by 1861 India had 12 spinning mills, increasing to 27 by 1875. "In 1897, there were 102 mills in the Bombay Presidency alone. The number of spindles exploded, from 1.5 million in 1879 to nearly 9 million in 1929." Beckert further notes that "by the 1890s 80 percent of the yarn exported from Bombay went to China" (2015, 410–411).

Chapter Six

1. H. D. Fong (1933, 20–28) outlines a range of handcraft textiles produced by women and girls in the 1930s.

2. Recall that data are not reliable for estimating the amounts of work that girls performed. The decade of their lives when they began to learn handwork, became proficient, and worked full time includes many variables that cannot be pinned down. The amount of work per day, per season, per year, or even in particular years or at particular ages and tasks is unmeasurable for informal work. Girls' work at home doing hand labor was informal; it did not leave any formal records of its existence: no time clocks; no fixed hours or labor laws; no direct tax requirements, pay stubs, or receipts. We cannot assume that it was part-time or voluntary just because it was performed within the household. With time unmarked by clocks or years of formal education, girls had few benchmarks to link work hours or stages in their work capacity with particular ages. The decades in which they grew up experienced changing market prices, government regimes, raids, takeovers, new technologies, and famines. China's young, rural girls had few ways to link their local experiences to a twentieth-century chronology of years or national events until after 1949, when formal primary education was instituted.

3. Sewing clothes, making cloth shoes, and embroidering were basic skills found among nearly all women.

4. James Scott (1999) uses the concept of "legibility" to refer to state efforts to create knowledge categories and standards to simplify economic and political administration and control. In the informal sector and within the family, work done by women and children tends to be invisible, uncounted, essentially off the map. In our usage, the lack of legibility of girls' labor means that it goes unrecognized and is not counted by scholars or the state; its value either is ignored or attributed to others.

5. Survey questions about work done for sale or wages probably underestimated exchanges in kind and gift exchange because the village idioms tend to be anticommercial. For example, in the 1990s whenever Bossen attempted to pay for

room and board with rural families during fieldwork, women, even if poor, were reluctant to set any price and often forcefully returned money multiple times, preferring kinship and friendship to commercial exchange. Gifts, however, were accepted with pleasure. Perhaps women were not comfortable in establishing a monetary value for services when they did not know reasonable market prices, whereas they understood gifts. Work for one's neighbors was often performed in return for goods in kind or similar labor.

6. Although the dichotomy will not capture all cases in which a girl devoted most of her time to handwork, it is a reasonable proxy for differentiating intense from casual hand labor. Similarly, the dichotomy might occasionally misclassify someone who did little handwork but occasionally sold a few handmade items.

7. "Disguised unemployment" refers to the situation in which people continue to work for meager returns because they lack access to other earning opportunities. It does not mean people are idle or that their output has zero value.

8. Chao describes the operation of putting-out firms in the 1920s and 1930s: "They clearly knew that it was impossible to compete successfully with factory cloth in the nationwide market if they had to pay subsistence wages to hand weavers" (1977, 214).

9. Our hypothesis would be falsified if data showed that girls who did very little handwork for income usually had bound feet or girls who worked intensively at handcrafts did not have bound feet.

10. Going further back in time to those born in the earlier years of the twentieth century, more women with bound feet remained bound into adulthood, their feet permanently transformed. Some girls were only temporarily compressed into "cucumber feet" or half-bound feet without breaking the major bones. Those born later were more likely to be bound for shorter periods, a number of years or a few months, when the tightest binding no longer seemed necessary or when the family division of labor was overridden by collectivization in the 1950s. Unbinding occurred under many different circumstances: some unbound during the 1920s or 1930s after just a few months; others stayed bound for years after Communist victory in 1949 and the establishment of communes during the Great Leap Forward. Women with permanently bent arches often needed the support of bindings to walk. Some women reporting binding, unbinding, and rebinding, as government policies, parental needs, and local customs vied with one another.

11. We have only to note the way modern toys for girls often include handcrafts: potholder kits, miniature looms, knitting machines, beading kits, and the like.

12. Finnane comments, "By the late thirties, then, a large number of people outside the big cities, living in little towns far from the coast, were probably buying machine-made cloth to make their clothes. Much of this cloth was produced in Shanghai, or arrived from abroad via Shanghai" (2008, 108).

13. "Logistic regression is a statistical method for analyzing a dataset in which there are one or more independent variables that determine an outcome.

The outcome is measured with a dichotomous variable" (MedCalc 2016). See Pampel 2000 for an accessible instruction manual. The introduction by the series editor, Michael S. Lewis-Beck, begins, "Logistic regression has pretty much come to replace ordinary least squares (OLS) regression as the data analytic tool of choice when the equation to be estimated has a dichotomous dependent variable" (Pampel 2000, v). The form of the equation fitted by a logistic regression means that predicted probabilities approach either 0 or 1 asymptotically, never reaching either limit.

14. "Value" here is the relevant logistic regression coefficient (see Pampel 2000 for details).

15. The mean birth year was 1934 for the Eight Provinces survey and 1919 for the Sichuan survey.

16. See, for example, Moser 1930.

17. Describing nineteenth-century European views, Finnane writes, "Footbinding, it is true, was regarded as barbaric, but in this respect, the agency of Chinese women was hardly admitted. Their feet were the fault of their culture" (2008, 40).

18. Colette Simon, an expert hand spinner and weaver in Montreal, told Bossen that it was virtually impossible for a woman with children to spin yarn because of the interruptions. She stressed that the term "spinsters" referred to unmarried women who were not encumbered by children and could therefore work efficiently.

19. Chao refers to H. B. Morse's statistics as "admittedly not highly accurate" (1977, 50). One *picul* equals 36 bolts, so 1.6 million bolts equal to 44,444 *piculs*; multiply by 133.33 to determine pounds/*picul*: 5,925,777 pounds (Chao 1977, 45–51). Later, Chao uses figures from H. D. Fong (1934, 322) that are roughly comparable but in different units. Chao's table 1 shows that cloth exports during 1801–1805 peaked at roughly 39,000 *piculs* (about 5.2 million pounds), but by the 1830s they had dropped to 3,888 *piculs* (785,047 pounds) (Chao 1977, 50, 82).

20. Feuerwerker reported in *piculs*, here converted to pounds. Imported factory yarn came from India and Japan as well as Europe and North America (Feuerwerker 1995a, 36; Gates 2015). From 1870 to 1910, the estimated value of yarn and thread imports increased fifteenfold from around four to sixty million *taels*; imports of cotton piece goods increased less rapidly, less than fourfold, from around nineteen million taels in 1870 to just over seventy million in 1901–1910 (Chao 1977, 89, table 4).

21. See Chao 1977, 232, table 26, and Feuerwerker 1995a, 34. Thomas Rawski (1989, 93, table 2.10), drawing on Feuerwerker (1970, 350, 355, 372) and Kraus (1980, 65, 143, tables 3-5, 6-1), estimates that hand-spun yarn in 1901–1910 was about 41 percent of total domestic supply (including net imports) and 71 percent of total domestic production (hand spun and factory spun).

22. The two railways were the Luhan (a.k.a. Jinghan, from Beijing to Hankou) and the Jinpu (connecting Tianjin and Pukou, near Nanjing). The Manchurian railways were built in the 1890s (Feuerwerker 1995a, 72).

23. By 1917, China had 9,244 kilometers of completed railways, with more than a third in Manchuria (Feuerwerker 1995a, 70).

24. See also *Zhonghua Minguo gonglu luxian tu* 1936.

25. Hamilton and Chang describe China's textile merchant organizations: "Merchants typically went to regional markets in the producing areas and bought cloth from commission agents or petty merchants who had collected the cloth in smaller markets from producing households in the region. Merchants then delivered the cloth to groups specializing in finishing the cloth through dyeing and calendering" (2003, 196–197). According to Craig Dietrich, "Since the activities of the innumerable spinners and weavers were not integrated with one another in any organizational structure, it was the merchants, both local and regional, who held the industry together and allowed it to function as a system" (1972, 131, quoted in Hamilton and Chang 2003, 197). Hamilton and Chang argue that regionally organized merchant networks "controlled all the links in the cotton textile commodity chain" in the late Qing (198).

26. Bray, Chao, Elvin, and Feuerwerker are among those who note that China's early innovations and developments in textile technology did not spread among the peasantry.

27. Chao did not specify evidence, time, place, or his source for this claim.

28. Even when a thirty- or forty-spindle iron hand-spinning machine requiring three people to operate it appeared before the war, "no one wanted to buy it" (Chao 1977, 332n28).

29. Net yarn imports rise from 1870 to 1910 and then fall to near nil, while factory yarn rises continuously from 1871 to 1936 (Rawski 1989).

30. Various authors provide estimates. Chao (1977, 114) mentions 31 mills for 1912; Tang Chi Yu (1924, 442), 73 mills in 1922; and Lai (1967, 87, 125), 118 for 1925 and 140 for 1936.

31. Mill counts given by Chao (1977, 114), Tang Chi Yu (1924, 442), and Lai (1967, 87, 125) are similar with respect to the overall rising trend from 1912 to 1936.

32. See Gates 2015, chap. 7. For the relocation of cotton industries to Sichuan and Yunnan during the Japanese occupation, see T'ien 1944 and Howard 2013.

33. The single mechanized mill was the Sanxi zhiran chang (Three Gorges Weaving and Dyeing Factory) established by Lu Zuofu in 1930. Between 1938 and 1941, four large mills were relocated to Chongqing from Shanghai, Zhengzhou, Hankou, and Shashi (Hunan) to supply cloth for the military and growing refugee population after the Japanese military blockade cut off supplies from the east (Howard 2013, 1896–1897).

34. Rawski (emphasizing the modernizing market forces of the Republican economy) calculates that the total output of hand-spun yarn increased in the 1920s, suggesting that handcraft industries did not decline as precipitously as implied by an inability to respond to market forces (1989, 95). The calculation seems to be drawn from estimates of the cotton supply, factory yarn, factory cloth output, to estimate hand-spun yarn and hand-loomed output. Chao (1977, 234) calculates yarn consumption for use on handlooms as yarn available for cloth production minus yarn used on power looms. As far as we know, no one has reliable direct data on hand-spun yarn output or even the distribution of different kinds of hand spinning wheels for China's diverse regions.

35. Chao (1977, 180) gives a ratio of 44:1.

36. Hand spinning persisted mainly in villages that grew their own cotton and employed it for a narrow range of uses, such as to give a thicker weft when handweaving with machine-spun warp (Chao 1977, 180). Warfare, trade blockades, and bombed factories revived home spinning temporarily out of necessity, but industrialized spinning resumed once the war ended, so hand spinning disappeared from most areas by the 1950s. Eyferth (2012) describes the revival of handloom weaving as informal, illegal activity during the first three decades of the planned economy.

37. Rawski cites Feuerwerker for 1871–1910 and Kraus's cotton supply and input-output data for 1923–1936. He notes that "these data are subject to considerable margins of error" and "rough estimates of handicraft production for 1923–24" as well as "painstaking sifting of evidence and verification of assumptions by Feuerwerker and Kraus" (Rawski 1989, 95). Rawski's (1989, 96) estimates (shown in Figure 6.5) differ from Chao's (1977, 232, table 26) in that Rawski estimates on the basis of cotton supply that total hand-spun yarn increased temporarily in 1922–1923.

38. While speed depended on the use of one's hands, the warp strands were raised and lowered by a foot pedal (Kraus 1980, 132). In the case of the iron-gear loom, the foot treadles "controlled the flying shuttle, raised and lowered the warps, and activated the take up roller which rolled up the cloth as it was woven. . . . [It was] the pinnacle of hand-technology. The only effective difference between it and the power-loom was that it lacked power. Indeed, the 'iron-gear' loom itself was often adapted and used for power weaving. When weaving the same types of cloth the power-loom had only a 50% productive advantage over the 'hand' [foot] driven iron-gear loom" (133).

39. According to Howard, "The introduction of the foot-pedal loom in 1905, the substitution of wooden pull shuttles for cast shuttle looms, and the use of iron wheel looms . . . spurred the concentration of labour into larger 'factories'" (2013, 1896). Kathy Le Mons Walker gives reason to believe that improved looms, possibly the flying-shuttle type, were in use in Nantong and the Yangzi delta area even before the 1884 crisis, when foreign competition had caused many cloth firms to close (1999, 89).

40. Tianjin artisan metalworkers copied the technology from a Japanese manufacturer (Hershatter 1983; 1986, 87; Chao 1977, 184) and began to produce for the Chinese market.

41. These ratios apply to the 1930s, not to fully automatic looms (Chao 1977, 185).

42. Kraus's source (1980, 135n29) is China Maritime Customs (1924, 2:109, 336, 395). The original spelling of place-names is Pakhoi (Guangdong), Chinhai (Zhejiang), and Tengyue (Yunnan).

43. See Gates 2015 and Bourne 1898 regarding expansion of weaving in Yunnan and Guizhou.

44. There is no quantitative information on improved loom distribution by region.

45. As we discuss in Chapter 5, in the late nineteenth century, weaving centers in Hexi, Xinxing, and Qujing in Yunnan, as well as in Xingyi in Guizhou, also developed using imported yarn. See Bourne 1898, 206–262, and Oakes 1998, 99.

46. Wei Xian (Shandong) on the Jiaozhou-Jinan railway near Qingdao rose as a handweaving center with the 1920 establishment of a local machine shop that produced seven thousand sets of iron-gear looms annually, with a credit system for purchase. Wei Xian "plus a few villages in neighboring districts had installed a total of about 100,000 looms, forming the largest hand-weaving center in North China" (Chao 1977, 195–196). "During the peak years about 150,000 persons were involved in the production of native cloth, with a maximum annual output of ten million bolts." This was "the wide type, ranging from 2 to 2.8 feet" (196). Wei Xian products had a "nationwide market" with the bulk shipped through "railway freight and post offices to major cities in Henan Anhui, and Shaanxi" (194; place-names changed to pinyin).

47. See Gates 2015, chap. 7, and Schran 1976 regarding wartime expansion of homemade cotton textile production.

48. Linda Grove observes that women operated iron-gear looms in Japan and the Yangzi delta workshops in the 1920s and 1930s and suggests that a crucial difference is that Gaoyang practiced family production in which men wove on their own looms, whereas in Japan and Jiangnan, the women worked for wages in workshops owned by employers (2006, 83). "The iron gear loom required a much larger investment, and those costs could only be justified if the loom was in constant use. . . . Accompanying this professionalization of weaving was a shift in the organization of household labor. . . . In the new family workshops men became the weavers, with women and children assigned to reeling and other preparatory tasks" (2006, 20). Also, Grove argues that "the shift from a women-centered production system to one managed by men, in which men held what came to be seen as the central technical role of operating the loom, was directly associated with the adoption of the iron gear loom and the use of machine-spun yarns" (82).

49. Weaving households usually were family operated: the man was the weaver, and women and children did reeling, sizing, and warping (Grove 2006, 80).

50. A wide range of possibilities from field labor to lace making or factory work existed, but access was difficult because of the sheer numbers of underemployed laborers seeking new forms of livelihood (Walker 1999; H. D. Fong 1933).

51. Grove (2006, 82–83) suggests that men more commonly took over handloom weaving in North China, while Walker (1993) reports that women played a greater role in handweaving in the Jiangnan region. "In North China . . . women entered the cotton mills later and in smaller numbers than their southern counterparts" (Hershatter 1986, 55). Most of the modern textile mills started up in or near Shanghai, while Tianjin initially competed with iron-gear looms. In Shanghai large supplies of factory thread put an early stop to hand spinning by girls. Shanghai's young women could have moved from home textile work into the mills one or two decades earlier than women in Tianjin, where the success of men weaving with iron-gear looms may have kept women spinning and practicing footbinding longer than in Shanghai.

52. Chao noted that for a young daughter aged seven or eight, apart from spinning it would be a long time "before she was old enough to learn any other technique of handicraft production" pertaining to weaving (1977, 182).

53. Hershatter (1986, 258n42) reports on a study by Wu Ao (1931).

54. Honig cites a report that cotton-mill managers did not want to hire old, footbound, or pregnant women, the "three don't wants" (1986, 191).

55. H. D. Fong also compares the loss of employment for women and children in China to a similar process in England "a century earlier": "Where is the distaff and spindle? . . . Where is the employment for women and children, formerly carrying comfort and independence to the home of every cottager?—all absorbed by machinery, or sacrificed to the cry of 'cheap'" (1933, 13).

56. Cliver (2010, 118), Hershatter (1986), and Honig (1986) note that factory owners did not want footbound women in their mills. Arno Pearse reports child laborers "of eight years or even less are running about among the machines" (1932, 644).

REFERENCES

Gazetteers

These *difangzhi* (administrative reports) are listed by gazetteer title abbreviation and title, publication year, editor, and place and name of publisher.

ASFZ (*Anshun fu zhi* [Anshun Prefecture gazetteer]). 2007. Edited by Anshun shi difangzhi bianzuan weiyuanhui. Guiyang: Guizhou renmin chubanshe.

ASSZ (*Anshun shi zhi* [Anshun City gazetteer]). 1995. Edited by Anshun shi difangzhi bianzuan weiyuanhui. Guiyang: Guizhou renmin chubanshe.

CCZZXZ (*Chongxiu Zhouzhi xianzhi* [Revised Zhouzhi County gazetteer]). 1925. Shaanxi Provincial Library.

FYXZ (*Anhui sheng difang congshu Fuyang xianzhi* [Anhui Province collected local gazetteer, Fuyang County]). 1994. Edited by Fuyang xianzhi difangzhi bianzuan weiyuanhui. Hefei, Anhui: Huangshan shu she.

JCXZ (*Jiangchuan xianzhi* [Jiangchuan County gazetteer]). 1994. Compiled by Yunnan sheng Jiangchuan shi zhi bianzuan weiyuanhui. Kunming: Yunnan renmin chubanshe.

KFXZ (*Kaifeng xianzhi* [Kaifeng County gazetteer]). 1992. Edited by Kaifeng xianzhi bianji weiyuanhui. Zhengzhou, Henan: Zhongzhou guji chubanshe.

LAXZ (*Liu'an xianzhi* [Liu'an gazetteer]). 1993. Edited by Liu'an xian difangzhi bianzuan weiyuanhui. Hefei, Anhui: Huangshan chubanshe.

LCXZ (*Luochuan xianzhi* [Luochuan County gazetteer]). 1994. Edited by Luochuan xian difang zhi bianzuan weiyuanhui. Xi'an, Shaanxi: Shaanxi renmin chubanshe.

LFXZ (*Lufeng xianzhi* [Lufeng County gazetteer]). 1997. Edited by Yunnan sheng Lufeng difangzhi bianzuan weiyuanhui. Kunming: Yunnan renmin chubanshe.

LLXZ (*Luliang xianzhi* [Luliang County gazetteer]). 1991. Edited by Yunnansheng Luliang xianzhi bianzuan weiyuanhui. Shanghai: Kexue puji chubanshe.

LLZZ (*Luliang Zhouzhi* [Luliang Department gazetteer]). 1844. Daoguang edition.

LXZ (*Lin xianzhi* [Lin County gazetteer]). 1994. Edited by Lin Xianzhi editorial committee. Beijing: Haichao chubanshe.

MGLQXZ (*Mingguo Linquan xianzhi* [Republican China Linquan gazetteer]). (1936) 1998. Revised by Liu Huandong (刘焕东). Nanjing: Jiangsu guji chubanshe; Shanghai: Shanghai shu dian; Chengdu: Ba shu shushe.

QZSZ (*Qingzhou Shi Zhi* [Qingzhou City gazetteer]). 1989. Tianjin: Nankai daxue chubanshe.

THXZ (*Tonghai xianzhi* [Tonghai County gazetteer]). 1992. Edited by Yunnan sheng Tonghai xian shizhi gongzuo weiyuanhui. Kunming: Yunnan renmin chubanshe.

XSZZ (*Xiushan zhen zhi* [Xiushan Township gazetteer]). 1994. Edited by Zhong gong Xiushan zhen weiyuanhui. Kunming: Yunnan renmin chubanshe.

YSRP (*Yunnan sheng 2000 nian renkou pucha* [Yunnan Province 2000 population census]). 2002. Edited by Yunnan sheng renkou pucha bangongshe [Yunnan Province population census office]. Kunming: Yunnan keji chubanshe.

ZZXZ (*Zhouzhi xianzhi* [Zhouzhi County gazetteer]). 1993. Edited by Wang Anquan (王安泉), Zhouzhi xianzhi editorial committee. Xi'an, Shaanxi: San Qin chubanshe.

Other Sources

Allen, Robert C., Jean-Pascal Bassino, Debin Ma, Christine Moll-Murata, and Lan Luiten Van Zanden. 2011. "Wages, Prices, and Living Standards in China, 1738–1925: In Comparison with Europe, Japan, and India." *Economic History Review* 64 (S1): 8–38.

Anderson, Aeneas. 1795. *A Narrative of the British Embassy to China in the Years 1792, 1793, and 1794*. London: J. Debrett.

Andors, Phyllis. 1983. *The Unfinished Liberation of Chinese Women, 1949–1980*. Bloomington: Indiana University Press.

Appiah, Kwama Anthony. 2010a. "The Art of Social Change." *New York Times Magazine*, October 22, p. MM22.

———. 2010b. *The Honor Code: How Moral Revolutions Happen*. New York: W. W. Norton.

Aylward, Gladys, with Christine Hunter. 1970. *The Little Woman*. Chicago: Moody.

Avery, Martha. 2003. *The Tea Road: China and Russia Meet Across the Steppe*. Beijing: China Intercontinental Press.

Banister, Judith. 1987. *China's Changing Population*. Stanford, CA: Stanford University Press.

Barclay, George, Ansley J. Coale, Michael Stoto, and T. James Trussell. 1976. "A Reassessment of the Demography of Traditional China." *Population Index* 42:606–635.

Beckert, Sven. 2015. *Empire of Cotton: A Global History*. New York: Alfred A. Knopf.

Bello, David. 2003. "The Venomous Course of Southwestern Opium: Qing Prohibition in Yunnan, Sichuan, and Guizhou in the Early Nineteenth Century." *Journal of Asian Studies* 62 (4): 1109–1142.

Benedict, Carol. 1996. *Bubonic Plague in Nineteenth-Century China*. Stanford, CA: Stanford University Press.

Beresford, Lord Charles. 1899. *The Break-up of China, with an Account of Its Present Commerce, Currency, Waterways, Armies, Railways, Politics, and Future Prospects*. New York: Harper.

Blackburn Chamber of Commerce. 1898. *Report of the Mission to China of the Blackburn Chamber of Commerce, 1896–7*. Blackburn, UK: North-East Lancashire Press.

Blake, C. Fred. 1994. "Foot-Binding in Neo-Confucian China and the Appropriation of Female Labor." *Signs: Journal of Women in Culture and Society* 19 (3): 676–712.

Blunden, Caroline, and Mark Elvin. 1983. *Cultural Atlas of China*. New York: Facts on File.

Bonavia, David. 1995. *China's Warlords*. Oxford: Oxford University Press.

Bossen, Laurel. 2002. *Chinese Women and Rural Development: Sixty Years of Change in Lu Village, Yunnan*. Lanham, MD: Rowman and Littlefield.

———. 2005. *Zhongguo funu yu nongcun fazhan: Yunnan Lucun liushi nian de bianqian* [Chinese women and rural development: Sixty years of change in Lu Village, Yunnan]. Translated by Yukun Hu. Nanjing: Jiangsu People's Publishing House.

———. 2007. "Village to Distant Village: The Opportunities and Risks of Long-Distance Marriage Migration in Rural China." *Journal of Contemporary China* 16 (50): 97–116.

———. 2008. "Hand und Fuß gebunden: Frauenarbeit und das Binden der Füße im China des frühen 20. Jahrhunderts" [Bound hand and foot: Women's work and footbinding in early twentieth-century China]. Translated by Mareile Flitsch. *Technikgeschichte* 75:117–140.

———. 2011. "Women's Labor and Footbinding in Early 20th Century Rural China." Paper presented at the annual conference of the Association for Asian Studies, Honolulu, Hawaii, April 1.

Bossen, Laurel, Wang Xurui, Melissa Brown, and Hill Gates. 2011. "Feet and Fabrication: Footbinding and Early 20th Century Rural Women's Labor in Shaanxi." *Modern China* 37 (4): 347–383.

Bourne, Frederick Samuel Augustus. 1898. *Report of the Mission to China of the Blackburn Chamber of Commerce, 1896–7: F.S.A. Bourne's Section*. Blackburn, UK: North-East Lancashire Press.

Bramall, Chris. 2009. *Chinese Economic Development*. New York: Routledge.

Bray, Francesca. 1997. *Technology and Gender: Fabrics of Power in Late Imperial China*. Berkeley: University of California Press.

———. 2013. *Technology, Gender and History in Imperial China: Great Transformations Reconsidered*. New York: Routledge.

Brenner, Robert, and Christopher Isett. 2002. "England's Divergence from China's Yangzi Delta: Property Relations, Microeconomics, and Patterns of Development." *Journal of Asian Studies* 61 (2): 609–662.

Broadwin, Julie. 1997. "Walking Contradictions: Chinese Women Unbound at the Turn of the Century." *Journal of Historical Sociology* 10 (4): 418–443.

Brown, Melissa J., ed. 1996. *Negotiating Ethnicities in China and Taiwan*. Berkeley: Institute of East Asian Studies, University of California.

———. 2004. *Is Taiwan Chinese? The Impact of Culture, Power, and Migration on Changing Identities*. Berkeley: University of California Press.

Brown, Melissa J., L. Bossen, H. Gates, and D. Satterthwaite. 2012. "Marriage Mobility and Footbinding in Pre-1949 Rural China: A Reconsideration of Gender, Economics, and Meaning in Social Causation." *Journal of Asian Studies* 71 (4): 1035–1067.

Buck, John L. (1937) 1964. *Land Utilization in China: A Study of 16,786 Farms in 168 Localities, and 38,256 Farm Families in Twenty-Two Provinces in China, 1929–1933*. Vol 1. New York: Paragon Books.

———. 1937. *Land Utilization in China*. Vol. 2, *Atlas*. Chicago: University of Chicago Press.

Burgess, Alan. 1957. *The Small Woman*. London: Evans Bros.

Chao, Kang (Zhao Gang). 1977. *The Development of Cotton Textile Production in China*. Cambridge, MA: Harvard University Press.

Chau, Adam-Yuet. 2006. *Miraculous Response: Doing Popular Religion in Contemporary China*. Stanford, CA: Stanford University Press.

Chen Han-seng and Miriam S. Farley. 1937. "Railway Strategy in China, New Style." *Far Eastern Survey* 6 (15): 165–173.

Chen Minglu. 2011. *Tiger Girls: Women and Enterprise in the People's Republic of China*. New York: Routledge.

Chen, Jack. 1973. *A Year in Upper Felicity: Life in a Chinese Village During the Cultural Revolution*. New York: Macmillan.

Chen, K., ed. 1989. *Guizhou sheng nongcun jingji quhua* [Agricultural economic plan for Guizhou Province]. Guiyang: Remin chubanshe.

Chen, Y., F. Kuang, and J. Wang, eds. 1993. *Guizhou sheng jingji dili* [Economic geography of Guizhou Province]. Beijing: Xinhua.

Cheng Biding (程必定), ed. 1989. *Anhui jindai jingji shi* [Anhui modern economic history]. Hefei: Huangshan shushe.

Chesneaux, Jean, Françoise Le Barbier, and Marie-Claire Bergère. 1977. *China from the 1911 Revolution to Liberation*. Translated by Paul Auster and Lydia Davis. New York: Pantheon Books.

Chi Hsi-sheng (Qi Xisheng). 1969. "The Chinese Warlord System." PhD diss., University of Chicago.

———. 1976. *Warlord Politics in China, 1916–1928*. Stanford, CA: Stanford University Press.

China Maritime Customs. 1887. *Report on the Trade of China and Abstracts of Statistics: Reports for the Year 1886*. Pt. 1. Shanghai: Statistical Department of the Inspectorate General of Customs.

———. 1888. *Returns of Trade and Trade Reports for the Year 1887*. Pt. 1. Shanghai: Statistical Department of the Inspectorate General of Customs.

———. 1892. *Trade Reports*. Vol. 2. Shanghai: Statistical Department of the Inspector General of Customs.

———. 1924. *Decennial Reports on the Trade, Industries, etc., of the Ports Open to Foreign Commerce, and on the Condition and Development of the Treaty Port Provinces, 1912–21*. 2 vols. Shanghai: Statistical Department of the Inspectorate General of Customs.

Clapp, Frederick. 1922. "The Huang Ho, Yellow River." *Geographical Review* 12 (1): 1–18.

Cliver, Robert. 2010. "China." In *The Ashgate Companion to the History of Textile Workers, 1650–2000*, edited by Lex Heerma van Voss, Els Hiemstra-Kuperus, and Elise Van Nederveen Meerkerk, 103–141. Amsterdam: Ashgate.

Cohen, Myron. 2005. *Kinship, Contract, Community, and State: Anthropological Perspectives on China*. Stanford, CA: Stanford University Press.

Colquhoun, Archibald R. 1883. *Across Chrysê, Being the Narrative of a Journey Through the South China Border Lands from Canton to Mandalay*. Vol. 1. London: Samson Low, Marston, Searle and Rivington.

Cong Xiaoping. 2013. "From 'Freedom of Marriage' to 'Self-Determined Marriage': Recasting Marriage in the Shaan-Gan-Ning Border Region of the 1940s." *Twentieth-Century China* 38 (3): 184–209.

Croll, Elisabeth. 1995. *Changing Identities of Chinese Women: Rhetoric, Experience and Self-Perception in Twentieth-Century China*. Hong Kong: Hong Kong University Press.

Davies, Major H. R. (Henry Rodolph). (1909) 1970. *Yun-nan: The Link Between India and the Yangtze*. Cambridge: Cambridge University Press. Reprint, Taibei: Ch'eng Wen.

Davin, Delia. 1975. "Women in the Countryside of China." In *Women and Chinese Society*, edited by Margery Wolf and Roxanne Witke, 243–276. Stanford, CA: Stanford University Press.

———. 1976. *Woman-Work: Women and the Party in Revolutionary China*. Oxford: Clarendon Press.

Derks, Hans. 2012. *History of the Opium Problem: The Assault on the East, ca. 1600–1950*. Boston: Brill.

De Vries, Jan. 2011. "The Great Divergence After Ten Years: Justly Celebrated yet Hard to Believe." *Historically Speaking* 12 (4): 13–15.

Dietrich, Craig. 1972. "Cotton Culture and Manufacture in Early Modern China." In *Economic Organization in Chinese Society*, edited by W. E. Willmott, 109–136. Stanford, CA: Stanford University Press.

Dikotter, Frank. 2006. *Exotic Commodities: Modern Objects and Everyday Life in China*. New York: Columbia University Press.

———. 2010. *Mao's Great Famine: The History of China's Most Devastating Catastrophe, 1958–1962*. New York: Walker.

Drake, Samuel B. 1897. *Among the Dark-Haired Race in the Flowery Land*. London: Religious Tract Society.

Eastman, Lloyd E. 1988. *Family, Fields, and Ancestors: Constancy and Change in China's Social and Economic History, 1550–1949*. Oxford: Oxford University Press.

Ebrey, Patricia. 1993. *The Inner Quarters: Marriage and the Lives of Chinese Women in the Sung Period*. Berkeley: University of California Press.

Edgerton-Tarpley, Kathryn. 2008. *Tears from Iron: Cultural Responses to Famine in Nineteenth-Century China*. Berkeley: University of California Press.

Elliott, Mark C. 2001. *The Manchu Way: The Eight Banners and Ethnic Identity in Late Imperial China*. Stanford, CA: Stanford University Press.

Elvin, Mark. 1972. "The High-Level Equilibrium Trap: The Causes of the Decline of Invention in the Traditional Chinese Textile Industries." In *Economic Organization in Chinese Society*, edited by W. E. Willmott, 137–172. Stanford, CA: Stanford University Press.

———. 1973. *The Pattern of the Chinese Past*. Stanford, CA: Stanford University Press.

Engelen, Theo, and Ying-Hui Hsieh. 2007. *Two Cities, One Life: Marriage and Fertility in Lugang and Nijmegen*. Amsterdam: Aksant.

Esherick, Joseph. 1988. *The Origins of the Boxer Uprising*. Berkeley: University of California Press.

———. 1994. "Deconstructing the Construction of the Party-State: Gulin County in the Shaan-Gan-Ning Border Region. *China Quarterly* 140:1052–1079.

Esposito, Vincent. 1959. *The West Point Atlas of American Wars*. Edited by Fang Guoyu. New York: Frederick A. Praeger.

Eyferth, Jacob. 2009. *Eating Rice from Bamboo Roots: The Social History of a Community of Handicraft Papermakers in Rural Sichuan, 1920–2000*. Cambridge, MA: Harvard University Asia Center.

———. 2012. "Women's Work and the Politics of Homespun in Socialist China, 1949–1980." *International Review of Social History* 55 (4): 365–391.

Fang Guoyu (方国瑜), ed. 1998. *Yunnan shi liao cong kan* [Collection of historical materials on Yunnan]. Kunming: Yunnan daxue chubanshe.

Fei Hsiao-tung (Fei Xiaotong). 1983. *Chinese Village Close-up*. Beijing: New World Press.

Fei Hsiao-tung (Fei Xiaotong) and Chang Chih-I (Zhang Zhiyi). 1948. *Earthbound China: A Study of Rural Economy in Yunnan*. London: Routledge and Kegan Paul.

Feuerwerker, Albert. 1970. *Handicraft and Manufactured Cotton Textiles in China, 1871–1910*. Ann Arbor: University of Michigan Center for Chinese Studies.

———. 1995a. *The Chinese Economy, 1870–1949*. Ann Arbor: University of Michigan Center for Chinese Studies.

———. 1995b. "Handicraft Industry in Ming and Ch'ing China: 'Proto-Industrialization, ca. 1550–1850.'" In *Studies in Economic History of Late Imperial China: Handicraft, Modern Industry, and the State*, edited by Albert Feuerwerker, 88–122. Ann Arbor: University of Michigan Center for Chinese Studies.

Finnane, Antonia. 2008. *Changing Clothes in China: Fashion, History, Nation*. New York: Columbia University Press.

Fong, Grace. 2004. "Female Hands: Embroidery as a Knowledge Field in Women's Everyday Life in Late Imperial and Early Republican China." *Late Imperial China* 25 (1): 1–58.

———. 2008. *Herself an Author: Gender, Agency and Writing in Late Imperial China*. Honolulu: University of Hawaii Press.

Fong, H. D. (Fang Xianting) 1933. *Rural Industries in China*. Tianjin: China Institute of Pacific Relations.

———. 1934. *Zhongguo zhi mian-fang zhiye* [China's cotton textile industry]. Shanghai: Shangwu yinshuguan.

Forbes, Andrew D. W. 1987. "The 'Cin-Ho' (Yunnanese Chinese) Caravan Trade with North Thailand During the Late Nineteenth and Early Twentieth Centuries." *Journal of Asian History* 21 (1): 1–47.

"Foreign Parents and Their Adopted Chinese Babies." 2003. *China Through a Lens*, December 17. http://www.china.org.cn/english/2003/Dec/82748.htm.

Fortune, Robert. (1847) 1972. *Three Years' Wanderings in the Northern Provinces of China, Including a Visit to the Tea, Silk, and Cotton Countries*. 2nd ed. Reprint, Taibei: Chengwen.

Franck, Harry Alverson. 1923. *Wandering in Northern China*. New York: Century.

Gamble, Sidney D. 1954. *Ting Hsien: A North China Rural Community*. New York: Institute of Pacific Relations.

Gao Chunping (高春平). 2006. *Zu huai xun gen: Shanxi Hongdong da huai shu yi min xun zong* [Common ancestral origin: A probe of the great migration from Hongtong County of Shanxi Province in the Ming dynasty]. Taiyuan: Shanxi renmin chubanshe.

Gao Huan. 2011. *Women and Heroin Addiction in China's Changing Society*. New York: Routledge.

Gao Xiaoxian. 2006. "'The Silver Flower Contest': Rural Women in 1950s China and the Gender Division of Labor." Translated by Yunxi Ma. *Gender and History* 18 (3): 594–612.

Gates, Hill. 1989. "The Commoditization of Chinese Women." *Signs: Journal of Women in Culture and Society* 14 (4): 799–832.

———. 1996. *China's Motor: A Thousand Years of Petty Capitalism*. Ithaca, NY: Cornell University Press.

———. 1997a. "Footbinding, Handspinning, and the Modernization of Little Girls." In *Constructing China: Economy and Culture in China*, edited by Kenneth G. Lieberthal, Shuen-fu Lin, and Ernest P. Young, 177–192. Ann Arbor: University of Michigan Center for Chinese Studies.

———. 1997b. "On a New Footing: Footbinding and the Coming of Modernity." *Jindai Zhongguo funu shi yanjiu* [Research on Women in Modern Chinese History] 5:115–136.

———. 2001. "Footloose in Fujian: Economic Correlates of Footbinding." *Comparative Studies in Society and History* 43 (1): 130–148.

———. 2005. "Girls' Work in China and Northwestern Europe: Of Guniang and Meisjes." In *Marriage and the Family in Eurasia: Perspectives on the Hajnal Hypothesis*, edited by Theo Engelen and Arthur P. Wolf, 319–342. Amsterdam: Aksant.

———. 2008. "Bound Feet: How Sexy Were They?" *History of the Family* 13:58–70.

———. 2015. *Footbinding and Girls' Labor in Sichuan*. Oxford: Routledge.

George Philip and Son, Ltd. 1948. *Philips' Commercial Map of China*. London: London Geographical Institute.

Giersch, C. Patterson. 2001. "'A Motley Throng': Social Change on Southwest China's Early Modern Frontier, 1700–1880." *Journal of Asian Studies* 60 (1): 67–94.

———. 2006. *Asian Borderlands: The Transformation of Qing China's Yunnan Frontier*. Cambridge, MA: Harvard University Press.

Gillin, Donald G. 1960. "Portrait of a Warlord: Yen Hsi-shan in Shanxi Province, 1911–1930." *Journal of Asian Studies* 19 (3): 289–306.

Goodman, David S. G. 1994. "JinJiLuYu in the Sino-Japanese War: The Border Region and the Border Region Government. *China Quarterly* 140:1007–1024.

Graham, Gael. 1994. "Exercising Control: Sports and Physical Education in American Protestant Mission Schools in China, 1880–1930." *Signs: Journal of Women in Culture and Society* 20 (1): 39.

Grove, Linda. 2006. *A Chinese Economic Revolution: Rural Entrepreneurship in the Twentieth Century*. London: Rowman and Littlefield.

Hamilton, Gary, and Wei-An Chang. 2003. "The Importance of Commerce in the Organization of China's Late Imperial Economy." In *The Resurgence of East Asia: 500, 150, and 50 Year Perspectives*, edited by Giovanni Arrighi, Takeshi Hamashita, and Mark Selden, 173–213. London: Routledge.

Han Min. 2001. *Social Change and Continuity in a Village in Northern Anhui, Chiba: A Response to Revolution and Reform*. Osaka: National Museum of Ethnology.

Hanson, Haldore, 1939. *"Humane Endeavour": The Story of the China War*. New York: Farrar and Rinehart.

Harrison, Henrietta. 2005. *The Man Awakened from Dreams: One Man's Life in a North China Village, 1857–1942*. Stanford, CA: Stanford University Press.

Hayford, Charles W. 1990. *To the People: James Yen and Village China*. New York: Columbia University Press.

Hayhoe, Ruth. 2007. *Portraits of Influential Chinese Educators*. Hong Kong: University of Hong Kong Springer and Comparative Education Research Centre.

Hershatter, Gail. 1983. "Flying Hammers, Walking Chisels: The Workers of Santiaoshi." *Modern China* 9 (4): 387–419.

———. 1986. *The Workers of Tianjin, 1900–1949*. Stanford, CA: Stanford University Press.

———. 2007. *Women in China's Long Twentieth Century*. Berkeley: University of California Press.

———. 2011. *The Gender of Memory: Rural Women and China's Collective Past*. Berkeley: University of California Press.

Hinton, Carma, and Richard Gordon. 1984. *Small Happiness: Women of a Chinese Village*. Brookline, MA: Long Bow Group. DVD, 58 min.

Hinton, William. 1966. *Fanshen: A Documentary of Revolution in a Chinese Village*. Berkeley: University of California Press.

Honig, Emily. 1986. *Sisters and Strangers: Women in the Shanghai Cotton Mills, 1919–1949*. Stanford, CA: Stanford University Press.

Hosie, Alexander. 1890. *Three Years in Western China: A Narrative of Three Journeys in Ssŭ-ch'uan, Kuei-chow, and Yün-nan*. London: George Philip and Son.

———. 1914. *On the Trail of the Opium Poppy*. 2 vols. London: George Philip and Son.

Howard, Joshua. 2013. "The Politicization of Women Workers at War: Labour in Chongqing's Cotton Mills During the Anti-Japanese War." *Modern Asian Studies* 17 (6): 1888–1940.

Hsu, Francis. (1948) 1967. *Under the Ancestor's Shadow: Kinship, Personality and Social Mobility in Village China*. Reprint, Garden City, NY: Doubleday Anchor and American Museum of Natural History.

Huang, Philip C. C. 1985. *The Peasant Economy and Social Change in North China*. Stanford, CA: Stanford University Press.

———. 1990. *The Peasant Family and Rural Development in the Yangzi Delta, 1350–1988*. Stanford, CA: Stanford University Press.

———. 2002. "Development or Involution in Eighteenth Century Britain and China? A Review of Kenneth Pomeranz's 'The Great Divergence: China, Europe and the Making of the Modern World Economy.'" *Journal of Asian Studies* 61 (2): 501–538.

———. 2003. "Further Thoughts on Eighteenth-Century Britain and China: Rejoinder to Pomeranz's Response to My Critique." *Journal of Asian Studies* 62 (1): 157–167.

———. 2011. "The Modern Chinese Family: In Light of Economic and Legal History." *Modern China* 37 (5): 459–497.

Huang Zhenglin (黄正林). 2006. *Shaan-Gan-Ning bianqu shehui jingji shi (1937–1945)* [Shaan-Gan-Ning Border Region social and economic history (1937–1945)]. Beijing: Renmin chubanshe.

Jacka, Tamara. 1997. *Women's Work in Rural China: Change and Continuity in an Era of Reform*. Cambridge: Cambridge University Press.

Jackson, Beverley. 1997. *Splendid Slippers: A Thousand Years of an Erotic Tradition*. Berkeley: Ten Speed Press.

Jenks, Robert. 1994. *Insurgency and Social Disorder in Guizhou: The "Miao" Rebellion, 1854–1873*. Honolulu: University of Hawaii Press.

Jiang Quanbao, Li Shuzhuo, Marcus Feldman, and Jesus J. Sanchez-Barricate. 2012. "Estimates of Missing Women in Twentieth-Century China." *Continuity and Change* 27 (3): 461–479.

Jing Su and Luo Luo. 1978. *Landlord and Labor in Late Imperial China: Case Studies from Shandong*. Cambridge, MA: Harvard University Council on East Asian Studies.

Johnson, Kay Ann. (1983) 2009. *Women, the Family and Peasant Revolution in China*. Reprint, Chicago: University of Chicago Press.

———. 1993. "China's Orphanages: Saving China's Abandoned Girls." *Australian Journal of Chinese Affairs* 30:61–87.

Johnson, Linda Cooke, ed. 1993a. *Cities of Jiangnan in Late Imperial China*: Albany: State University of New York Press.

———. 1993b. "Shanghai: An Emerging Jiangnan Port, 1683–1840." In *Cities of Jiangnan in Late Imperial China*, edited by Linda Cooke Johnson, 151–181. Albany: State University of New York Press.

Johnston, Reginald F. (1910) 1986. *Lion and Dragon in North China*. Reprint, Hong Kong: Oxford University Press.

Karlbeck, Orvar. 1957. *Skattsokare I Kina* [Treasure seeker in China]. Translated by Naomi Walford. Stockholm: Cresset Press.

Ke Jisheng (柯基生). 2003. *Qianzai jinlian fenghua: Chanzu wenwu zhan* [A thousand years of golden lotus elegance: Footbinding exhibition]. Taibei: National Museum of History.

Keating, Pauline. 1994a. "The Ecological Origins of the Yan'an Way." *Australian Journal of Chinese Affairs* 32:123–153.

———. 1994b. The Yan'an Way of Co-operativization. *China Quarterly* 140:1025–1051.

———. 1997. *Two Revolutions: Village Reconstruction and the Cooperative Movement in Northern Shaanxi, 1934–1945*. Stanford, CA: Stanford University Press.

Ko, Dorothy. 1994. *Teachers of the Inner Chambers: Women and Culture in Seventeenth-Century China*. Stanford, CA: Stanford University Press.

————.1997. "The Body as Attire: The Shifting Meanings of Footbinding in Seventeenth-Century China." *Journal of Women's History* 8 (4): 8–27.

————. 1998. "The Emperor and His Women: Three Views of Footbinding, Ethnicity, and Empire." In *Proceedings of the Denver Museum of Natural History: Life in the Imperial Court of Qing Dynasty China*, edited by Chuimei Ho and Cheri A. Jones, 37–48. Denver, CO: Denver Museum of Natural History.

————. 2005. *Cinderella's Sisters: A Revisionist History of Footbinding.* Berkeley: University of California Press.

Kraus, Richard A. 1980. *Cotton and Cotton Goods in China, 1918–1936.* New York: Garland.

Kung, James Kai-Sing, Nansheng Bai, and Yiu-Fai Lee. 2011. "Human Capital, Migration, and a 'Vent' for Surplus Rural Labour in 1930s China: The Case of the Lower Yangzi." *Economic History Review* 64 (S1): 117–141.

Lai, David Chuen-yan. 1967. "The Cotton Spinning and Weaving Industrialization of China, 1890–1957: A Study in Industrial Geography." PhD diss., Harvard University.

Lavely, William. 1989. "The Spatial Approach to Chinese History: Illustrations from North China and the Upper Yangzi." *Journal of Asian Studies* 48 (1): 100–113.

Lavely, William, and R. Bin Wong. 1998. "Revisiting the Malthusian Narrative: The Comparative Study of Population Dynamics in Late Imperial China." *Journal of Asian Studies* 57 (3): 714–748.

Lee, James. 1982. "The Legacy of Immigration in Southwest China, 1250–1850." *Annales de Démographie Historique* [Annals of Historical Demography] 1:279–304.

Lee, James, Cameron Campbell, and Wang Feng. 2002. "Positive Checks or Chinese Checks?" *Journal of Asian Studies* 61 (2): 591–607.

Lee, James, and Wang Feng. 1998. "Malthusian Models and Chinese Realities: The Chinese Demographic System, 1700–2000." *Population and Development Review* 24:33–65.

————. 1999. *One Quarter of Humanity: Malthusian Mythology and Chinese Realities, 1700–2000.* Cambridge, MA: Harvard University Press.

————. 2002. "Positive Checks or Chinese Checks." *Journal of Asian Studies* 61 (2): 591–607.

Leland, John. 2011. "For Adoptive Parents, Questions Without Answers." *New York Times*, September 16. http://www.nytimes.com/2011/09/18/nyregion/chinas-adoption-scandal-sends-chills-through-families-in-united-states.html.

Levitt, Steven. 2011. "Adopting My Daughter." *YouTube*, September 8. http://www.youtube.com/watch?v=7Fw3lEMFofY.

Levy, Howard. 1966. *Chinese Footbinding: The History of a Curious Erotic Custom.* Taiwan: SMC.

Li Bozhong. 1998. *Agricultural Development in Jiangnan, 1620–1850.* New York: St. Martin's Press.

———. 2000. *Jiangnan de zaoqi gongyehua* [Proto-industrialization in the Yangzi delta]. Beijing: Shehui kexue wenxian chubanshe.

———. 2009. "Involution and Chinese Cotton Textile Production: Songjiang in the Late Eighteenth and Early Nineteenth Centuries." In *The Spinning World: A Global History of Cotton Textiles: 1200–1850*, edited by Giorgio Riello and Prasannan Parthasarathi, 387–398. Oxford: Oxford University Press.

Li Jinghan (李景漢, a.k.a. Franklin C. H. Lee). 1929. *Village Families in the Vicinity of Peiping*. Peiping: Social Research Department, China Foundation.

———. 1933. *Dingxian shehui gaikuang diaocha* [Ding County survey of social conditions]. Beijing: University Press.

Li, Lillian. 2007. *Fighting Famine in North China*. Stanford, CA: Stanford University Press.

Lim, Louisa. 2007. "Painful Memories for China's Footbinding Survivors." *NPR*, March 19. http://www.npr.org/templates/story/story.php?storyId=8966942.

Little, Daniel. 2010. "The Involution Debate." In *New Contributions to the Philosophy of History*, edited by Daniel Little, 171–193. New York: Springer.

Litton, George. 1903. *Report on a Journey in North and North-west Yunnan, Season 1902–1903*. Shanghai: Shanghai Mercury.

Lu Yu (路遇) and Teng Zezhi (滕泽之). 2006. *Zhongguo fensheng qu lishi renkou kao* [Chinese province and population history]. Jinan: Shandong renmin chubanshe.

Luo Yu (罗钰) and Zhong Qiu (钟秋). 2000. *Yunnan wuzhi wenhua, fangzhi juan* [The material culture of Yunnan, spinning and weaving volume]. Kunming: Yunnan jiaoyu chubanshe.

Ma Junya and T. Wright. 2010. "Industrialisation and Handicraft Cloth: The Jiangsu Peasant Economy in the Late Nineteenth and Early Twentieth Centuries." *Modern Asian Studies* 44 (6): 1337–1372.

Mackie, Gerry. 1996. "Ending Footbinding and Infibulation: A Convention Account." *American Sociological Review* 61 (6): 999–1017.

Mann, Susan. 1992. "Women's Work in the Ningbo Area, 1900–1936." In *Chinese History in Economic Perspective*, edited by Thomas G. Rawski and Lillian M. Li, 243–270. Berkeley: University of California Press.

———. 1997. *Precious Records: Women in China's Long Eighteenth Century*. Stanford, CA: Stanford University Press.

———. 2007. *The Talented Women of the Zhang Family*. Berkeley: University of California Press.

Mao Zedong (Mao Tse-tung). 2004. "Economic and Financial Problems in the Anti-Japanese War." In *Selected Works of Mao Tse-tung*, vol. 6. Hyderabad, India: Kranti. https://www.marxists.org/reference/archive/mao/selected-works/volume-6/mswv6_35_2.htm.

Matthews, James J. 1999. "The Union Jack on the Upper Yangzi: The Treaty Port of Chongqing, 1891–1943." PhD diss., York University, Toronto.

McLaren, Anne E. 2008. *Performing Grief: Bridal Laments in Rural China.* Honolulu: University of Hawaii Press.

MedCalc. 2016. "Logistic Regression." https://www.medcalc.org/manual/logistic_regression.php.

Metford, Beatrix. 1935. *Where China Meets Burma: Life and Travel in the Burma-China Border Lands.* London: Blackie and Son.

Moser, Charles K. 1930. *The Cotton Textile Industry of Far Eastern Countries.* Boston: Pepperell.

Mueggler, Eric. 1998. "The Poetics of Grief and the Price of Hemp in Southwest China." *Journal of Asian Studies* 57 (4): 979–1008.

Mungello, D. E. 2008. *Drowning Girls in China: Female Infanticide Since 1650.* Lanham, MD: Rowman and Littlefield.

Oakes, Timothy. 1998. *Tourism and Modernity in China.* New York: Routledge.

Osgood, Cornelius. 1963. *Village Life in Old China.* New York: Ronald Press.

Pampel, Fred C. 2000. *Logistic Regression: A Primer.* Thousand Oaks, CA: Sage.

Pasternak, Burton, and Janet Salaff. 1993. *Cowboys and Cultivators: The Chinese of Inner Mongolia.* Boulder, CO: Westview Press.

Pearse, Arno S. 1929. *Cotton Industry of Japan and China.* Manchester, UK: Taylor, Garnett, Evans.

———. 1932. "The Cotton Industry of Japan, China, and India and Its Effect on Lancashire." *International Affairs* 11 (5): 633–657.

Perry, Elizabeth J. 1980. *Rebels and Revolutionaries in North China, 1845–1945.* Stanford, CA: Stanford University Press.

Peyrefitte, Alain. (1992) 2013. *The Immobile Empire.* Reprint, New York: Knopf.

Pomeranz, Kenneth. 2000. *The Great Divergence: China, Europe and the Making of the Modern World Economy.* Princeton, NJ: Princeton University Press.

———. 2002. "Beyond the East-West Binary: Resituating Development Paths in the Eighteenth Century World." *Journal of Asian Studies* 61 (2): 539–590.

———. 2003a. "Facts Are Stubborn Things: A Response to Philip Huang." *Journal of Asian Studies* 62 (1): 167–181.

———. 2003b. "Women's Work, Family, and Economic Development in Europe and East Asia: Long-Term Trajectories and Contemporary Comparisons." In *The Resurgence of East Asia: 500, 150, and 50 Year Perspectives*, edited by Giovanni Arrighi, Takesi Hamasita, and Mark Selden, 124–172. London: Routledge.

———. 2005. "Women's Work and the Economics of Respectability." In *Gender in Motion: Divisions of Labor and Cultural Change in Late Imperial and Modern China*, edited by Bryna Goodman and Wendy Larson, 239–264. Lanham, MD: Rowman and Littlefield.

Pruitt, Ida. 1945. *A Daughter of Han: The Autobiography of a Chinese Working Woman.* Stanford, CA: Stanford University Press.

Qian Chengrun, Shi Yueling, and Du Jinghong. 1995. *Fei Xiaotong Lufeng cun nongtian wushi nian* [Fei Xiaotong's Lufeng Village farmland, fifty years]. Kunming: Yunnan renmin chubanshe.

Rawski, Thomas. 1989. *Economic Growth in Prewar China*. Berkeley: University of California Press.

Richards, Timothy. 1916. *Forty-Five Years in China*. London: T. Fisher Unwin.

Rocher, Emile. 1879. *La province Chinoise du Yun-nan* [The Chinese province of Yunnan]. 2 vols. Paris: Ernest Leroux.

Rofel, Lisa. 1999. *Other Modernities: Gendered Yearnings in China After Socialism*. Berkeley: University of California Press.

Schran, Peter. 1976. *Guerrilla Economy: The Development of the Shensi-Kansu-Ninghsia Border Region, 1937–1945*. Albany: State University of New York Press.

Scott, James. 1999. *Seeing like a State: How Certain Schemes to Improve the Human Condition Have Failed*. New Haven, CT: Yale University Press.

Selden. Mark. 1971. *The Yenan Way in Revolutionary China*. Cambridge, MA: Harvard University Press.

Shepherd, John S. 2012. "The Practice of Footbinding: Neglected Evidence from the Censuses of Taiwan." Unpublished manuscript.

———. 2014. "Footbinding and Manchus: Footnotes." Unpublished manuscript.

Skinner, G. William. 1964. "Marketing and Social Structure in Rural China, Part I." *Journal of Asian Studies* 24 (1): 3–43.

———. 1965. "Marketing and Social Structure in Rural China, Part II." *Journal of Asian Studies* 24 (2): 195–228.

———. 1977. "Regional Urbanization in Nineteenth-Century China." In *The City in Late Imperial China*, edited by G. William Skinner, 211–252. Stanford, CA: Stanford University Press.

Smith, Arthur H. 1899. *Village Life in China: A Study in Sociology*. New York: Feming H. Revell.

———. 1901. *China in Convulsion*. New York: Feming H. Revell.

Snow, Edgar. 1938. *Red Star over China*. New York: Grove Press.

Snow, Helen Foster. 1984. *My China Years*. New York: William Morrow.

Sommer, Matthew. 2010. "Abortion in Late Imperial China: Routine Birth Control or Crisis Intervention?" *Late Imperial China* 31 (2): 97–165.

———. 2015. *Polyandry and Wife-Selling in Qing Dynasty China: Survival Strategies and Judicial Interventions*. Berkeley: University of California Press.

Stacey, Judith. 1983. *Patriarchy and Socialist Revolution in China*. Berkeley: University of California Press.

Steele, Valerie, and John S. Major. 1999. *China Chic: East Meets West*. New Haven, CT: Yale University Press.

Stockard, Janice. 1989. *Daughters of the Canton Delta: Marriage Patterns and Economic Strategies in South China, 1860–1930*. Stanford, CA: Stanford University Press.

Stranahan, Patricia. 1981. "Changes in Policy for Yanan Women." *Modern China* 7 (1): 83–112.

———. 1983. "Labor Heroines of Yan'an." *Modern China* 9 (2): 228–252.

Tang Chi Yu. 1924. "An Economic Study of Chinese Agriculture." PhD diss., Cornell University.

Tang Zhiqing (唐致卿), ed. 2004. *Jindai Shandong nongcun shehui jingji yanjiu* [Modern Shandong rural social economic research]. Beijing: Renmin chubanshe.

Teichman, Eric. 1918. "Notes on a Journey Through Shensi." *Geographical Journal* 52 (6): 333–351.

T'ien Juk'ang (Tian Rukang). 1944. "Supplementary Chapter: Female Workers in a Cotton Textile Mill." In *China Enters the Machine Age*, edited by Kuoheng Shih, 178–198. Cambridge, MA: Harvard University Press.

Tong Shuye. 1981. *Zhongguo shougongye shangye fazhan shi* [History of the development of handcrafts and commerce in China]. Jinan: Jilu Press.

Tschiang Wei-guo (Jiang Weiguo). 1986. *Die chinesisch-japanesicheKrieg, 1937–1945: Wie mein Vater Tschiang Kaishek die Japaner beseigt* [The Sino-Japanese War, 1937–1945: How my father, Chiang Kai-shek, drove out the Japanese]. Osnabrück, Germany: Biblio Verlag.

Turner, Christena. 1997. "Locating Footbinding: Variations Across Class and Space in Nineteenth and Early Twentieth Century China." *Journal of Historical Sociology* 10 (4): 444–479.

Valenze, Deborah. 1995. *The First Industrial Woman*. New York: Oxford University Press.

Van Slyke, Lyman. 1988. *Yangtze: Nature, History, and the River*. New York: Addison Wesley.

Vermeer, Edward. 1988. *Economic Development in Provincial China: The Central Shaanxi Since 1930*. Cambridge: Cambridge University Press.

Walker, Kathy Le Mons. 1993. "Economic Growth, Peasant Marginalization, and the Sexual Division of Labor in Early Twentieth-Century China: Women's Work in Nantong County." *Modern China* 19 (3): 354–365.

———. 1999. *Chinese Modernity and the Peasant Path: Semicolonialism in the Northern Yangzi Delta*. Stanford, CA: Stanford University Press.

Wang Heming (王鶴鳴) and Shi Liye (施立业). 1991. *Anhui jin dai jingji guiji* [Anhui modern economic trajectory]. Hefei: Anhui People's Press.

Wang Zheng. 1999. *Women in the Chinese Enlightenment*. Berkeley: University of California Press.

Wolf, Arthur P. 1964. "Aggression in a Hokkien Village: A Preliminary Description." Paper presented at a seminar on personality and motivation in Chinese society, Bermuda, January.

———. 1985. "Fertility in Pre-revolutionary Rural China." In *Family and Population in East Asian History*, edited by Arthur P. Wolf and Susan B. Hanley, 154–185. Stanford, CA: Stanford University Press.

———. 2001. "Is There Evidence of Birth Control in Late Imperial China?" *Population and Development Review* 27 (1): 133–154.

Wolf, Arthur, and Theo Engelen. 2008. "Fertility and Fertility Control in Pre-revolutionary China." *Journal of Interdisciplinary History* 38 (3): 345–375.

Wolf, Margery. 1970. "Child Training and the Chinese Family." In *Family and Kinship in Chinese Society*, edited by M. Freedman, 37–62. Stanford, CA: Stanford University Press.

———. 1972. *Women and the Family in Rural Taiwan*. Stanford, CA: Stanford University Press.

Wou, Odoric Y. K. 1994. *Mobilizing the Masses: Building Revolution in Henan*. Stanford, CA: Stanford University Press.

Wright, Tim. 2000. "Distant Thunder: The Regional Economies of Southwest China and the Impact of the Great Depression. *Modern Asian Studies* 34 (3): 697–738.

Wu Ao. 1931. *Tianjin shi shehui ju tongji huikan* [Statistical issue of the Tianjin Bureau of Social Affairs]. Tianjin: Tianjin shehui ju.

Yang, Bin. 2009. *Between Winds and Clouds: The Making of Yunnan (Second Century BCE to Twentieth Century CE)*. New York: Columbia University Press.

Yang, Martin C. 1945. *A Chinese Village: Taitou, Shantung Province*. New York: Columbia University Press.

Yang Yang (杨杨). 2001. *Xiaojiao wudao: Dian-nan yige xiangcun de chanzu gushi* [Dancing on small feet: Stories of footbinding from a south Yunnan village]. Hefei: Anhui wenyi chubanshe.

———. 2004. *Yaohuang de Linghun: Tanfang zhongguo zuihou de xiaojiao bu-luo* [Swaying spirits: Seeking China's last small foot tribe]. Shanghai: Xuelin chubanshe.

Ye Weilie. 2001. *Seeking Modernity in China's Name: Chinese Students in the United States, 1900–1927*. Stanford, CA: Stanford University Press.

Yen Chung-p'ing (Yan Zhongping). 1963. *Zhongguo mianfangzhi shi gao* [Draft history of China's cotton textile industry]. Beijing: Kexue chubanshe.

Zhang Chengde (张成德) and Sun Liping (孙俪萍), eds. 2005. *Shanxi kangri kou-liao shi, san bu* [Oral history of the Anti-Japanese War in Shanxi, 3 vols.]. Taiyuan: Shanxi renmin chubanshe.

Zhang Guoxiang (张国祥), ed. 2005. *Shanxi kang ri zhanzheng tuhua shi* [Illustrated history of the Anti-Japanese War in Shanxi]. Taiyuan: Shanxi renmin chubanshe.

Zhang Hongming (张宏明). 2005. *Tu di xiang zheng: Lucun zai yan jiu* [Land as symbol: Lu Village restudied]. Beijing: Shehui kexue wenxian chubanshe.

Zhang Qizhi and Shi Nianhai. 1997. *Shaanxi tongshi, Minguo juan* [Shaanxi general history, Republican China volume]. Xi'an: Shaanxi shifan daxue chubanshe.

Zhang Shiwen (张世文). (1936) 1991. *Dingxian nongcun gongye diaocha* [An investigation of rural industries in Ding County]. Reprint, Chengdu: Sichuan renmin chubanshe.

Zhang Zhengming (张正明). 2001. *Jin shang xing aishi: Chengxiong shangjie 500 nian* [The sad history of Shanxi merchant prosperity: 500 years of commercial dominance]. Taiyuan: Shanxi guji chubanshe.

Zhonghua Minguo gonglu luxian tu [National highway map of China]. 1936. [Nanjing?]: Quan guo jingji weiyuanhui gong lu ju.

Zurndorfer, Harriet. 2009. "The Resistant Fiber: Cotton Textiles in Imperial China." In *The Spinning World: A Global History of Cotton Textiles, 1200–1850*, edited by Giorgio Riello and Parthasarathi Parsannan, 43–62. Oxford: Oxford University Press.

———. 2011. "Cotton Textile Manufacture and Marketing in Late Imperial China and the 'Great Divergence.'" *Journal of the Economic and Social History of the Orient* 54 (5): 701–738.

decline of, 76, 174; distribution of, 3, 5–7, 14–17, 135, 138, 185n1, 187n14; eyewitness observation of, 3, 5, 36–37; and factory work, 168; and farmwork, 10, 15, 74, 103, 124–125, 128, 148, 171, 209n65; fines to deter, 52, 79, 113, 200–201n14, 206n38; government bans on, 6, 87, 113; history of, 3, 13–17, 23; as identity marker, 187n12; incentives for, 9, 15, 24, 87–88, 98, 109, 128–129, 135, 209n65; and marriage chances, 8–10, 14, 147, 174; odds and probability of, 142–146, 183; and physical mobility, 8, 146; and sedentary handcrafts, 8, 9, 11, 67, 105, 117, 135, 140, 149, 153; shapes of bound feet, 2, 37, 74, 124, 211n10; temporary versus permanent, 33, 37, 74, 111, 117, 171, 173, 200–201n14, 206n38, 211n10; traditional explanations for, 3, 5, 8, 14, 36, 175, 188n24, 192n50, 207n42; and unbinding, 2, 7, 32, 37, 52, 73–74, 86, 167, 172, 198n44, 200–201n14, 201n16, 206n38, 211n10; as a variable, 37, 140–142, 145. *See also* Anti-footbinding movement; *names of specific counties*
Forbes, Andrew D. W., 101
Foreign commerce, 26–27, 44–45, 98, 101, 150–151; imports, 57, 69–70, 74, 78, 106; influence of, 46, 57, 59, 79. *See also* Cotton cloth; Textile mills; Yarn, cotton

Gamble, Sidney, 29, 47–48, 50–53, 195nn9, 14, 17, 195–196n18, 196n20
Gansu Province, 87, 89, 96, 185n3, 186n8
Gaoyang, Hebei, 51, 60, 164–166, 197n30, 215n48
Gates, Vera Neill, 201n26
Gender, 42, 174; and disguised unemployment, 147; and division of labor, 8, 21, 99–101, 113, 117, 129, 146; gender ideology, 35. *See also* Biases; Women's and gender studies
Germany: railroad building by, 57; textiles from, 59, 82
Girls' ages: in factory work, 168; at footbinding, 1, 9, 22, 31, 36, 60–61, 66, 73–74, 145

Girls' labor, 4, 8–10, 12–14, 17–27, 29–30, 34–35, 37, 41–42, 44, 47, 61, 147; ages at start of hand labor, 8, 19, 22, 50–52, 70, 73, 80, 81, 108–109, 117–119; harsh conditions of, 173–174; before marriage, 34, 50, 60, 65, 70, 80–81, 83, 108, 113, 116; unawareness of, 147; in textile mills, 18, 168, 172; vulnerability of, 173. *See also* Handcrafts; Labor; *names of specific counties*
Gordon, Robert, 200n13
Government. *See* Communism; Guomindang (GMD; Nationalist Party); Qing dynasty; Qing period; Republican government
Grain crops, 42, 43, 46, 80, 90, 94. *See also names of specific crops*
Grand Canal, 42, 43, 57, 62, 198n47
Grandmothers, 30, 37, 42, 60, 74, 109, 115, 178, 185n1
Great Depression, 66, 201n26, 205n26
Great Leap Forward, 64, 72, 193n14, 199n59, 204n18, 211n10; famine of, 33
Grove, Linda, 215n48, 216n51
Guangdong Province, 104, 120, 156, 162, 186n7, 192n3; Hakka in, 186n9
Guangxi Province, 99, 120, 127, 186n7, 192n3
Guangzhou (Canton), 7, 18, 27, 53, 58, 116, 120, 151, 159
Guanzhong, Shaanxi, 89, 91–93, 95–96, 201nn19, 24
Guizhou Province, 38–40, 98–104, 125–132, 134, 136, 154, 177, 180, 186n7, 192–193n4, 193n13, 202nn1, 3–4, 203n12; colonization of, 99; ethnic minorities in, 203n8; footbinding in, 129–130; girls' and women's work in, 126–128, 208n63, 215n43; lack of cotton in, 101–102, 208n58; opium in, 126, 208n59; rebellions in, 100–101, 208n57. *See also* Anshun, Guizhou
Guomindang (GMD; Nationalist Party), 44, 47, 57, 74, 133, 147, 201n24; anti-footbinding action by, 112, 202n31; army of, 44, 57, 74; Chongqing taken as China's capital by, 133, 135; handcraft textile promotion by, 95; and need for women in labor force, 147; opium ban by, 132

Lightning Source UK Ltd.
Milton Keynes UK
UKHW011610251118
332942UK00009B/337/P